The Cycling Year 90

VETEMENTS
KENWOOD
COUPE DU MONDE Perrier WORLD CUP
BBV

The Cycling Year

A record of the 1990 cycle racing season

by:
Phil Liggett
John Wilcockson
Rupert Guinness

photography:
Graham Watson
Cor Vos

SBL Springfield Books Limited

Published by Springfield Books Limited,
Norman Road, Denby Dale, Huddersfield
HD8 8TH, West Yorkshire, England

British Library Cataloguing in Publication Data
Liggett, Phil
The cycling year: a record of the 1990 cycle racing season.
1. Bicycles. Racing, history
I. Title II. Wilcockson, John III. Guinness, Rupert
796.62

ISBN 0 947655 21 2

Design: Douglas Martin Associates
Typesetting: Armitage Typo/Graphics Ltd, Huddersfield
Printed and bound in Great Britain by Butler & Tanner Ltd

Acknowledgements

The publishers are grateful to the following people for supplying additional material for use in this book:

ASL of Lausanne, for the pictures of the Tour of Romandie on pages 54-55

Carpress of Brussels, for the maps of Het Volk, Paris-Nice, Tirreno-Adriatico, Milan-San Remo, Tour of Flanders, Ghent-Wevelgem, Paris-Roubaix, Flèche Wallonne, Liège-Bastogne-Liège, Amstel Gold, Vuelta a España, Dauphiné Libéré, Giro d'Italia, Tour of Switzerland, Tour de France, Championship of Zürich, World Championship road circuit, Paris-Brussels, Paris-Tours and Tour of Lombardy

Stewart Clarke of ActionPact, for the pictures of the Milk Race on pages 74-75, and the pictures of the Grundig and World Mountain Bike Championships on pages 112-115

Cycling Weekly, for the lists of British teams

Luke Evans, for writing the account of the Milk Race on pages 74-75

A J Geisser, for the picture of the Tour of Switzerland on page 79 (bottom)

Pierre Hamel, for the account of the Grand Prix des Amériques on pages 134-135 (translated from French by John Wilcockson)

Julia Ingersoll, for the account of the NORBA series on pages 110-111

Willie Mathews, for the pictures of the NORBA series on pages 110-111

Sergio Penazzo, for the pictures of the Giro d'Italia which appear on pages 67 (top right) and 70 and of the Championship of Zürich on page 108

Photosport International, for the pictures of the Tour of the Americas which appear on pages 8, 10 and 11

Presse Sports, for the pictures of the Critérium International (pages 24-25), Four Days of Dunkirk (pages 46-47), Dauphiné Libéré (pages 62-65) and Championship of Zürich (pages 108-109)

Mike Randolph, for the pictures of the Grand Prix des Amériques on pages 134-135

Ranier P Rentas, for the picture of the Tour of the Americas on page 9

Beth Schneider, for the pictures of the Tour de Trump on pages 50-51

Karen Schulenberg, for the pictures of the Tour de Trump on pages 48-49 and 52-53, and of the CoreStates Championship on pages 76-77

SportCom AG, for the World Cup classification on page 160

Wolfgang Straüli, for the pictures of the Tour of Switzerland on pages 78 and 79 (top)

John Swanda, for the pictures of the Tour of Texas on pages 32-33

VeloNews, for the team listings and results information

Cover pictures:

Front: Champs Elysées, Paris: Greg LeMond on his way to a third successive Tour de France win

Back: The Tour of Spain peloton swarms up the Alto de Los Leones during the last stage into Madrid

Endpapers: The lines of poplar trees guide the riders south in the Paris-Tours classic

Frontispiece: A light-hearted moment at the Clasico San Sebastian for two of the most successful riders of the season: Greg LeMond and Gianni Bugno

Contents

Foreword: by Greg LeMond

Although I've now been a professional cyclist for 10 years, I'm still excited to begin a new season . . . and relieved when it ends. And like most riders, I experience plenty of highs and lows during the cycling year. The 1990 season was a particularly memorable one for me, especially as I was wearing the rainbow jersey as world champion. Yet I struggled for many weeks during the first half of the year. My winter training schedule was really disrupted by the demands of the media – it seemed like everyone wanted to interview America's *Sportsman of the Year.* Then a virus stopped me racing in April. So my season didn't really get under way until early May.

But despite the problems, the cycling fans always made me feel good. Even when I finished half an hour behind the leaders on the more difficult stages of the Trump race, and the Giro d'Italia, they were still waiting with their autograph books. It was sometimes hard for me to keep up my morale, but the fans really helped. And so it was a thrill to be able to repay all their support, and the support of my Z team, by winning the Tour de France for a third time.

People tend to forget that cycling is a team sport; there's a great sense of camaraderie on a team like Z. We have a lot of good French riders, including Ronan Pensec, Jérôme Simon and Gilbert Duclos-Lassalle, as well as climbers like Robert Millar of Scotland, Atle Kvalsvoll of Norway, and Miguel Arroyo of Mexico. These guys make you realize how international cycling has become since I first turned pro in 1981. Back then, most of the teams and riders came from France, Belgium and Italy, and all the big races were on the Continent. That's changed. Today, we travel all over the world to race. Besides the traditional events in Europe, there are also big races like the Tour de Trump in my country, the Nissan Classic in Ireland, and the World Cup races in Canada, England and Spain. And this year, the World championships were held in Japan. It can sometimes be tough coping with jet lag, but all the new races and racers have helped cycling become a much more popular sport than ever before.

With so much going on, it can be hard to remember who won what race, and how they won it. That's why this new book is so useful. Starting with the Tour of the Americas in February, we can read (and see) what happened in every major event through the season, right up to the World Cup final in late October. Seeing the photos of Paris-Nice and the spring classics reminds me how rugged these races are, and how much faster they've become in recent years. The reason, of course, is the battle to finish in the top 50 at each race to qualify for FICP points – which now determine which teams take part in the World Cup events and the Tour de France.

The new system has certainly changed the way we race. For instance, there was the unexpected, early break in Milan-San Remo, which saw me and most of the race favourites left behind. And a similar thing happened on the first stage of the Tour de France, when my team-mate Pensec, my old friend Steve Bauer and the Italian Claudio Chiappucci stole a 10-minute lead, because none of the other teams wanted to chase. I hardly knew Chiappucci – except for his winning the best climber's prize at the Giro – but he turned out to be my biggest rival for the Tour.

It was a great year for the Italians, with Gianni Bugno, particularly, enjoying a phenomenal season. He has seemed like a new rider since winning Milan-San Remo in March. He couldn't have done any better than he did in the Giro – winning three stages and wearing the pink leader's jersey for the whole race. As a consequence of this success in the Giro, Bugno took over the FICP ranking as world number one from Laurent Fignon, whose season was wrecked by injuries. I know how Fignon feels, and I'm sure he'll come back and be a strong contender for the big races in 1991.

Another rider who figured in the Italian success story was an old rival of mine, Moreno Argentin. He was unbeatable in April, taking both the Tour of Flanders and the Flèche Wallonne to head the Perrier World Cup standings. But a bad crash in the Tour de France stopped Argentin racing for a few weeks, and Bugno took over the World Cup lead after he won the Wincanton Classic in England.

I couldn't compete in the English race because of a saddle sore acquired during the Tour, but I was able to take part in the World Cup races at San Sebastian, Spain, and Zürich, Switzerland. Again, it was a disappointment to get beaten in the sprint at Zürich by Frenchman Charly Mottet. However, I hoped my good form would allow me to win the world Championship again. The road race in Japan was gruelling because of the heat and high humidity, and the US team rode really well – until they got beaten by the distance. I then had to rely on the other teams, like the Italians, to chase down the breaks. But the final chase was just too late and the Belgians Rudy Dhaenens and Dirk De Wolf took the top two medals. And Bugno outsprinted me to get on the podium.

Besides coverage of all the big road races, you'll also find stories here about the top off-road races. These include the first ever official World Mountain Bike Championships, which took place in Colorado and were dominated by the Americans, who won eight of the 10 titles. Mountain biking is a lot of fun, and on my return from Japan I was really pleased that I was able to take part in (and win) my first off- road race – at the Chequamegon Festival in Wisconsin. It was a lot of fun (as well as pretty exhausting) racing in an event with more than 1300 riders, most of whom were what we call citizen racers. There should be more events like this, because with greater numbers of riders taking part in bike races, the sport can only continue to grow.

Greg LeMond

Tour of the Americas: 16-25 February

With a versatile performance that befitted the 1988 world track points champion, Daniel Wyder of Switzerland won the third Tour of the Americas that took place in Florida, Puerto Rico and Venezuela. As in previous years, the race had to be split into two sections because the UCI refuses to sanction races longer than six days until they have taken place for five years, and the 28-year-old Swiss, riding for the Italian team Selle Italia-Eurocar, won both the Florida-Puerto Rico and Venezuela sections of the Tour, overcoming strong challenges from Colombian Hector Patarroyo (Postobon) and Britain's Malcolm Elliott (Teka) to take the combined classification, known as the Super Series.

The revised format for the Tour – three days each in Florida, Puerto Rico and Venezuela – was a sporting success, despite some annoying, but not unexpected, delays transporting 15 teams and their equipment around the Caribbean. One of the ten European sportswriters who followed the race, standing at the finish of the final stage in Caracas amidst a joyous gathering of about 200,000 spectators, enthused, 'This is superb. Really fabulous. It's exactly what cycling needs to extend its internationalization.'

Tour of the Americas, Florida (251.6km), Puerto Rico (537.6km) and Venezuela (431.5km)

Florida, 16-18 February: 251.6km

English rider Keith Reynolds of the Banana-Falcon team won the first of the three Florida circuits in hot, blustery weather at West Palm Beach, and he retained the yellow jersey for the next two days despite excellent stage wins by Andrea Tafi (Wyder's twenty-three-year-old Italian team-mate) at Fort Lauderdale, and Elliott at Miami Beach.

The opening stage of the Tour was a thirty-lap, 57km race, but despite its brevity, it provided some unexpected drama – including a first-lap crash for Spanish race favourite Pedro Delgado of Banesto, which put him three minutes behind the leaders. 12 laps from the finish Reynolds launched a sharp counterattack, followed by the Americans Roy Knickman (7-Eleven) and Michael Carter (AC-Pinarello), Spaniard Herminio Diaz-Zabala (ONCE) and Patarroyo. A chase was started by Elliott, American Thomas Craven (7-Eleven) and Australian Stephen Hodge (ONCE), but their efforts came too late to affect the outcome, and Knickman was outfought by Reynolds in an exciting dash for the line.

Reynolds takes the first stage at West Palm Beach, with Diaz-Zabala (right) in third place

At the end of the second day, race promoter German Blanco seemed to be as happy as stage winner Tafi and race leader Reynolds. 'We tried for three years to get this course on the Fort Lauderdale strip,' said Blanco. 'The police said they would never approve it, but it went very well today.' Indeed, the 35-lap, 112km circuit race beside Fort Lauderdale Beach was, with continuous attacks and chases, the most competitive of the race's three Florida legs.

One of the chief animators of the race was 7-Eleven's Dane, Jens Veggerby. With nine of the 35 laps remaining, Veggerby and Tafi dashed away from the pack. They had a 40-second lead with three laps left when Delgado's Banesto team started a concerted chase. The gap closed to 20 seconds as the bell rang for the final round. But then Tafi stopped pulling, and Veggerby had a difficult choice. 'I could also have stopped pulling, and lost everything; or I could carry on going hard and know that I'd finish second. I chose to pull . . . but second place is worth nothing.' Tafi easily won the eventual sprint, but his gamble only just paid off – metres behind the two leaders, Elliott led in the pack for third place.

Elliott proved he was the strongest rider of the Florida section of the race by impressively winning a sprint

Rayner and Mejia lead the decisive break through the Puerto Rican jungle

finish to the third stage at Miami Beach. He led a four-man break for the last 44km of the stage, with the pack catching them in the final lap. 'Malcolm was awesome,' commented Canadian Alex Stieda of 7-Eleven, another of the four breakaways. The other two were overall third-placed Diaz-Zabala and the talented Belgian, Johan Museeuw (Lotto-Superclub). The four were still together when Diaz-Zabala punctured with just two laps to go. The Spaniard was swallowed up by the pack, closing to within nine seconds of the Elliott trio as the bell sounded. Said Stieda: 'We were caught just going into the final turn. Roberto Gaggioli (the Italian Coors Light rider) went past us in the corner. Malcolm took his wheel, while Tom (Craven) came around me and past Gaggioli.' Elliott accelerated away to win the stage by five lengths over Craven, while Museeuw held on for third place.

Puerto Rico, 19-21 February: 537.6km

The hot and humid Caribbean island of Puerto Rico – witnessing professional cycling for the first time – provided superb terrain and weather for this early season event. Elliott went on to win two more stages in this first, six-day section; but he conceded overall victory by one second to the other Puerto Rico stage winner, Wyder.

When Tafi and Wyder, along with the Venezuelan amateur Yussen Monsalve, dashed away on the first break of stage four (the first in Puerto Rico), a sleepy peloton didn't bother to chase. And by the time the pack woke up, about 40km from the finish of this 146km road race, the trio was more than six minutes ahead.

Tafi went on to win his second stage of the Tour with a vigorous solo over the final 18km of the flat, expressway circuit, and took over the race lead from Reynolds by more than two minutes – a dramatic turnabout explained partly by the stultifying, tropical heat of Puerto Rico.

Starting the fifth stage, Wyder was ready to show his true strength – if team-mate and overnight leader Tafi should falter. The fast early pace wore out most of the field, leaving them no time to admire the stunning views of the ocean to their left or the cloud-covered mountains to their right, beyond the tobacco and sugar plantations. Among the casualties were the powerful Coors Light and 7-Eleven teams, who both failed to place a man in the big group that split from the pack when the real climbs began. On roads slicked by sudden tropical downpours, the constant accelerations of the Postobon team – and particularly its leader, Colombian Alvaro Mejia – drew 20 or so riders clear of the pack, and Tafi was one who missed out on the selection.

Of the chasers, only Patarroyo managed to catch up with the leaders before the tricky, slippy, winding drop to the island's south coastal plain. But with nearly everyone in the bunch taking extra care on the descent, the skilful Wyder threw caution to the winds and went charging across the one-minute gap with the surprising English sprinter, David Rayner.

Behind, Tafi was desperately trying to cut his losses, but despite a 48 kph, with-the-wind pursuit, this group was still a hefty 2:35 behind the regrouped breakaways at the finish line in Ponce. The stage provided an easy victory for the confident Elliott. It was his second stage win of the race, and he was now in second place overall, only 11 seconds down on the new yellow jersey, Wyder.

A strong east wind blowing against the peloton for most of the final stage in Puerto Rico discouraged every

attempt to upset the status quo established at Ponce. Over five hours, only three attacks succeeded in breaking clear of the pack, and the last of these was absorbed with an hour's racing still to go. The resultant field sprint was won, inevitably, by the fast-finishing Malcolm Elliott.

However, his third stage victory of the six-stage race wasn't quite enough to give Elliott an overall win. His 10-second time bonus left the 28-year-old Briton a single, frustrating second behind Daniel Wyder. It was a tough result for Elliott, who a year ago lost the Florida section of the Tour by only two seconds to Michel Vaarten.

Venezuela, 23-25 February: 431.5km

After a tiring 10-hour transfer from Puerto Rico, the Venezuela section of the Tour started with a time trial which was expected to decide the outcome of this three-day concluding leg. It was not a particularly challenging course – a straight, almost flat 20.5km along a well-surfaced freeway – but a strong headwind and suffocating heat made the test both mentally and physically tough.

The Florida-Puerto Rico sector winner, Wyder – riding a low-profile time trial bike fitted with a rear disc wheel and triathlon bars – recorded 28:05, to give him the first time trial win of his seven-year pro career. He came in ahead of Museeuw (28:34), Patarroyo (28:41)

The course along Fort Lauderdale Beach provided one of the most competitive days' racing of the Tour

At the end of the Puerto Rican section of the race – Andrea Tafi, Daniel Wyder and Malcolm Elliott

and Wyder's Venezuelan team-mate Leonardo Sierra (28:46). The crowds lining the finish area had expected Delgado to challenge the best times, but they were shocked when he was caught by and overtaken by Carter, who recorded 29:03.

Although the 1988 Tour de France champion had been keeping a low profile in the race so far, he showed his quality in the second stage: a 19-lap, 99km circuit race in Valencia. 'I'm feeling very strong,' said Delgado, 'so I thought it natural to help one of my team riders win.' The team-mate in question, Carlos Gonzales, had already come close to winning several stages, and now his team leader decided he would lend a hand.

With four laps (21km) left of the day's second stage, a dangerous break including the Colombians Patarroyo and William Pulido (Postobon), and top twelve riders Carter and Tafi, got 1:16 ahead of the group. Delgado then took over, closing the gap to 17 seconds as he pulled the peloton through the start-finish area with two laps remaining. The break disintegrated on a short climb, and a new attack formed. Delgado was there to control things as Stieda and Italian Antonio Fanelli (Selle Italia) joined two riders from the original break: Rayner and Tafi. Delgado and Tafi dropped back to aid the chase as Rayner and Stieda redoubled their efforts in front, shadowed by Fanelli. The three were caught 1.4km from the finish, Delgado leaving Gonzales ideally placed to make his final, uphill charge to the line and win from Fanelli and Elliott.

There were tremendous expectations for the only point-to-point stage in Venezuela, which would take the 79 survivors over the mountains to Caracas. At the start line in Valencia's Avenida Bolivar on a hot, breezy morning, the top climber from the race's Puerto Rico section, American rider Andy Bishop, summed up the feelings of the peloton. 'If Wyder can get over the first climb with the front group, then he's won the race,' he observed.

But when the riders topped that first climb, the 7.5 kilometre long Los Colorados, the race still appeared to be in the balance. Wyder was indeed in the front group of thirty-four riders, but the Swiss had only one team-mate with him: local man Sierra. Wyder was saved by the fact that the group also contained five Venezuelan amateurs – who had already shown their willingness to help him and his Selle Italia squad. With six friendly faces alongside, Wyder was understandably confident about his situation. Talking about it later, he said, 'I was never afraid of losing contact with the group. In any case, the Colombians controlled the race.'

As the pace eased momentarily after the first mountain prime, the Colombians hesitated when the aggressive ONCE rider, Santos Hernandez of Spain, sped away. The chase was taken up (on Wyder's behalf?) by one of the amateurs, impressive 20-year-old Venezuelan climber, Alexis Mendez . . . and Delgado. Postobon sent Colombian Oscar Vargas with them to shadow the break. The three caught Hernandez, and they crossed the summit of the next climb with a 50-second advantage. It seemed that this four-man break could completely change the course of the race, but the four Colombians in the Wyder group now started to chase in earnest. They led their thirty-strong group up to the break just beyond the last of the four climbs, but with less than 20km of the stage remaining, and such redoubtable sprinters as Elliott and Museeuw in the lead group, their stage hopes looked slim. But when the elegant Colombian rider Pulido made a speculative break on the long, winding downhill into Caracas, few of the riders in the group saw him go: 26 seconds after Pulido cruised across the line, Spaniard Juan Martinez-Oliver of Banesto came racing up Caracas's Avenida Bolivar, celebrating what he believed was his first win for his new team.

With his lead secure, Wyder and team-mates easily contained the few attacks on the final circuit race in Caracas, which was taken in a field sprint by 7-Eleven's Irishman, John Brady.

Blanco and his fellow promoter Erwin Vasquez had improved the race organisation, and this contributed greatly to the smoother operation, particularly in Venezuela. But they know that many improvements still need to be made. Staying at four- and five-star hotels, with excellent meals and the warmth of Caribbean hosts, winner Wyder and the other participants agreed that this event is an excellent way to start the season. However, only time will tell if it can become a permanent fixture in the international racing calendar.

Malcolm Elliott receiving advice from his assistant directeur sportif, Julio San Emeterio

Het Volk: 4 March

By winning the European calendar's first major one-day race, the 198km Het Volk, Belgian Johan Capiot caused a major upset. Known as the sprinting specialist of Australian Phil Anderson's TVM team, Capiot was nevertheless not expected to win the final sprint of this Belgian classic. Pre-race favourites were his compatriots the defending champion, Etienne De Wilde (Histor-Sigma), Eddy Planckaert (Panasonic-Sportlife), or even the promising Johan Museeuw (Lotto), who took third place in the great Paris-Tours bunch finish in late 1989. The 26-year-old Capiot – whose last major wins were the back-to-back victories in the two Flèche Brabançonne semi-classics – was at best considered a long shot.

Capiot (left) was always prominent, as in this attack with Vanderaerden

With the finish almost in sight, Capiot leads the winning break from Criquielion (left), Lammerts and Holm

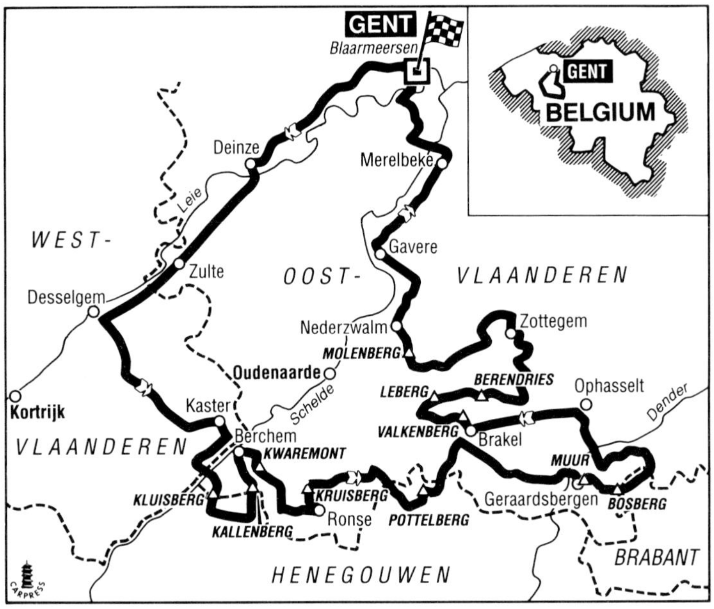

Het Volk, Belgium: 198km

Yet not only did Capiot win, it was his aggression and determination that characterised this new, shorter version of the race. The shortening of the Het Volk route from 244km to 198km was expected to draw criticism from all sides. Yet, while some purists disapproved of the easier route, others saw the change as an element that helped to create the action – most of which started after the notorious Mur de Grammont, the sixth of the eleven sharp, cobbled climbs which characterise Belgian races.

In the earlier stages, including the infamous climbs of the Kluisberg, the Old Kwaremont, and the Kruisberg, the peloton remained largely intact. At the Mur, Dutchman John Talen (Panasonic-Sportlife) attacked, and although he was caught before the next climb he triggered off several more strong moves. The first of these was a breakaway, on the Bosberg at 116km, of six riders – Belgians Marc Sergeant, Henrik Redant (both Lotto), Edwig Van Hooydonck (Buckler) and Luc Roosen (Histor-Sigma) and Dutchmen Eddy Schurer (TVM) and Gerrit Solleveld (Buckler). But of these only Solleveld made any headway. Demonstrating once again his time-trialling prowess – a talent he revealed when he won last year's Ghent-Wevelgem, sharing a marathon move with Englishman Sean Yates of 7-Eleven – Solleveld escaped alone for 30km before being reeled in by the peloton. A barrage of counter-attacks was launched, reducing Solleveld's lead from two minutes at the Valkenberg, to 0:50 with 39km to go, and finally catching him five kilometres further on.

Capiot first stepped into the limelight when, with 34km still remaining, he inspired the initial break of twelve riders on the last of the race's eleven climbs, the Molenberg. Then, with 25km left, he stopped for a rear wheel change, after enduring the frustration of racing for two kilometres with a flat tyre before his team car arrived.

Undaunted, Capiot set off on a successful 4km solo chase of the leaders, a group which included De Wilde,

Capiot made a late charge to win from Van Hooydonck (left), De Wilde (right), Museeuw and Planckaert

Planckaert and Museeuw; five other Belgians, Sergeant, Eric Vanderaerden (Buckler), Carlo Bomans (Weinmann), Claude Criquielion (Lotto) and Van Hooydonck; Denmark's Brian Holm (Histor-Sigma); and the Dutch duo of Johann Lammerts (Z) and Adrie Van der Poel (Weinmann). The break would have been even stronger had Irishman Sean Kelly's PDM team been racing; PDM had, however, withdrawn from the event following the sudden death of team member Johannes Draaijer early in the week. Even so, it was as star-studded a break as you could expect in any Belgian classic, let alone an early season race, in which the stars usually prefer to take a back seat and save their energies for the bigger spring events.

It was clear from the outset that despite the relative ease with which the break had got clear from the peloton – most of the big teams being represented – the eventual winner would have to fight every inch of the way, as Capiot, who had successfully latched on to the leaders after his post-puncture chase, discovered. With 11km remaining he had to pull out all the stops to make the final cut when the twelve leaders made the decisive split. It was De Wilde who threw down the gauntlet, attacking from the outside on a right turn – as he did in Het Volk last year, although then it had been closer to the finish and far more successful. Along with the former Belgian champion went Van Hooydonck, Planckaert and Museeuw. And then, with the four starting to get away, Capiot, Lammerts and Van der Poel followed suit.
At this juncture, Capiot's already slim chances of beating the better-known sprinters seemed to reach vanishing point. A solo attack in the final kilometres was obviously not going to work; Lammerts, Van der Poel and Van Hooydonck had all made such attacks without success. Rather, it was the exhilarating and aggressive tussle between Planckaert and De Wilde as they charged down the last 300 metres to the line that looked certain to produce the winner; clearly former Het Volk winner Planckaert had taken on De Wilde on this basis. However, such single-subject focus often leaves other doors wide open, and such was the case at Het Volk. Planckaert's aggressive blocking tactics – swerving from his right to his left where De Wilde's line stood – left Planckaert's right wide open.

It was an open invitation for Capiot. Van der Poel and Lammerts had both been counted out after trying early lead-out sprints with 350 metres left, and De Wilde and Planckaert were racing themselves out of contention. That left only Van Hooydonck and Museeuw for Capiot to deal with. He seized the opportunity and burst towards the line, with Van Hooydonck on his wheel and Museeuw trying to pass through on his left. But the doggedness he had already demonstrated so many times in this race did not desert him now, and he crossed the line just ahead of Van Hooydonck and De Wilde, with Museeuw in fourth place and Planckaert fifth.

Johan Capiot

Paris-Nice: 4-11 March

Fifty-eight years ago, French journalist Jean Leulliot was summoned to the mayoral offices in Nice to discuss how that town could become involved in a race similar to the successful Tour de France. Thus the seeds were sown for one of the world's best-loved races – 'La Course au Soleil', the race to the sun, or simply Paris-Nice. When he died in 1982 Jean Leulliot – a familiar figure in the press rooms, cigarette permanently hanging from the corner of his mouth, his very English flat hat tilted to one side – left the cycling world a great legacy. It was a legacy accepted with enthusiasm by his two daughters, Josette and Jacqueline, who are still the only female organizers of a professional race. Josette Leulliot, a petite business-like lady, is dedicated to preserving what her father started. Amidst the changing demands of the sport, she has faced and won many a battle to protect Paris-Nice, and she has done it without allowing the eight-day race to the Côte d'Azur to lose any of its friendliness or charm.

This year, the race's fortieth anniversary celebrations brought together the best cyclists it has seen in a long time. The 144 riders in 18 teams contained five of the eight top world-ranked men, despite the annual clash with Tirreno-Adriatico. Some, like 1989 world champion and Tour de France winner Greg LeMond of the Z team,

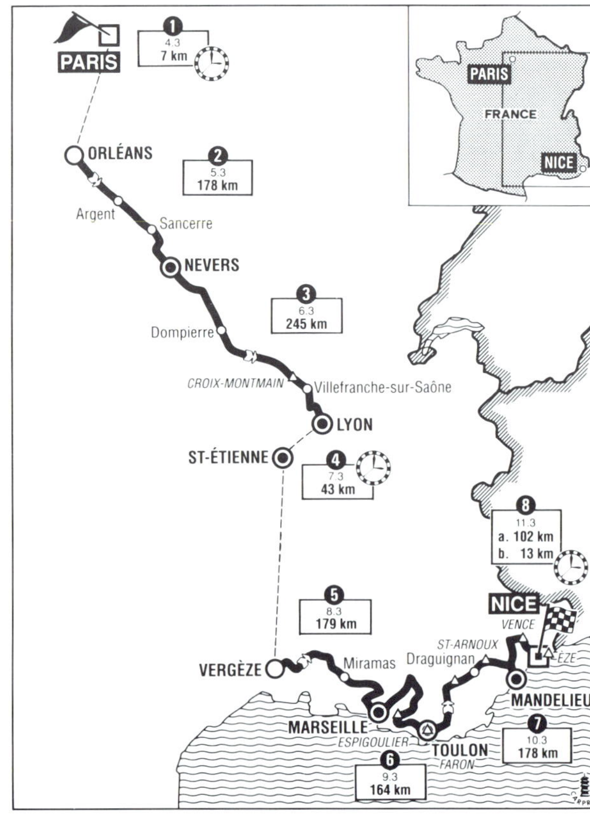

Paris-Nice, France: 1109km

Indurain attacked near the summit of the Tanneron, momentarily shaking off Fignon in an attempt to increase his race lead

use the 1109 kilometres to work off winter excess. Two riders came to Paris with a question mark over their form: Irishman Stephen Roche (Histor-Sigma) and Frenchman Jean-François Bernard (Toshiba). Bernard had been out of the sport for nine months with injured knee ligaments, while Roche, in between flashes of brilliance such as his great treble (the Giro d'Italia, Tour de France and world title) in 1987, has been for a number of years troubled by a knee injury. Both stars were back, saying that their problems were behind them; and as the race unfolded, they showed the world that they might be right.

Unlike Paris-Roubaix, Paris-Nice really does start in Paris, closing off a large part of the French capital on a March Sunday afternoon for its first stage. The 7km individual time trial raced from the Place Léon Blum, not far from the Bastille, across the Place de la Nation to the Place d'Italie on the opposite bank of the Seine. With a short, cobbled climb in the last kilometre, it demanded a lung-bursting effort that would hurt all the way.

At the start, Roche was clearly happy to be facing a new season free from injury and with a new team, Belgian Histor. 'I'm just going to see what happens,' he said. 'I have no pressure and I like my new team.' When the Dubliner left the Spanish team Fagor, he took with him the young Francis Moreau, and it was Moreau who secured the first victory of Paris-Nice, winning the time trial with 9:15. Spaniard Miguel Indurain of Banesto, last year's winner, and France's Laurent Fignon (Castorama-Raleigh) finished close behind, losing three seconds and ten seconds respectively. The big shock was Roche placing fourth and Bernard sixth: clearly, the 'invalids' were recovering.

After the opening time trial, the strategic stages are the team time trial at St Etienne, the mountain-top finish at Mont Faron, and the Col d'Eze time trial in Nice itself. In between these obvious battlegrounds, the riders must stay alert, making sure that their plans are not upset. So, Moreau had struck first, and on the next day the Frenchman successfully defended his jersey on the second stage of 178km from Orléans to Nevers. The course was a gentle one, and the first two hours rolled by at tourist speeds of less than 32kph. The sun was shining, the songbirds had found their voices, and Nice seemed a long way away. There were those who tried – such as Denmark's Brian Holm (Histor-Sigma), who had the form after his win in the GP Wielerrevue in Holland. But his attack with Jesper Worre (Café de Colombia) came to nothing, and the Chateau d'Ax team

The finish of the stage from Nîmes to Marseille: a jubilant Adriano Baffi

Even world champions suffer from cramp: Greg LeMond and the early-season blues

brought the race together, before passing through the finish line for the first time. After a finishing loop, the pack was still together. The last time a stage ended in Nevers was in 1968, when sprinters Walter Godefroot, Edouard Sels and Eddy Merckx led a Belgian clean sweep. So it was fitting that Etienne De Wilde of Histor-Sigma – who also won the first stage last year – kept up the Belgian tradition, and sprinted home ahead of 138 riders.

You could have assumed that the third stage, from Nevers to Lyon, would also see a bunch finish, were it not for the fact that its 245km ended on top of la Croix Rousse, in the city suburbs. But it did in fact turn out this way, with victory going to Belgian champion Carlo Bomans (Weinmann), ahead of the little Italian Claudio Chiappucci (Carrera), who would have been a major challenger for final victory if he'd been on a stronger team. It was a route that found the unfit legs, and only

Roche (right), riding here with new Soviet star Ekimov, took over the white jersey after the team time trial

fifty riders disputed the scramble to the top of the 2km climb. This proved to be an attacking stage over the last half, which included a number of climbs and a high spot of 750m on top of the Col de Croix-Montmain, 60km from the end. Bruno Bruyère (Lotto) was the early attacker, quickly joined by 'policeman' Laurent Biondi (Histor). By the climb, they had been ahead for 100 kilometres, and Bruyère was left by Biondi. The bunch, at one time 11 minutes behind, had their tails up once the hills started; and Chiappucci became the new leader in the mountains when he topped the Col de Croix-Montmain in second place behind Biondi – whose time out front was almost over. Chiappucci crashed on the descent, finishing up at the back of the field – but he recovered magnificently not only to catch up, but take second place in Lyon. Near the finish, Bernard tried a cheeky move and pulled away to catch Biondi, who was by now a very tired man. He left Biondi immediately, but even though there was only 20km to go, Bernard, who finished second in 1987, was not yet competition-fit, and was caught at the start of the climb to the finish. Histor's plans to keep Moreau in first place did not work out, and he lost his lead after being dropped approaching the finish, and losing 38 seconds. His white jersey passed to Indurain, last year's winner, who seemed to be as good as ever and once again the man to beat.

This season, the Banesto team hoped to keep Pedro Delgado fresh for the Tour de France, and instead use Indurain for possible victory in the Tour of Spain. Their plans, at this time, were on schedule. However, Paris-Nice was far from won: Indurain's overall lead was just 3 seconds over Chiappucci, 7 seconds over Fignon and 11 seconds over Roche; the next stage would be a crucial team trial, with the actual time of each team going to the individual classification of those riders finishing together in their formations. Roche and his Histor squad had been out around the 44.5km St Etienne course early, and had come back saying they had never seen anything like it. 'I doubt whether anyone will beat the hour on those hills,' declared Roche – two hours before the Histor team finished in 56:11, scoring the team's first team trial win in five years. The Irishman was all smiles as he went to receive the leader's jersey. He was back after injury, and judging by the way both the public and the press mobbed him, he was still as popular as ever. The big loser in the team time trial was Chiappucci, whose Carrera team (with whom Roche won the 1989 Tour de France) lost 1:48 to Histor – Chiappucci slumped to 27th, losing his overall chances. Fignon's Castorama-Raleigh team fared better – losing only 35 seconds to take second place for the team, and keeping Fignon in fourth place overall. Indurain's team lost 58 seconds and he slipped to seventh, 47 seconds behind Roche.

The sunlit peloton rolls by the Aqueduc de Roquefavour, north of Marseilles

Paris-Nice is always a battle of seconds as the leaders closely mark one another; and the following day's 179km stage from Nîmes to Marseille provided little opportunity to break the vigilance. Adriano Baffi (Ariostea) won the eventual field sprint along the quay in Marseille, while Roche turned his thoughts to Mont Faron, above Toulouse and only 24 hours away. 'Mont Faron does not frighten me,' he said, 'and if I lose the lead, I still have two more days to get it back.' And lose it he did, on the narrow climb of five kilometres that ended the 164km stage from Marseille; his 10th place, 62 seconds behind Indurain, still left room for hope. However, Roche suffered terribly on the climb, and it was clear that although he still had his natural talent, his form was not quite enough – as the Col d'Eze would highlight later. The 1987 world champion fell back to second overall, 15 seconds behind Indurain, who had hauled his tall body up the twisting, steep slope to nowhere to win by 35 seconds from Fignon, who said: 'I tried to follow Indurain, but he killed me – so I limited my losses.'

At next morning's start in Toulon, LeMond, wearing his world champion jersey, was in a talkative mood. Clearly enjoying the race, he was sad not to be among the leaders: 'Yesterday was the first time I felt like a racing cyclist, and then the percentages went up and I was struggling on the climbs. I really want to do well this season, but for the moment it's up to the rest of the team.' So it was clear as the race headed out of Toulon on the seventh stage to Mandelieu-La Napoule that only three riders were out for victory – Roche, Indurain and Fignon. The remaining stages, although certainly difficult, were well known by the leaders and surprise attacks would be unlikely. Chiappucci was becoming

Jean-François Bernard

unassailable in the mountains competition, but although the race toured the hills of Provence during this 178km stage, only the Col de St Arnoux and the narrow Tanneron counted for mountain points.

Robert Millar, the Scottish climber on the Z team, won the first climb as he tried desperately to improve his 12th place overall; but the race never allowed him a lead of more than 65 seconds, and it was Chiappucci who was first over the Tanneron, followed by Indurain and Frenchman Eric Boyer (Z). In fact, Millar crashed, and was lucky not to be run over by the Banesto team car, whose driver seemed not to see the fallen Z professional. 'I could smell his brakes,' said Millar – it had been that close.

In Mandelieu, the heads of state all finished together. The field came off the Tanneron in groups, and LeMond found elite company at the back with Charly Mottet (RMO) – both finishing in a group of 30 over 22 minutes behind.

The final stage of the race, from Mandelieu to Nice, takes 30 minutes by car along the Mediterranean. But for the 128 survivors, it was a 102km road race and then, for the top 70 overall, a 12km time trial up the Col d'Eze to decide the winner. The morning's road race decided nothing: Mottet went ahead with Brazilian team-mate Mauro Ribeiro over the top of the 900m Col de Vence (where a puncture two years ago robbed Roche of victory), and with 45km to go the pair raced to the Promenade des Anglais in Nice. It was touch and go along the windy seafront from Nice airport, but they survived by 27 seconds and Mottet gave the victory to his young team-mate, who crossed the line applauding Mottet. Yes, it was all very nice in Nice; but after a short break, the showdown at the Col d'Eze – on a course that climbs from sea level to 550m in its last ten kilometres – would decide the race.

Roche still hoped that 15 seconds would not be too much. After all, last year he had won the climb, beating Indurain by 32 seconds, although he lost the race by 13 seconds in the end. A similar ride this year would give him a clear victory. Fignon, Roche, Indurain, separated by two minutes, was the reverse starting order. It was quickly apparent that Fignon had nothing left: he suffered and slipped away to finish an unhappy fourth overall, after Luc Leblanc, his Castorama team-mate, produced an inspired ride to finish second on the climb, moving ahead of Fignon overall. The best time was done early on by Jean-François Bernard, reminding everyone of his similar time trial victory on Mont Ventoux in the 1987 Tour de France.

But fine as Bernard's victory was, there was only one battle to watch – that between Indurain and Roche, the top two for the past two years. Roche again had the disadvantage of starting two minutes ahead of Indurain; but he also had the confidence born of four previous wins on Eze and victory in the race itself in 1981. By half way, victory was possible: he passed through the check 12 seconds slower than Bernard but 5 seconds faster than Indurain. However, on the steepest part of the mountain Roche's progress slowed – and Indurain conceded only 2 seconds more before the line. The Irishman had lost Paris-Nice by 8 seconds – the exact time difference that took the Tour de France away from Fignon and gave it to LeMond last year. But unlike Fignon then, Roche was not unduly dismayed: he had known all long that Indurain was the better man, and the Col d'Eze had simply confirmed it. More importantly, his performance proved that he was back, and fitness would follow in due course – that was more significant than victory this time on the Côte d'Azur.

After losing a minute at Mont Faron, Roche was still optimistic about his chances with two days still to go

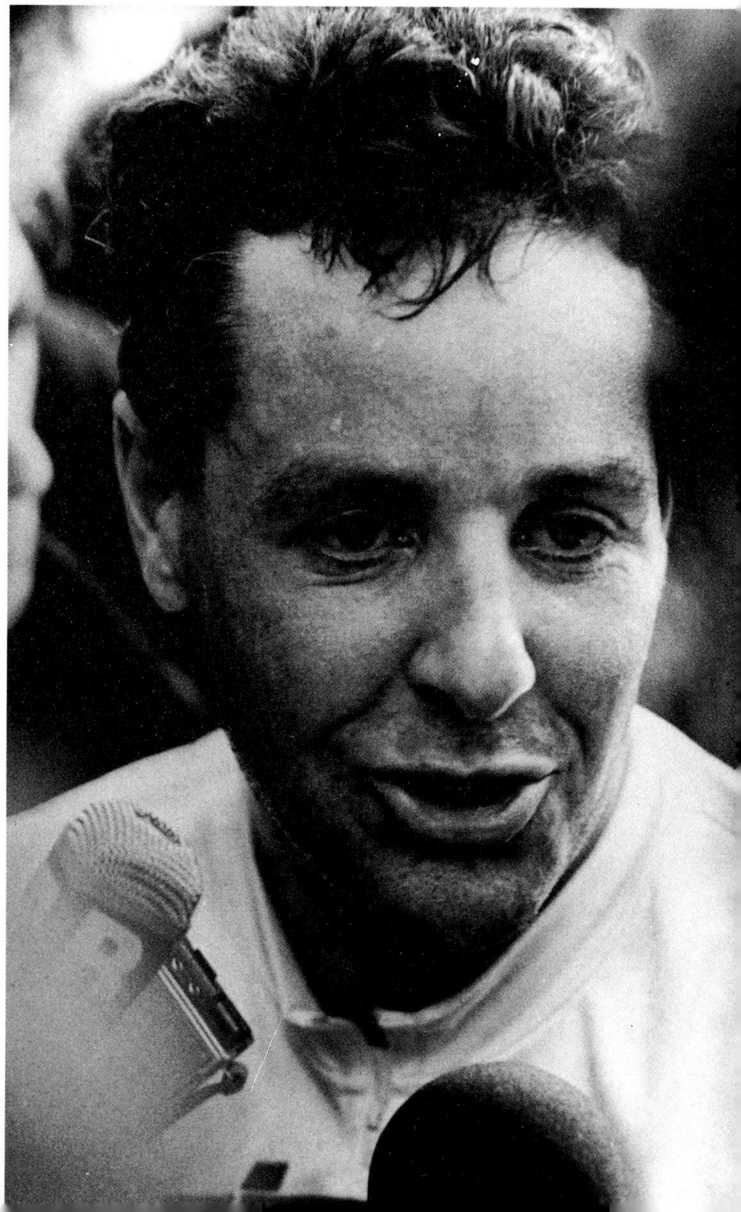

Tirreno-Adriatico: 7-14 March

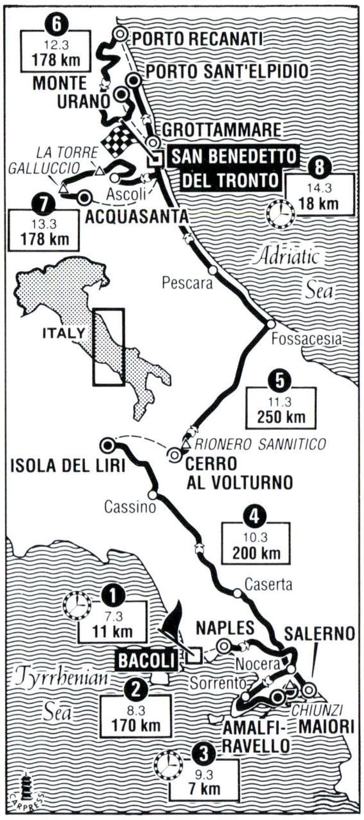

Tirreno-Adriatico, Italy: 1011km

The lucrative Tirreno-Adriatico stage race in Italy, 'sister' to Paris-Nice, failed to find a home winner for the fifth year running when Switzerland's Toni Rominger, the 1989 winner, once again finished triumphant. The consolation prize for the Italian fans was that Rominger rides for an Italian sponsor, Chateau d'Ax. But in 1988 Switzerland had claimed victory with Erich Mächler (Carrera), while in 1987 Denmark's Rölf Sorensen (Ariostea) carried off the spoils. This latest success provided confirmation that 29-year-old Rominger is indeed a rider with world-class ability, a talent he first revealed at the end of 1989, when he won the Tour of Lombardy and secured second place in the inaugural Perrier World Cup.

The critical leg in this year's edition of the 'Race of the two Seas' came as early as stage two, when Rominger virtually repeated his winning solo attack at Lombardy. On this 175km second stage from Naples to Maiori, the lanky, dark-haired Swiss attacked on the last climb and stayed away to the line, despite a strong chase from Ireland's Sean Kelly (PDM), Italy's Maurizio Fondriest (Del Tongo), Belgium's Luc Roosen (Histor-Sigma), Switzerland's Daniel Steiger (Frank), France's Gilles Delion (Helvetia-La Suisse) and new Polish sensation Zenon Jaskula (Diana-Colnago). In the end, Rominger finished the stage 1:47 clear of second-placed Delion, ironically his nearest rival at Lombardy as well. Yet, while Rominger's overall lead seemed safe, the six stages preceding the seaside finish at San Benedetto-del-Tronto did not pass without drama.

Rominger adding another winner's blue jersey to his collection

The stage three uphill time trial over a 6.8km route from Amalfi to Ravello posed the first threat to his lead. Heavy rain made the Italian roads – hardly renowned for their quality at the best of times – particularly dangerous. Fate could have turned nastier than it did; abating rain saw Jean-Claude Leclercq take the stage, but only by 0:09 from Rominger.

There were more exciting times ahead for Rominger and his Chateau d'Ax team-mates on stage four, when they were forced into a chase of six breakaways led by Jaskula after the second-placed Steiger's Frank team declined the opportunity to help in the pursuit. Ultimately, though, it was Steiger who paid the price. The break, reduced to three riders – Jaskula and the Italian duo of Massimiliano Lelli (Ariostea) and Giorgio Furlan (Diana-Colnago) – was reeled in to a safe margin for Rominger. But Jaskula's third place on the stage, behind Lelli and Furlan, was enough to oust Steiger from his overall second position.

Finishing stage four with a 2:23 overall lead on Jaskula, Rominger's battle for overall victory was overshadowed, on the 249km fifth stage from Al Volturno to Porto Sant'Elpidio, when a dramatic bunch sprint led to affairs being settled hot-headedly, both on and off the saddle. At the centre of the fracas was Italian Mario Cipollini (Del Tongo), who catapulted himself up to the front by grabbing the jersey of an angry Kelly and then impeded the line of East German Olaf Ludwig

Eddy Planckaert celebrates his return to the Panasonic fold by winning the penultimate stage of Tirreno-Adriatico

(Panasonic-Sportlife). The race jury, after hearing a protest, disqualified Cipollini from first place for illegal riding; the stage win went to Belgium's Eric Vanderaerden (Buckler), who crossed the line in second place, and Ludwig moved up to second position.

It was on the sixth stage, a 192km run from Porto Recanati to Monte Urano, that the 1990 Tirreno-Adriatico received its biggest shake-up, and Rominger returned to the limelight. Leclercq, building up for a strong spring classic campaign, attacked with only one kilometre to go on the steep ascent of the last circuit to the Monte Urano finish line. Rominger, aware that Leclercq was dangerously strong on such climbs, contained the assault – even though the Helvetia-La Suisse Frenchman notched up his second stage win here. Rominger finished at 0:08 in fifth place with three others – Italians Maurizio Fondriest (Del Tongo) and Lelli in third and fourth places, and Ireland's Martin Earley (PDM) sixth.

Rominger's overall lead was now 2:31 on Leclercq, who had ousted Jaskula from second place – thanks to his win by two seconds over Dutch champion Frans Maassen (Buckler). While Leclercq moved up from ninth to second place overall, Jaskula's stage finish, 0:38 after Rominger, saw him fall to sixth place overall, at 2:52. Luck also changed here for Leclercq's team-mate, Delion, who by finishing eighth at 0:15, moved from fourth to third overall.

After Monte Urano, Rominger's victory seemed inevitable. Belgian Eddy Planckaert, recently signed up with his old Panasonic team, edged out the Danish duo of Sorensen and Sören Lilholt (Histor-Sigma) in the bunch sprint finale to stage seven. But with a safe lead, and a time trial well suited to Rominger's talents still to come, not much could intervene between the Swiss and the winner's podium. And in fact not even an uncharacteristically 'poor' performance in the closing 18.3km race of truth prevented Rominger from winning. Finishing 11th on the stage, 0:40 short of an impressive Eric Breukink (PDM), Rominger still retained enough of a lead – 2:31 – to assure him of victory.

One of the remarkable aspects of this final time trial was the performance of the revitalised Jaskula. The neo-pro finished third on the stage at 0:19, just one second behind second placed Sorensen – but it was enough to reshuffle the overall order and put the blond Pole back up to second place. Leclercq, so aggressive throughout the week, was unable to muster the energy to defend his gains and fell back to fourth overall. But the highlight of the final day was the inspiring win of the Dutchman Breukink – who clocked his winning time with an average speed of 49.348 kph.

A brilliant time trial by Polish newcomer Zenon Jaskula earned him second place overall behind Rominger

Milan-San Remo: 17 March

Gianni Bugno of the Chateau d'Ax team, a 26-year-old Italian long deserving of a major victory, became the first 1990 Perrier World Cup leader with his victory in this Italian classic. Bugno won in record time with a solo break over the final 32km to defeat the late-chasing West German Rolf Gölz (Buckler) by 4 seconds.

It was not only the fastest Milan-San Remo on record but also one of the most extraordinary. What made the Italian classic so remarkable was the unprecedented abandonment of nearly every pre-race favourite with 100km still to go, when an early break by half the field left the stars floundering up to 15 minutes behind. The vital split happened when strong sidewinds hit the peloton after only 20km – the complacent heavyweights left joking at the back included Frenchman Laurent Fignon (Castorama), Ireland's Sean Kelly (PDM), Dutchmen Steven Rooks and Gert-Jan Theunnisse (both Panasonic), Belgian Claude Criquielion (Lotto), Australia's Phil Anderson (TVM), Belgians Eric Vanderaerden and Edwig Van Hooydonck (both Buckler), Italians Guido Bontempi and Claudio Chiappucci (both Carrera), and the Americans Greg LeMond (Z) and Andy Hampsten (7-Eleven).

Nevertheless, the absence of the top men from the anticipated battle over the crucial climbs – the Cipressa at 270km and the notorious Poggio at 290km – didn't lessen the worth of Bugno's victory, which was the first for an Italian since Francesco Moser's win in 1984. Bugno's time of 6:25:06 was the fastest in the 81-year history of the race: riding at an average speed of 45.806 kph, his performance significantly bettered that of seven-

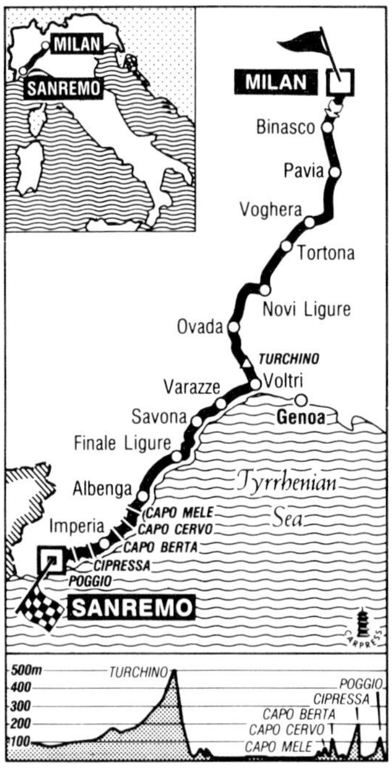

Milan-San Remo, Italy: 294km

Bugno's victory was all the more impressive because of the quality of the chasing group, seen here on the Poggio

At San Remo, Bugno became the first leader of the 1990 World Cup

time Milan-San Remo champion Eddy Merckx, whose record of 44.805kph had stood since 1967.

Additionally, many people would say that the dark-haired Italian, plus the six hardy chasers who came so close to reeling him in, and the rest of the 110 finishers, had taught their more exalted comrades a much-needed lesson. Viewed in the context of their loud complaints about the rigours and trials they suffer because of the demands of their sponsors, the media and the public, the withdrawal of so many stars two-thirds of the way through the race hardly improved their public image. Why did they let it happen? The question had everyone scratching their heads in the aftermath of this first of thirteen World Cup rounds. How did the stars get left behind? Why did they ride with so little conviction, allowing such a massive break to escape? And why did they leave it so long to chase?

From all the confusion there has emerged one factor very revealing of the changing state of professional cycling. It is now clear that riders with star billing are no longer guaranteed protected status within the peloton. With the growing emphasis on the accumulation of FICP ranking points for future contract security, the lowliest domestique is as hungry for victory as the stars, and just as opportunistic when he gets the chance. And at Milan-San Remo, we saw how.

Two other factors influenced the outcome. First, there was a strong initial tail wind which suddenly turned into a cross-wind when the race turned left at Binasco, breaking the peloton into four echelons, the last of which contained most of the favourites. And second, there was the lethargic mind set of the stars, who anticipated the traditional Milan-San Remo scenario – early breaks are 'always' caught, so they were safe to amble along at the back until the pressure was 'supposed' to come on, on the climbs of the Cipressa and the Poggio.

As the cycling world gathered for the start, under the majestic façade of Milan's Gothic cathedral, there was no doubting the sincerity of their ambition. Kelly, a former winner and the defending World Cup champion, said, 'If you ask me which classic I really want to win this year, I would say Milan-San Remo. It's a very prestigious race, and to win a race like that early in the season is great. This puts the year off to a great start and makes you feel so much more comfortable going into the Belgian classics.' Fignon, the top rider on the FICP-Perrier world rankings, and the winner in 1988 and 1989, was looking to score an unprecedented hat-trick in the Primavera. His major objective was still to prove himself in the 'tougher' Belgian classics, but no one could doubt his determination. 'I have the condition . . . and I know what I need to do.' And so continued the expression of ambitions doomed to be frustrated . . .

Not surprisingly, Milan-San Remo also provoked aspirations among the Italian contingent. Former world champions Moreno Argentin (Ariostea) and Maurizio Fondriest (Del Tongo) were expected to be in at the kill, as were such racers as Adriano Baffi (Ariostea), Chiappucci (Carrera) – and Bugno. Good performances were also expected from the Italian-based foreigners, including the Swiss Tony Rominger (Chateau d'Ax), fresh from winning Tirreno-Adriatico, and Rolf Sörensen of Denmark (Ariostea).

Leaving Milan, and beginning the 156km southward stage to the Mediterranean town of Voltri, the race was expected to be a simple procession to the coast, with the Turchino Pass, just outside Voltri, providing the only obstacle. However, the reality was very different. Experiencing crisp temperatures under the blue sky, the 213 starters were soon cruising along with the assisting wind, but seemed unprepared for the mighty gust from the left when the course turned to the south-east, splitting the peloton into echelons after the fashion of the Belgian classics. And while the first two echelons regrouped, the last two – about eighty riders, including most of the stars – failed to do so.

Milan cathedral

The well-placed Dag-Otto Lauritzen of Norway (7-Eleven) commented on the split: 'I never saw those guys. They must have been sitting in the back. Suddenly, about twenty guys went away up front and the rest of the group started to chase. After that , we looked around and there were none of the favourites. And we kept riding.'

Among the first twenty aggressors were Dutch riders Eddy Schurer and Jacques Hanegraaf and Jesper Skibby from Denmark (all TVM), Gölz and Dutchman Gerrit Solleveld (Buckler), Henk Lubberding (Panasonic), also from Holland, and the promising French rider Gilles Delion (Helvetia-La Suisse). After ten kilometres, the next echelon of eighty-eight riders bridged the gap, bringing with it names like Sorensen, Argentin, Fondriest, Baffi and Bugno. The Italians were inevitably intent on extending their lead on Fignon's group as far as possible. Also up there was a substantial 7-Eleven presence – Steve Bauer from Canada, Lauritzen, Americans Davis Phinney and Bob Roll and Englishman Sean Yates – along with Mexican PDM rider, Raúl Alcalá.

Behind, the third echelon of fourteen riders had been caught by the rear group, and the two tried vainly to bridge the gap. For nearly 100km, the margin hung at around 1:45. Phil Anderson of TVM was one of many in the field left wondering where the race would now go. 'At first, we (TVM) didn't chase because we had riders up front in the break,' he said. 'Then we started to work our butts off as the race started on. But we couldn't get closer than two minutes to them by the Turchino.'

The fact that many of the top men had riders from their teams up front, along with the extraordinary size of the group and the growing reluctance of any 'name' to chase and possibly benefit a rival, all contributed to the group becoming unmanageable. By the Turchino's windy summit, the gap was up to 4:30. And between the top of the Turchino and the first feed zone in Savona, 40km later, that deficit grew to 15 minutes. In Savona, the rear group rolled to a stop, as the lead group, driven by the Ariostea and Chateau d'Ax teams, sensed that the race was now in their control. Some riders, like Kelly, continued on for 'training' purposes to the next feed station at Alassio, 50km away; but they never looked like re-entering the stakes. 'For all of us, there just wasn't any point in going further,' said Anderson. 'They (the leaders) were away and working so hard.' Fignon's reaction emphasised the sense of incredulity felt by the stars. 'It's never been like that before,' he said. 'In Milan-San Remo, the pace is always irregular. There's an early push, then it's calm, and then the race begins. It's really surprising that so many big leaders have been left behind like this. We didn't know what was going on up front. And when we started to chase, we got closer, but in the end it was impossible.'

For the next 90km, the leading group of about 125 riders prepared for the expected onslaught on the Cipressa – the second last climb of the race, which last year saw the PDM team of Kelly and Alcalá dominate the race until the winning attack by Fignon and Dutchman Frans Maassen. But this year, there was no Fignon and no Kelly. What there was, though, was Bugno. Along with Italy's Angelo Canzonieri (Gis-Benotto), he attacked at Imperia, with 33km to go, and 8km before the foot of the Cipressa. They reached the obstacle with a small lead, but after only a kilometre of steady climbing, Canzonieri faded. Bugno sensed his rival's weakness and upped the ante with a strong surge. Canzonieri dropped his head and wilted in Bugno's wake with 3km left to climb and 24km still to go. Behind Bugno – who was then lying 18th on the FICP rankings – a series of heavy counter-moves was taking place. Roll was one of the first to make a challenge, albeit unsuccessfully. Then Rolf Gölz got away with five others – Fondriest, Argentin, Delion, Skibby and Frenchman Jean-Claude Colotti of RMO. Down the Cipressa, the chasers were never far behind – just 20 seconds with 20km remaining. But on the 10km stretch along the coast road before the Poggio, Bugno's steady cadence never faltered, and as he swung up onto the Poggio, his lead was still 15 seconds.

News of the stars all jumping ship had filtered back to the finish line at San Remo, along with reports that the *Primavera* was under Italian control. Local spectators waiting at the top of the Poggio, and furiously downing cheap wine and salami, seemed to revel in the prospect of Fignon's misfortune.

One kilometre from the top of the Poggio, nearing a level stretch, this already startling Milan-San Remo

While Criquielion, Kelly and Fignon reminisced at the back, the race was happening without them . . .

. . . Van Hooydonck and his team-mates also missed the bus to San Remo

Gölz chasing Bugno on the Poggio

caught light again when Gölz, who had had Bugno in his sights for most of his courageous 32km break, set off in pursuit of the Italian leader. With a 5-second deficit before the corkscrew, 3.2km descent to the flat, finishing 800m straight, the West German seemed to be within reach of his prey. With Bugno leading, Gölz a few seconds behind, and the five remaining pursuers at 15 seconds, it only needed an untimely spill or puncture to throw the race into further disarray – and it very nearly happened. Bugno misjudged a switchback right turn with two kilometres left, and would certainly have come to grief had he not been able to brake and adjust his line. But in any case, Gölz was unable to take advantage of Bugno's mishap, the lack of straight stretches making it difficult for him to pick up the necessary chasing speed. His descent was no more confident than Bugno's, which made it inevitable that Bugno would hold his narrow lead. A huge roar from the Italian crowds lining the roadside greeted the dark-eyed Bugno as he pedalled for the finish, looking round for Gölz five times in those final 800 metres. But the West German had blown his last chance on the descent, and Bugno finished 4 seconds clear of Gölz, 20 seconds ahead of a points-hungry Delion, anxious to prove that his second place in last year's Tour of Lombardy was more than good fortune, and 31 seconds clear of Argentin, Fondriest, Colotti and Skibby, in that order.

The main group of 59 riders came in at 1:02 and a further group of 15 at 7:44. With just 110 finishers from 213 starters, one can only imagine what the outcome would have been had the laggards – if riders like Laurent Fignon can be called laggardly – been more alert in the early stages.

Bugno's solo charge to San Remo heralded the start of a brilliant season for the Italian

Criterium International: 24-25 March

The frustration of the notorious mass abandonment during Milan-San Remo by stars like Frenchman Laurent Fignon (Castorama) and Ireland's Sean Kelly (PDM) still rankled when they signed up for the Criterium International one week later, and this two-day stage race in southern France provided an opportunity for the stars to come up with the performances they had so signally failed to produce at the *Primavera*.

Organized by the Société du Tour de France, the Criterium International has become a popular race in its fifty-nine years. Comprising a rolling flat road stage, a mountain leg and a short time trial, this weekend event requires that its winner possesses true all-round ability. Relatively short, yet difficult, stages make for a fast, hard race. The Criterium International is also ideal preparation for the Tour of Flanders the following week.

This year's Criterium International had plenty of worthy candidates to field against Fignon and Kelly. There were two other former winners, Irishman Stephen Roche (Histor) and Spaniard Miguel Indurain (Banesto), along with strong contenders like Indurain's Spanish team-mate Julian Gorospe and the French riders Charly Mottet (RMO), Jean-Claude Leclercq and Gilles Delion (both Helvetia-La Suisse) – Delion's stage-racing potential having been revealed by his third place in Tirreno-Adriatico only ten days before. However, little was known about the early season form of world champion Greg LeMond (Z), his fellow American Andy Hampsten (7-Eleven), and the Soviet newcomer Viatcheslav Ekimov (Panasonic-Sportlife).

The race began under its customary sunny blue skies with a 200.5km first stage from Pertuis to Apt. The high standard of racing the Criterium International demands from its participants was immediately evident: Greg LeMond, struggling to keep up with the pace, eventually dropped off the back. He was still out of shape, fighting a viral infection, and abandoned after only 100km. Five

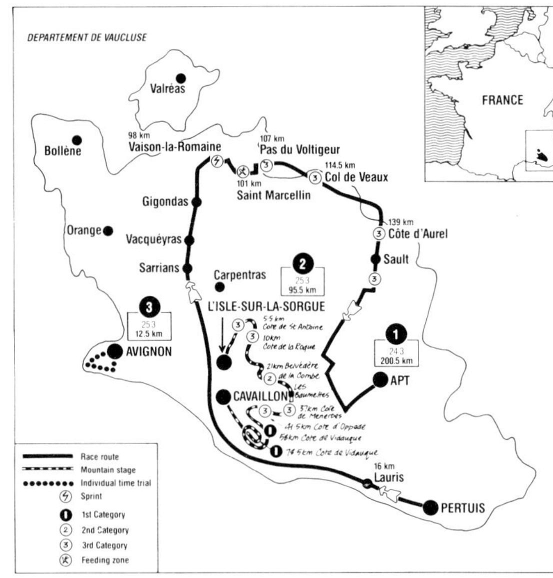

Criterium International, France, 308.5km

kilometres later the pace increased again when American Ron Kiefel (7-Eleven) formed a fourteen-man breakaway including Indurain and Delion, Frenchmen Jean-François Bernard (Toshiba), Ronan Pensec (Z) and Eric Caritoux (RMO), and the ONCE team-mates Johnny Weltz of Denmark and Stephen Hodge of Australia. But the break had no more than a minute's lead before the peloton, led by Fignon's Castorama team, began to reel them in, achieving a regroupment 20km from the finish. On the rolling hills approaching Apt, it was Fignon who made the initial contact for the peloton: his intentions were clear.

A barrage of attacks followed, but nothing of consequence until the three-man assault of Kiefel, Frenchman Pascal Lino (RMO) and Norwegian Atle Kvalsvoll (Z), with six kilometres to go. The peloton reacted quickly and, with two kilometres left, it looked

The Criterium is a mini-Tour de France in March

Kiefel was an easy winner of the first stage

as though the leaders' hopes were doomed.

Passing the red 'kite' denoting one kilometre to go, Kiefel bolted from the rear of the break to attack alone. Winding his way through the narrow streets of sandstone houses, the hardy American milked every advantage he could from the complex approach to the finish. And despite the Kelly-led peloton hot on his heels, he finished first, with two seconds to spare. Kiefel's defence of his tenuous leadership became even more difficult when Hampsten, whom he could have expected to be his strongest team-mate, abandoned in the aggressive 92.5km stage from l'Isle-sur-Sorgue to Cavaillon – no doubt affected by the seven mountain primes and the gusty cold tailwind.

After several breaks, the vital move came on the first of two climbs up the narrow, twisting 8km Tête des Buisses. All the favourites were massed up front. After the race passed the barren summit, where a small lead group had formed, an attack was launched by the Swiss Niki Rüttimann (Helvetia-La Suisse) and Mottet, pursued by Fignon, Delion, Roche, Kelly and several others, including Kiefel.

Delion, hungry for a stage win if not overall victory, counterattacked immediately – but although he gained a strong advantage, he was quickly caught by Leclercq and Fignon, who knew any lead on the expert time triallists like Roche or Indurain would be a valuable advantage later. Going up the last climb, it was again Delion who set the fast pace to give them a 0:40 lead on the chasing Roche and Lino – themselves 0:35 ahead of the main group – and by the summit the leaders were a minute clear. Just as impressive was Delion's lightning pace on the descent, which nearly took out Fignon as he missed a turn and took a short-cut through the shrubbery! But all Fignon had to do now was stay away from Roche and Indurain – stage wins were not on his agenda, and he knew he could beat Delion and Leclercq in the time trial.

A rare moment of serenity for Laurent Fignon

The stage ended with a win for Delion, a second place for Leclercq which took him to first overall with Fignon second overall at 0:02; most significantly, however, Fignon's main rivals finished 1:11 in arrears. And the closing 12.5km time trial in Avignon proved that Fignon had played his cards well – Leclercq produced a disappointing 29th at 1:21, which took him to third overall; Delion's 19th at 1:06 secured him second place overall; but Fignon's fifth place at 0:37 to the fancied winner, Ekimov, gave him overall victory. For Fignon, the bitterness of Milan-San Remo had been sweetened by the more familiar taste of victory.

Delion leads Leclercq and Fignon on the winning break

Tour of Flanders: 1 April

As the hot sun beat down on the 194 starters in the 73rd Tour of Flanders, one could have been forgiven for imagining it was midsummer. In fact it was April, but with temperatures expected to soar to 24° Celsius it was curious weather for a race that has previously been notorious for its cold, wet and often snowy conditions. But despite the heat, a large crowd was present in the imposing setting of the market square of St Niklaas, where most of the stars had gathered for this second rendezvous in the Perrier World Cup series.

The 'Ronde' is 262km long, and its thirteen bergs, that come in the last 100km through deepest Flanders, invariably decide the outcome of this most revered of Belgian classics. Over the years, the race has been kindest to its home nation, according Belgium fifty-five wins. The Netherlands, with nine wins, comes a poor second, and other countries consider themselves lucky if they manage more than one winner; there has never, since its inception in 1913, been a winner from outside Europe. Irishman Sean Kelly (PDM) was one foreigner hoping for a victory before retirement, but this brilliantly sunny day was destined to go down as a black one in his career. There were also two Italians causing early-season blues amongst the rest – Maurizio

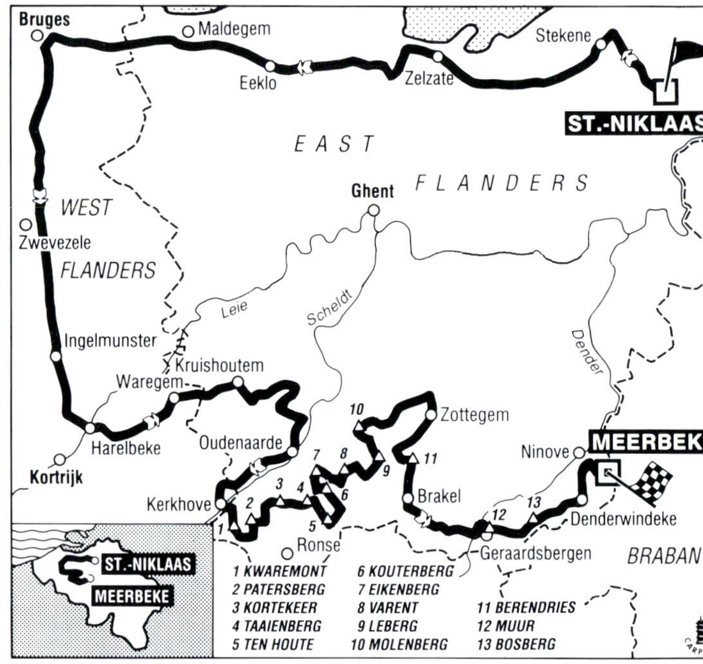

Tour of Flanders, Belgium: 262km

The race started, as always, in the market square at St Niklaas

Fondriest (Del Tongo) and Moreno Argentin (Ariostea). Argentin had been talked about as the man to beat ever since Paris-Nice, which seemed to herald his return to a lead role after two seasons playing bit parts.

Belgians fans are weaned on cycling, and plenty of noise seems to be essential to the atmosphere. Pre-race commentators, introducing former winners on the high platform erected in the centre of the town square, were sometimes barely audible over the band, and the riders themselves had to push through dense, noisy crowds to take their places for the long day ahead: the finish at Meerbeke is only a brisk 90-minute cycle ride away – unless, of course, you have entered for the Ronde, in which case seven hours is a better estimate.

Bauer and Bontempi on the Patersberg

Argentin and Peiper setting the pace at the head of the break

Frustrated by the failure of his many attacks, Fignon eventually quit

There were no challenges to break the rhythm of the peloton during the opening four hours, as the race headed away from Ostend before turning to the hills – in such pleasant weather, few riders tried to steal a lead that they knew would be taken back in the final three hours of racing. Once the race left St Niklaas, the Belgian fans were off in the opposite direction, speeding away in cars to the first of the thirteen climbs – the Old Kwaremont, a 12 per cent cobbled gradient which marks the start of the race's final phase, 98km from the end. But by the time the race arrived among the cobbled corrugations Sean Kelly was already in hospital. He had sustained a badly broken right collarbone in a crash on the very first stretch of cobbles, in the village of Lede. Kelly, three times second in this race, is now thirty-three, and with only two more seasons left before retirement, his chances of winning it look slim. More importantly, the likeable Irishman – whose consistency has made him the most respected rider on the circuit – would be out of competition for at least four weeks, and out of the World Cup series until round six – the Wincanton

Fignon climbing with Van der Poel

Classic – in July. In short, he had lost his World Cup without having the chance to defend it.

Kelly described the crash that left him lying on the cobblestones after 136km: 'I was in the first 25 riders when we arrived at the first stretch of cobblestones; as usual, the pace was fast, and there were the usual fights to get to the front. There was a corner in the village slightly uphill, and as the road narrowed, someone slowed at the front. I rubbed a cyclist and then I was hit from behind: I couldn't get my hand out and fell directly onto my right shoulder. I wasn't going fast, but it was such a heavy fall . . .' He acknowledged that he was 'disappointed, after putting so much into my early season preparation in January and February, but what can you do? Hopefully, I'll be back to do well in my last Tour de France.'

At about the same time that Kelly was in trouble, there was another event of significance when Argentin punctured and rejoined. It was then that the Italian realised that he could win this year's Tour of Flanders: 'I got back to the race with incredible ease,' Argentin reported. 'I knew then I was very strong.' But there was still a lot of work to be done. Ahead were the three early leaders – Italian Fabio Roscioli (Del Tongo) and Belgians Chris Scharmin (LA-William) and Noel Szostek (SEFB).

Once into the hills, Scharmin faltered and then, after yo-yo-ing on each climb, Roscioli also left Szostek to the chasers behind. Constantly under pressure, the field split and regrouped after each of the early climbs, but after the Taaienberg, with 83km to go, a group of some fourteen riders – including Fondriest, Belgian Eddy Planckaert and Australian Allan Peiper (both Panasonic) and Belgian Rudy Dhaenens (PDM) tried to break away. Roscioli's lead, once in double figures, had tumbled to a couple of minutes when, with 80km to go, he punctured and lost a further 15 seconds. Eleven kilometres later, on the Eikenberg, he managed to find the strength to hang on to the back of an advance party of six that caught and overtook him.

The damage had been done by Belgian Michel Dernies (Weinmann), a rider who can spring the occasional surprise. Dernies had forced the pace up the Eikenberg, splitting off Peiper, Dhaenens, Italian Giuseppe Calcaterra (Chateau d'Ax), Per Pedersen of Denmark (RMO) and Switzerland's up-and-coming Rolf Järmann (Frank). Argentin, clearly worried by the move, got no help from the field and bridged the gap alone, and a puncture to Dernies helped Frenchman Laurent Fignon (Castorama) join the leaders; Dernies, with a fresh rear wheel, had just got back on his bike when Fignon came by, and together they caught up with the break.

With 52km to go, this nine-man lead group now tackled the 14 per cent climb of the Molenberg. Their lead grew to a minute, but the chase behind was never less than intense, and the leaders had no time to hesitate – especially with the fearsome Mur de Grammont to come. Fignon, on his best-ever early season form, tried to rip the breakaway apart, but his violent acceleration – which took him clear with Pedersen – only worked to Argentin's advantage: as Fignon and Pedersen slowed,

Argentin and Dhaenens were never likely to be caught

the Venetian attacked and went by them both.

This happened towards the top of the Berendries climb, with 31km and two climbs to go, and a lot of riders still frisky enough to spoil the result. The six riders around Fignon would not help him chase Argentin and Dhaenens, who were building up a tenuous 40-second lead, and his frustration was underlined by his now pointless accelerations. And the field, constantly reforming, was never out of contention; more than a hundred would reach the finish line in Meerbeke, and the two hoping to be there first were Dhaenens and Argentin.

Dhaenens, a Flemish-speaking Belgian in his eighth season as a professional, had previously finished second and third in Paris-Roubaix, but he was still looking for one big win, and surely – over roads he knew so well – it was now. He was stronger than Argentin on the climbs, thundering – or clattering – up the Mur de Geraardsbergen ahead of the Italian. The climb is narrow and cobbled and, with its 18 per cent gradient, so steep that all following cars are diverted to minimize the risk of blocking the road. But the crowds are as big as ever, and with a Belgian in the lead, their voices echoed around the narrow corridor of the Mur.

The Geraardsbergen also marked the end of Fignon's race; worn out by his constantly frustrated attacks, he retired on the climb after he and the rest of the breakaway – including the brave Roscioli – had been swept up in the streets of Geraardsbergen. But there was a new urgency now: with only the Bosberg climb to come before the final dash for Meerbeke, the Panasonic team took up the chase. Belgian champion Carlo Bomans (Weinmann), the Dutch Panasonic rider John Talen, Swiss Niki Rüttiman of Helvetia-La Suisse, the East German Olympic and world team trial champion Jan Schur (Chateau d'Ax) and Fondriest made a last-ditch attempt to catch Argentin and Dhaenens.

At this point, Dhaenens' team manager told him not to lead Argentin at all in the final kilometre. Argentin was ready for that, however; he manoeuvred Dhaenens into the lead and left him there, only passing him in the sprint finish. The Italian had won his first classic – two years after winning his third Liège-Bastogne-Liège and the Tour of Lombardy. He was clearly delighted at his comeback: 'To win this Tour of Flanders was more important to me than to win Liège-Bastogne-Liège for a fourth time,' he said later. 'My change of teams this winter has been good for me, and I get on better with my manager Giancarlo Ferretti than I did with Felice Gimondi, my former boss at Bianchi . . . I am only the third Italian to win.' His victory, with his fourth place in Milan-San Remo, also gave him the lead in the Perrier World Cup.

Third place went to Talen, who finished just eleven seconds behind, outsprinting Bomans, and Fondriest tailed off to take fifth place. The Italian Del Tongo team had ridden well, but Fondriest had been unable to finish what Roscioli had started. But after being out front practically all day, Roscioli still managed to finish only 67 seconds behind, in 38th place: if there had been a 'man of the match' award, the 24-year-old Italian would certainly have won it.

Ghent-Wevelgem: 4 April

After seeing foreigners carry off the first round of Belgium's Flemish classics, local riders looked to Ghent-Wevelgem as their last chance to win some glory. And to the relief of the worried crowds of Flemish spectators, disillusioned by the unsuccessful performances of Belgian riders in the early classics, to say nothing of sponsors and teams, all waiting at the finish in Wevelgem, the day had a happy ending. It was the blond Belgian Herman Frison, of Histor-Sigma, who won the mid-week race from compatriot Johan Museeuw (Lotto-Superclub) and Italy's Franco Ballerini (Del Tongo).

Victory in Ghent-Wevelgem – his 21st win in seven years as a professional – marked Frison's greatest success since he won the fourth stage of the 1987 Tour de France. Not that this 28-year-old Flemish rider is not a worthy participant in Belgium's classics; this year, along with his team-mates in Histor-Sigma, he has been active in several important breaks, and last year, Frison finished second in the Tour of Flanders.

At 204km, this year's Ghent-Wevelgem covered a course 72km shorter than last year, but the race pattern was barely affected. The omitted sector was only the flat terrain in the northern part of the route, so that instead of hitting the coast at northern Knokke-Heist, the race headed straight down from Bruges to Ostend.

Held on an extraordinarily sunny day – giving the lie to weather forecasts of snow – the race encountered a strong cross-tailwind, rather than a pure crosswind, at Ostend. So it wasn't until the race veered left at Nieuwport, away from the coast and towards the French border, that any split occurred. Here, an acceleration by the Russian 1989 world championship silver medallist, Dmitri Konyshev of Alfa Lum, temporarily split the peloton into two groups. By Poperinge, 138km into the race, the first group of twenty-six riders, which included 7-Eleven's Canadian Steve Bauer, had gained 50 seconds on the following peloton.

Five kilometres further on the race approached Schomminkel and the first of seven short climbs. As

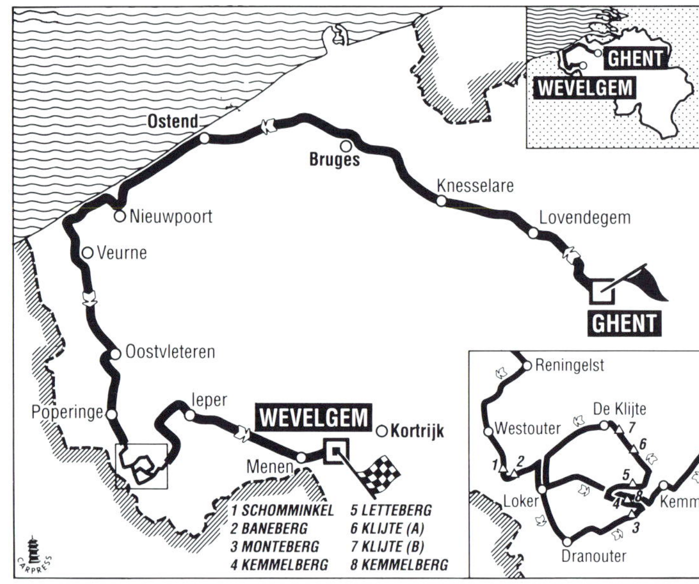

Ghent-Wevelgem, Belgium: 204km

Crosswinds split the peloton on the road to Poperinge

expected, the field was split into five groups by the time the riders reached the fourth climb, the abrupt, 22 per cent, cobbled Kemmelberg. It was Belgian Rudy Dhaenens (PDM), proving his legs were still in good working order after his second place in the Tour of Flanders, who initiated the break with his Dutch team-mate Nico Verhoeven. Approaching the 500-metre-long ascent, their attack was joined by nine others – the Panasonic-Sportlife duo of Belgian Jean-Marie Wampers and Swiss Urs Freuler, Belgian Etienne De Wilde (Histor-Sigma), Poland's Marek Kulas (Diana-Colnago), Konyshev, Bauer, Frison, Ballerini and Museeuw.

It was the type of move Steve Bauer had expected. 'I was watching for a break before the Kemmel. Just when I knew there would be a crosswind, I went [with it] . . . and tagged along,' he said later. With the second peloton of about fifty riders at 10 seconds, and the third group, including Frenchman Laurent Fignon (Castorama) about one minute behind, the following three climbs were taken just as aggressively by the leaders.

Soon after the climbs – whose highlight was the ascent of the Kemmelberg's southern approach, the 23 per cent Kemmeltop – four chasers caught the eleven leaders. They were Frans Maassen from Holland (Buckler), Denmark's Brian Holm (Histor-Sigma), and the Panasonic-Sportlife team-mates, East Germany's Olaf Ludwig and Belgium's Marc Sergeant. With 40km to go, Panasonic's chances of dominating the race were good, given its four riders in the front group of 15, now 0:50 ahead of the main group. However, an attack by Ballerini – reaching for some glory after his Del Tongo leader Maurizio Fondriest crashed on the Kemmelberg – caught out the hesitant Panasonics with 16km to go. Ludwig would have been a near certainty to beat De Wilde in a sprint finish, so this last-minute split must have left Panasonic boss Peter Post fuming.

Ballerini's attack was followed through by Frison, Museeuw, Maassen, Holm and Wampers. The lone

The persistent Herman Frison finally got a classic victory

Panasonic representative, Wampers, was the only one not taking his turn up front, probably hoping that the nine discards would catch his group and produce a sprint win by Ludwig. And that outcome appeared likely when at five kilometres to go there was only a 13-second difference between the two lead groups, with a charging peloton not far adrift and sensing the possibility of a regroupment before the finish.

Bauer, with the group of nine, reflected on his predicament afterwards: 'There was a big group coming back to us, and no one in our group wanted to ride. So I attacked and started everything going again. And then I counterattacked – and that worked, to keep us away from the peloton.' But his acceleration wasn't enough to catch the six leaders, and Frison, aided by team-mate Holm, sprinted clear for the coveted Flemish win ahead of Museeuw and Ballerini, with Wampers in fifth place. Four seconds later, as if to demonstrate what *should* have happened for Panasonic, Ludwig won the sprint for seventh place, ahead of Konyshev, Bauer and Dhaenens.

With Paris-Roubaix approaching, ninth place was a reassuring result for Bauer, who was depending on the Hell of the North to salvage something from an unsuccessful spring season.

Eric Vanderaerden and Uwe Raab on the Kemmelberg

Tour of Texas: 30 March–8 April

Showing surprising all-around ability, 28-year-old American pursuit champion Chris Huber of Coors Light became the first rider in the event's eight-year history to lead the Tour of Texas from first day to last. Huber won the brief prologue time trial at Round Rock, near Austin, and fought off every attack over the following eight stages to keep his four-second advantage. Huber was a worthy winner, taking not only the prologue but also the race's hilliest stage, at Leakey. His minimal lead was seriously endangered only once – on the penultimate stage in Dallas, when the 7-Eleven team pulled out all the stops to protect a late break by their new member, Thomas Craven, but their manoeuvres resulted only in the disqualification of Roy Knickman for 'unsportsmanlike conduct'.

Huber, in his second year with Coors Light, finished the snaking, 3.5km prologue time trial in 4:25.80, an average speed of 18.6kph. In second place, two seconds slower, came world amateur 100km record holder, Kent Bostick of Team Shaklee. Knickman was third, a further second behind. The 7-Eleven team riders were all well placed, with defending champion Alex Stieda in ninth place, only four seconds down.

In 1989, the twisting Zilker Park criterium course in Austin was the scene of a dramatic last-stage smash-and-grab victory by Stieda, who displaced Alexi Grewal of Coors Light from the overall lead. There were no similar manoeuvres this year, but 7-Eleven's Irish sprinter John Brady took the stage for the team over Coors Light's latest fast man, Italian Roberto Gaggioli.

Although the first long stage, from Austin to Boerne, reached into the Texas hill country, the climbs were only moderate, and the giant Dutch sprinter, Michel Zanoli of Coors Light, won two of the three hill sprints from Team Crest's Steve Speaks. At the finish, American track veteran Harvey Nitz of Subaru-Montgomery displayed some of his former power in an early sprint, to take the stage from Brady.

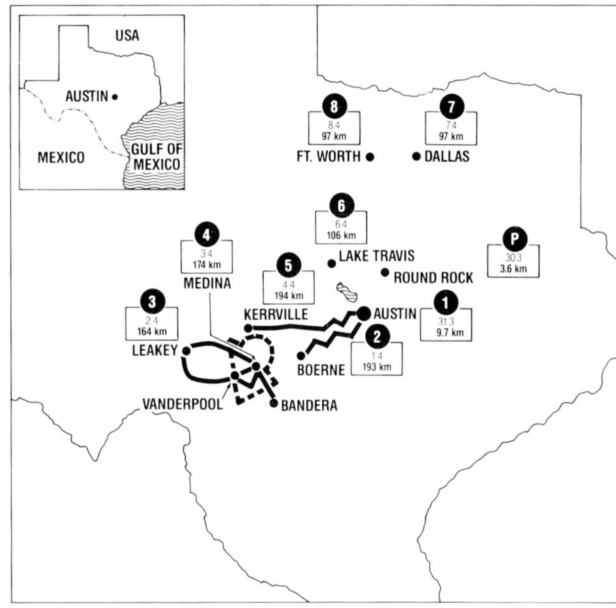

Tour of Texas, USA: 1125km

Early rain gave way to warm sunshine by the end of the stage from Bandera to Leakey. The rain caused many problems, starting with a series of 70 punctures and culminating with two dramatic crashes on a steep descent. Spago professional Doug Smith, who was leading the race at the 64km point, skidded on a slick turn and smashed his bike. Seconds later another experienced pro, Steve Tilford, came down when he tried to avoid hitting the motorbike that had stopped to help Smith, and had to quit the race with a broken arm.

With an 80km loop remaining eleven men broke clear, including professionals Grewal, Knickman and Randy

Racing through the Texas hill country

Chris Huber established his winning margin in the prologue time trial

Whicker of AC-Pinarello. At the feed zone, 54km from the finish, their one-minute lead had dropped to 200 metres, and Subaru team leader Thurlow Rogers cleverly bridged the gap. With Rogers' team blocking, the break moved 2:20 clear, but the peloton finally got itself organised, and 43 riders came together for the long, downhill run to the finish. With most of the sprinters behind, the stage looked a good bet for the fast amateur Czech rider, Jan Svorada, but also looking for a stage win was Huber, who attacked first. 'The Czech came by me, but I took it up from the corner, and managed to stay clear for the win,' he said later.

Although the 7-Eleven team wasn't very successful in chipping away at Huber's narrow overall lead, they did manage to propel Brady to a second victory in the fourth stage, based on the tiny town of Medina. In a field sprint that involved most of the 140 survivors, the 25-year-old Irishman easily beat the 19-year-old West German amateur Alex Dörper.

On the longest stage, 192km back to Austin, the well-placed Knickman, Andy Bishop (American Commerce) and Mike Engleman (AC-Pinarello) spearheaded a break from the gun. They gained more than six minutes, and the Coors Light team had to chase for 64km to save Huber's magenta-and-white leader's jersey. In a mass finish, Dörper won the sprint from Svorada. The chief victim of the stage was Knickman, who paid for his earlier efforts by coming home 4:28 behind the pack.

Much was expected from the 15-lap, 105km circuit race at Inn on Lake Travis, but no break was able to gain more than 10 seconds. With two laps left Chris Boardman, representing Great Britain, powered away from the peloton with Peter Verhesen, representing Canada. They just managed to stay clear on the final lap, and Boardman scored a well-deserved win.

In what proved to be the most exciting and controversial leg of the Tour, Nate Sheafor of Team Shaklee won an opportunistic stage victory in the 50-lap, 96km stage seven criterium in White Rock Lake Park, Dallas. The controversy began when some strong riders allowed themselves to be lapped so that they could help pull team-mates who were attacking off the front of the peloton. One rider who benefitted from this strategy was 7-Eleven's Thomas Craven, who was only four seconds behind overall. His team-mate Knickman dropped back and pulled him to a 30-second lead before officials eventually decided to pull lapped riders from the race, and going into the final lap, Craven still had nine seconds in hand. Sheafor managed to pass the leader and stayed ahead to win the stage, but more significant were the changes to the overall standings: Bostick, Speaks and Engleman dropped from second, third and fourth respectively, and Zanoli moved up to second.

All eyes were on the rival Coors Light and 7-Eleven teams going into the final stage, a flat, 80-lap, 64km criterium in Fort Worth. With Knickman disqualified, 7-Eleven had their work cut out, but with three laps remaining Craven made a determined effort. Huber inched his way up to the 7-Eleven aggressor, caught him with two laps to go . . . and everyone came together for a mass sprint. The determined Svorada finally won the stage victory he'd been seeking, but it was Huber, rolling across the line in 16th place, who finished the race still wearing that magenta-and-white leader's jersey.

Knickman leads Engleman, Bishop and Gogulski on their long stage 5 break

Paris-Roubaix: 8 April

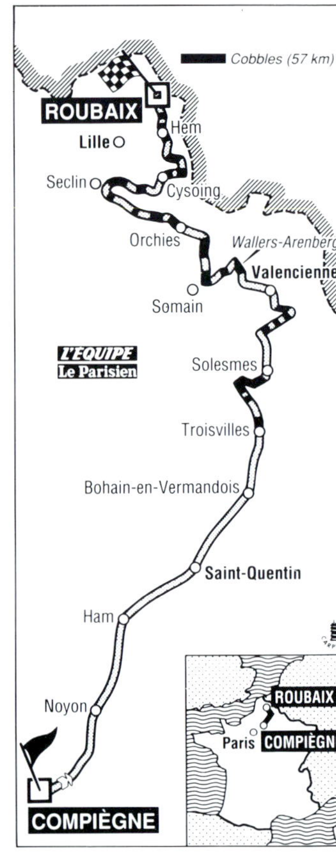

Paris-Roubaix, France: 265km

Officially, it was a millimetre, but to those who saw it, half a millimetre would have been more accurate.

The 88th edition of 'la Pascale' produced the closest finish in the history of the sport, and to many who stood in the centre of the ancient velodrome last April, a dead heat would have been the sporting decision. But cycling has never been a sport for the village-green attitudes of cricket, and there is no room for such niceties in classic racing. So who won the Queen of the Classics on that cold, sunny afternoon – Steve Bauer of 7-Eleven or Panasonic's Eddy Planckaert?

Like two defeated boxers, Bauer and Planckaert slumped in the centre of the velodrome at Roubaix, oblivious to the shouts of congratulation: in limbo for five long minutes while the photo-finish film was developed. Only one man was sure of the winner, and made no secret of it: Walter Planckaert, Eddy's elder brother and Panasonic assistant director, immediately said, 'It's you, Eddy, it's you by a centimetre!' Eddy wasn't impressed; he continued on tenterhooks, asking periodically, 'C'est qui, qui gagne?' Then it came, the announcement that silenced the stadium: 'The winner is Eddy Planckaert.'

Steve Bauer, no stranger to such body blows of disappointment, took the news stoically, and on to the podium walked Eddy Planckaert, having earned the ultimate honour for this famous Belgian cycling family. 'This has been my goal for ten years, since I turned professional,' he said. 'I've always felt I've been the rider for Paris-Roubaix, and even after Bauer came up to me, I felt I could still win. This victory means more to me than the Tour of Flanders two years ago, and it is the equivalent to me of what Fignon must have felt when he won his first Tour de France.'

The Planckaert name has been synonymous with cycling in Belgium since Eddy's father Gaston turned professional in 1954. Gaston was Belgian champion in 1962, and he went on to win Liège-Bastogne-Liège – but not Paris-Roubaix. Then came Eddy's brother Willy, one of the fastest ever roadman sprinters, who won 159 races as an amateur, including 44 in one season. Willy finished second in the 1964 world road championship and, as a

Despite aggressive racing, Fignon finished in 27th place

professional, came second in Paris-Brussels; but he never won Paris-Roubaix. The mantle passed to brother Walter, who won the Amstel Gold (1972) and the Tour of Flanders (1976); but again, never Paris-Roubaix. Now, while Willy's son Jozef is becoming known as Belgium's best amateur rider, Eddy has brought home the ultimate reward for his family's dedication to the sport. And the huge embrace from Walter said it all.

For Bauer, the quiet Canadian from Fenwick who seems to be a magnet for disaster and controversy, this must have seemed the ultimate misfortune. In the 1984 Olympics Bauer lost the road race almost on the finish line, because he underestimated the will power of the seemingly exhausted American Alexi Grewal. Then, in 1988, he collided with Belgian ace Claude Criquielion in the last 75 metres of the world championship road race. Criquielion fell and Bauer was disqualified – although blame was disputed – and Bauer suddenly found himself needing police protection from Criquielion's angry Belgian fans. Paris-Roubaix completed Bauer's hat-trick of almost-victories in the world's three most important one-day races. But with commendable reserve he said only, 'Obviously, it's disappointing to lose by so little. I did a lot of work near the end – and Planckaert didn't. One day, I'm going to win this race.'

Paris-Roubaix has always left indelible memories – mostly bad – on the minds of the men who have ridden it. The 265km from Compiègne, 80km north of Paris, to the Roubaix velodrome, is full of traps. The majority of the riders know that they will not finish; and no one likes to be called a favourite, as form rarely decides the outcome – fate does that. Between Troisville, 98km into the race, and the finish lie 22 sectors of broken road – partly cobbled, partly sand and soil, and often covered with sharp granite chippings ready to rip a rider's flesh

Bauer's unrelenting pressure finally pulled Planckaert and Van Hooydonck away to contest the finale

Never-say-die Martial Gayant almost caused an upset in the final kilometres

The Wallers-Arenberg Forest claimed its usual quota of victims

Riding the pavé is an exercise in acrobatics as much as athleticism

Planckaert made a long-range bid for victory

apart if he falls. From Troisville, the race is a latter-day Charge of the Light Brigade, with the strong holding front position until fate robs them of it; then – dirty, damaged, and often riding damaged bicycles – they fight back to the front again. These atrocious roads, fewer each year, have survived since Napoleonic days; some, like those in the Forest of Arenberg, are carefully preserved, open to motor vehicles on race day only.

This year, the riders faced a cold, cruel headwind, and had to spend nearly eight hours in the saddle after leaving Compiègne, so as they battled through the wooded countryside towards St Quentin there was no great urgency to rendezvous with 'the Hell of the North'. The first attack came after 19km, when the TVM team spring-boarded Dutchmen Rob Kleinsman and Peter Pieters ahead, with Swiss Stephan Joho (Ariostea) for company. Two years ago, a similar move proved decisive, and Dirk DeMol won the race against all the odds (and has won little since). However, it seemed the favourites were taking the view that lightning would not strike twice in the same place, and by Troisville, and the first section of pavé, the trio had built up a gap of 16 minutes. By Preseau, 138km into the race, the pavé had claimed Kleinsman when he punctured, and the other two had their lead reduced to a little over 7 minutes – the chase was on.

Now the riders entered the long, straight, cobbled road of Wallers-Arenberg, where a huge crowd, thirsty for accidents, formed a narrow corridor. Here, twenty-one riders grouped at the front, including French favourite Laurent Fignon (Castorama), East German Olympic champion Olaf Ludwig (Panasonic), Italian favourite Maurizio Fondriest (Del Tongo), and Eddy Planckaert. At the front, Pieters dropped back, leaving Joho, always the strongest, alone. Meanwhile the field swelled to over a hundred riders, smoother roads out of the forest giving temporary relief to their jaw-rattling progress.

After the Tour of Flanders a week earlier, Planckaert had told Belgian journalists that he was on his best form, stronger than anyone. But when he attacked alone – into the headwind and with almost 90km to go – they shook their heads and muttered 'Planckaert has gone mad, his brain has gone, he's crazy . . .' Was he, or did he simply believe he *was* the best? Bouncing over the pavé, Planckaert caught Joho on sector 12 (the first sector is counted as 22, and they go down to sector 1, the last before the finish), and by Orchies, 190km into the race, he was alone with a lead of 1:15.

Meanwhile, Fondriest the hot favourite after a series of good results, but no wins – was not enjoying the race. Two punctures, broken gears, a crash and finishing 56th were the memories he took home, but he left saying 'I had my share of bad luck, but I love this race and I will come back next year with the same ambition.'

Riders never need reminding that nothing is certain in Paris-Roubaix, and with this in mind Frenchman Martial Gayant of Toshiba, the rider who has earned the sobriquet 'almost-won', attacked in pursuit of Planckaert. He was joined by the little-known Belgian rider Kurt Van Keirsbuik (Isoglass), in his second year as a professional, and together they caught Planckaert at Bersee after 201 kilometres. Van Keirsbuik was on a high; inspired by the example of two surprise winners in two years, he contributed well to the pace.

With the break 1:30 ahead, Fignon was launching fierce attacks from the field, but with the Panasonics – last year's winner Belgian Jean-Marie Wampers, Urs Freuler of Switzerland, Ludwig and Dutchman John Talen – dominating at the front, the French world number one was getting increasingly frustrated. But his constant attacks did erode the lead to just 40 seconds, and with only 40km left, the chasers were reduced to fifteen riders, including the Panasonic foursome and Bauer, last survivor of the 7-Eleven team. Edwig Van Hooydonck of Belgium (Buckler) attacked at Templeuve (230km), and two kilometres later was alongside the three leaders; then PDM's Dutch rider Van Den Akker and Bauer also bridged the gap, making it a six-man break with a much better chance of staying clear.

The strong wind and dry conditions caused constant dust storms around the riders, and as the race neared the Belgian border the route twisted and turned as it sought out the stretches of pavé that make this race the anachronism of the sport. The riders' dust-rimmed eyes squinted through the gritty air as they tried to find the smoothest path over the cobbles. Planckaert, in front for almost two hours, appeared to be suffering, while Bauer was firing the engine as he sensed a first-ever Canadian victory. Since turning professional Bauer had won only one classic, the Championship of Zurich last year; hoping now for a second, he began to force the pace. Knowing that the group behind had split and it was now every man for himself in the scramble to reach Roubaix, he attacked alone with 17km to go. Only Planckaert and Van Hooydonck found the reserves to catch Bauer, and with 15km to go, the three riders were set to fight out Paris-Roubaix.

In Roubaix now, Bauer was forced into the lead on the approach to the velodrome, but once into the stadium – and to a roar from the packed house – he tried to relinquish his front spot. The pace slowed, and in the blink of an eye Jean-Marie Wampers was alongside him, with the never-say-die Martial Gayant still hoping for a miracle, and his compatriot Gilbert Duclos-Lassalle of Z, who had fought his way back into contention after a late puncture. Wampers immediately sought his Panasonic team-mate Planckaert and, appearing not even to consider a second win for himself, attempted to lead Planckaert around the velodrome as his tired leader tried to finish off in style. But it was Van Hooydonck who started the sprint first; then Bauer reacted, passing the lanky Belgian on the inside. Going into the home straight, Bauer looked certain to win – until, riding high on the banked track, Planckaert made his run, just plucking victory from Bauer's grasp.

Of the 186 who started, 92 finished. Forty minutes after Planckaert crossed the line, new American professional John Tomac of 7-Eleven, gamely sticking it out to the end, arrived in the velodrome. The average speed of 34.805 kph was the slowest for 32 years, but it still provided a memorable battle, and the finish of the 1990 Paris-Roubaix will be remembered as one of the most dramatic ever.

Fignon was a marked man, particularly by Panasonic riders Freuler (right) and Ludwig

Superior numbers were not much help for De Wilde (right) and his Histor cohorts

The photo finish

Flèche Wallonne: 11 April

If anyone thought Moreno Argentin's new-found aggression at the Tour of Flanders might have been a flash in the pan, they had their doubts swept away conclusively at the Flèche Wallonne, ten days later. His victory in this restructured 207.5km Belgian classic was far more impressive than his win in the Flanders race.

Thirty-year-old Italian Argentin, leader of the Ariostea team, secured his win over former French champion and 1987 Flèche Wallonne winner, Jean-Claude Leclercq (Helvetia-La Suisse), and Dutch climbing star, Gert-Jan Theunisse (Panasonic) when he made a lightning uphill attack from the small lead group with only 200 metres to go. The finish, up the steep, narrow Mur de Huy where home favourite Claude Criquielion (Lotto) won last year after attacking Panasonic's Steven Rooks on the brutal 20 per cent climb, again provided a dramatic climax to one of the season's most exciting races to date.

Instead of completing its traditional opening loop through Stavelot and Verviers, the 54th Flèche Wallonne headed north from the start in Spa, in order to bring the distance down towards the UCI-recommended 200km. However, this more direct route allowed the organizers to insert a further lap of the 42km finishing circuit at Huy, taking the number of hills from 12 to 15. On the third of these climbs, the Côte de Tilff after 32km, the race was brought to life by an attack from Frenchman Laurent Pillon (Histor). Given the green light by his team leader, Irishman Stephen Roche, who had been impressed with Pillon's form at the Tour of the Basque Country, Pillon gained four minutes before reaching the infamous Mur de Huy for the first time. He was caught by Switzerland's Rolf Järmann (Frank) on the eighth ascent, the 2.4km Côte de la France, after 102km.

Steep climbs: the hallmark of the Flèche Wallonne

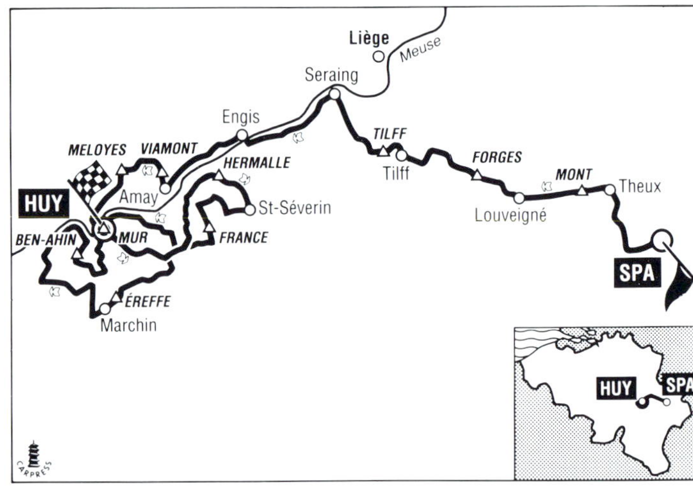

Flèche Wallonne, Belgium: 207.5km

Shortly before the second climb of the Mur de Huy, with two laps of the finishing circuit remaining, this duo had 3:00 on the peloton. But their lead became more precarious after passing the Mur when Scot Robert Millar (Z) and Switzerland's 1987 Milan-San Remo winner Erich Mächler (Carrera) began to chase; just how precarious was demonstrated when Millar and Mächler caught the two leaders on the Côte d'Ereffe with 73km, and five climbs, to go.

The finishing circuit is the traditional springboard for Flèche Wallonne drama. And this year's drama really got going after Millar, Mächler, Pillon and Järmann took a lead of 2:30 on the by now very active peloton, which was hopping with impatience. The first to counterattack was French rider Patrice Esnault (BH), who was quickly chased down by Italian Claudio Chiappucci (Carrera).

Going up the Mur de Huy for the third time, Millar's group had a minute's lead on the two pursuers and 2:20 on the peloton. Millar was the strongest rider, leading the three others over the top. And 10km later, the Z team's star climber dropped his companions, who were all absorbed by the pack after a series of chases from the peloton.

It was American Ron Kiefel who revived the chase after Millar, with a counterattack on the Côte de Ben-Ahin, with 13km to go. 'I was just feeling in good form and thought, why not?', said the blond 7-Eleven stalwart. 'This is a race suited to me, and since the Criterium International, I have felt more confident about my chances.' Kiefel, whose fine spring form had been rewarded by a stage win in the Criterium International, sprang from the regrouped peloton like a hare, followed by Theunisse and his Panasonic team-mate Viatcheslav Ekimov of the USSR. They were in turn marked by one of Argentin's Italian team-mates, Davide Cassani. At the summit of the 2.2km climb, with Kiefel's bid for freedom denied, Theunisse surged forward. And this time – with Millar now only 15 seconds ahead – he took with him Rooks, Mexican Raul Alcala (PDM), Argentin and Spain's Paris-Nice winner Miguel Indurain (Banesto). Within a minute they were followed by Leclercq, Cassani, Kiefel and Roche. So ten riders were in contention when, with six kilometres to go,

Millar's unexpected solo break almost brought him victory

Millar's 25km solo break was finally reeled in.

The Scot wasn't surprised: 'When I felt the other three [breakaways] were weakening, I decided to take some risks,' he said later. 'But we were always going to be caught. When it's that windy, it's virtually impossible to stay away from a chase group as strong as that.'

The peloton, now numbering a meagre thirty-five riders, was still closing as contingents from the Lotto, TVM and Banesto teams started to put in a belated effort. On the approach to the final climb of the Mur de Huy one chase even threatened to catch the leaders. Comprising TVM's Jesper Skibby of Denmark and Australian Phil Anderson, Frenchman Dominique Arnaud (Banesto) and Italian Franco Vona (Chateau d'Ax), it brought the field up to within 12 seconds of the leaders as the final ascent began.

Up front, it was Theunisse who was setting the tempo around the first, steeply banked turn of the 1.5km long Mur. He was followed by Indurain, Argentin, Leclercq, Roche, Rooks, Kiefel, Alcala and Millar. And it stayed that way: the long-haired Dutchman looked about to score a convincing win, as he surged twice more before the final 300 metres. But, miraculously, Argentin pulled up alongside the Panasonic rider, whose sudden turn to his left revealed the surprise every observer felt as well. Then, with a little glance down, a tightening of his hands on the handlebars and a determined glance at the finish line, Argentin attacked. Theunisse had no answer. Only Leclercq, the most consistent Frenchman this spring, came back; unable to catch Argentin, he still snatched second place from Theunisse.

Regarded as a dress rehearsal for Liège-Bastogne-Liège, four days later, the Flèche reintroduced to classic competition many of the climbing forces in the peloton. The American Andy Hampsten (7-Eleven) finished 5 minutes behind the leaders, among whom his team-mate Kiefel came in seventh at 0:22, an improving Alcala was eighth at 0:29, and in ninth place at 0:37 Robert Millar, whose enterprise almost won him his first victory in a classic.

Argentin packed too much power at the finish, eclipsing his rivals

Liège-Bastogne-Liège: 15 April

As well as a personal triumph for Eric Van Lancker, his victory in the 76th Liège-Bastogne-Liège marked the return to glory of his Panasonic-Sportlife team. The 28-year-old Belgian's solo victory – by 34 seconds over Frenchman Jean-Claude Leclercq (Helvetia-La Suisse) and his Panasonic team-mate, Dutchman Steven Rooks – was the second major classic win in eight days for team boss Peter Post and his riders.

In the early 1980s, the military precision of Post's Panasonic team was awesome . . . and highly successful. His riders seemed to be on every winner's podium, in every break and in every chase. In more recent years, though, there has been a question mark over the team's ability even to finish a Tour de France. But now, after Eddy Planckaert's win at Paris-Roubaix and Van Lancker's at Liège, where Panasonic had three riders – including the winner – in the top ten, this powerful Dutch team became a clear leader in the World Cup teams competition.

Run in wet, windy and freezing conditions on Easter Sunday, this hilly 256km classic – known as 'la Doyenne' because it is the oldest of the surviving classics, having first been held in 1894 – produced more than seven hours of hard racing. The first notable action came from Frenchman Jean-François Bernard (Toshiba), intent on proving that his comeback from a knee operation was on course; at 116km, on the Bois des Moines hill, he made a successful attack with the Soviet rider Dmitri Konyshev (Alfa Lum) and Frenchman Henri Abadie (Z). By the Côte de Lorcé, at 196km, Bernard had shed his two breakaway companions and was 2:57 up on the peloton; his break was, however,

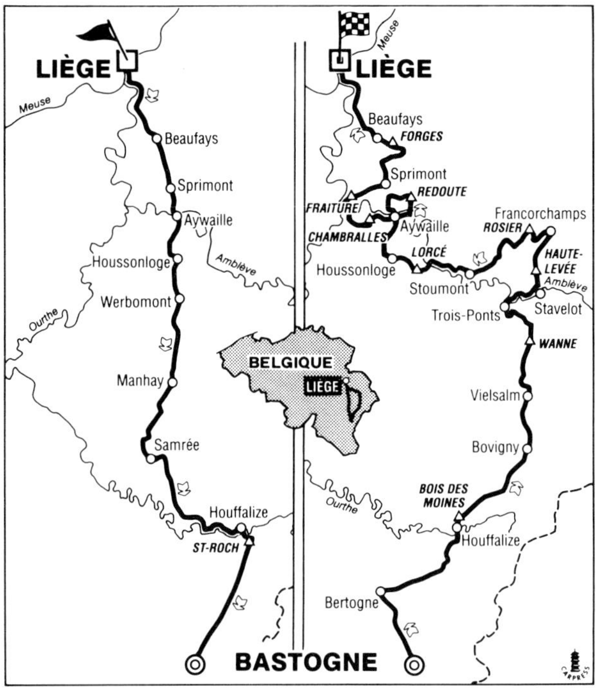

Liège-Bastogne-Liège, Belgium: 256km

intended more as conditioning for the forthcoming Tour of Spain than to secure a classic win, and against a relentless headwind his capture was always imminent.

Fifteen kilometres further on the race reached the Côte de la Redoute, and it was on this narrow, three-kilometre climb that Panasonic's Gert-Jan Theunisse launched a punishing acceleration in pursuit of Bernard, whose unsteady rocking and weaving near the top indicated that his long breakaway was almost over. The long-haired Dutchman, King of the Mountains in last year's

The early break was led by Konyshev, Abadie and Bernard, who then took off on his own

Eric Van Lancker attacked on the Forges climb . . . kept up the pace . . . and captured the glory in Liège

Second-placed Leclercq was unable to break free from Panasonic's powerful domination of the race

Tour de France, moved up to third position in the pack, waited a moment, then attacked down the peloton's right. With Theunisse went Italy's Moreno Argentin (Ariostea), jumping on Theunisse's wheel as if his life depended on it, followed by Rooks and the local favourite Claude Criquielion (Lotto). Then went two PDM riders, Mexican Raul Alcala and Belgian Rudy Dhaenens, with two Buckler men, Dutchman Peter Winnen and West Germany's Rolf Gölz, and finally they were followed by Panasonic's Dutch rider John Talen, East German Uwe Ampler of PDM, and three Frenchmen – Ronan Pensec of Z and the Helvetia-La Suisse riders Jean-Claude Leclercq and Gilles Delion. The result was a threatening 13-man break which quickly took care of Abadie, Konyshev already having been reeled in on the Côte du Rosier at 178km.

Several race favourites were badly positioned before this break, including two former top three Liège-Bastogne-Liège finishers, Ireland's Stephen Roche (Histor) and Australia's Phil Anderson (TVM), who had predicted that 'the critical part of the race will be the Redoute' – in fact, a crash at the foot of the hill left him positioned at the rear when the attack came. For Roche, whose sixth place in the Flèche Wallonne put him in contention, it was a case of poor positioning: 'I couldn't get to the front coming to the Redoute,' he said later. 'Normally, the race approaches it in a different way. But today, it wasn't hard enough beforehand, and kind of dangerous. I was on my own and couldn't get through.' He did, however, fight his way back up to the front, and embark with twenty other riders on a belated chase – heartening proof that his return to form was on schedule.

It was on the ascent of the Côte de Chambralles, 11km after the Redoute, that the Roche chase group started to close in on the leaders. Pensec, Delion, Gölz and Talen all dropped back to the peloton, which was now only 200m behind and 1:16 down on Bernard. Amongst those up there with Roche were Scotland's Robert Millar (Z), Italy's Gianni Bugno (Chateau d'Ax), the Spanish duo of Miguel Indurain and Pedro Delgado (both Banesto), Belgium's Luc Roosen (Histor), Ireland's Martin Earley (PDM) and, of course, Van Lancker.

The chasers continued to gain on the descent of Chambralles, and all hell was let loose on the next climb, the Côte de Fraiture, with 31km to go. Bernard's lone escape came to an end when he was caught – almost nonchalantly – by Theunisse, who continued setting the attacking tempo of the eight-strong group he led. Then, on a short plateau after the summit, Criquielion launched an attack, but was reeled in by Alcala – after Argentin, Theunisse and Rooks had all hesitated. Alcala then tried a break himself, but was just as quickly brought back by Rooks.

World Cup leader Argentin, who had been reluctant to reveal his hand, was finally forced into the open when he was attacked by Dutchman Peter Winnen (Buckler), who

Three-time winner Argentin (centre) was closely marked by Criquielion (left), Alcalá and Theunisse

Theunisse was perhaps the strongest climber in the hilly race . . .

had spent much of the previous five kilometres at the back of the group. The Italian chased down Winnen, taking the Norwegian Atle Kvalsvoll (Z) with him. These three went clear, but after a kilometre's freedom, they were joined first by Roosen and Van Lancker, then Earley and Millar, and finally Rooks and Theunisse.

The list of aspiring Doyenne champions was quickly being fined down under this barrage of attacks. With three Panasonics – Theunisse, Rooks and Van Lancker – now in the front group of nine, it was a good bet that one of them would produce the winning move. Of the three, the odds would probably have been longest on Van Lancker, but in fact it was he who bolted away at Sprimont, with 22km left, shortly before the last of the ten climbs, the infamous Côte des Forges.

All eyes turned to Argentin, who had come to Liège fresh from his victory in the Flèche Wallonne, intent on winning this Ardennes classic for the fourth time; but he refused to give chase, and as the others hesitated Van Lancker's sudden 25-second lead turned just as suddenly to 45 seconds. As the pace eased on the Côte des Forges, others joined the front group, and it was the newly arrived Leclercq who finally counterattacked, only to have Rooks jump on his wheel.

With 14km to go, Van Lancker was repeating his winning effort at last year's Amstel Gold. Out on his own, he raced with all his might, while Rooks played out his copybook defensive role with Leclercq. The French chaser was forced into doing all the work, and Rooks did not relent until his team-mate Van Lancker's lead had stabilized at 41 seconds.

What helped Rooks persevere, of course, was a strong desire to further extend his lead on the remaining chasers and ensure that he won the maximum number of World Cup and FICP points. He was successful, partly thanks to Theunisse, who was also following Panasonic team tactics and guarding every possible move by Argentin; not even a belated counterattack by Dhaenens and Roosen could prise him from his vigil over the fancied Italian. 'Argentin has been in such good form this year – particularly on Wednesday – that we knew he would be good today', said Theunisse, who had experienced Argentin's finishing strength first-hand in the previous week's Flèche Wallonne. But while Van Lancker finished a clear winner, by 34 seconds over runners-up Leclercq and Rooks, and 1:16 over Dhaenens and Roosen, Argentin could do no better than sixth place this time, sprinting in ahead of eleven riders who finished 1:20 in arrears.

For Van Lancker, ranked 63rd in the world before the race, the win came very appropriately just before his twenty-ninth birthday. 'It's the best present I could ever have given myself,' he said later. And, since the 1990 Liège-Bastogne-Liège had provided a showcase for a brilliant display of Panasonic team tactics, Peter Post would probably have said the same.

. . . but Panasonic team-mate Van Lancker was the beneficiary of his team's superiority

Amstel Gold: 21 April

For the first time in fourteen months, Dutchman Adrie Van der Poel found himself on the winner's dais after a major race when he won the Amstel Gold in one of the season's most aggressive finales. With credentials including Tour de France stage wins and victories in the Tour of Flanders and Liège-Bastogne-Liège, as well as a Dutch national championship, the Weinmann rider was a worthy recruit to the Amstel's roll of honour.

Van der Poel pipped Belgium's Luc Roosen (Histor) to the post after a day's racing highlighted by the Dutch star's feud with his compatriot and rival, the 1988 winner Jelle Nijdam (Buckler). Their aggressive behaviour towards each other reached a peak on two occasions. First, on the 22 per cent Keutenberg climb, with 30km to go, Nijdam elbowed Van der Poel when a crucial split in the regrouped field took place. The second incident took place in the closing minutes of the race, when Van der Poel pushed Nijdam as the two men tried to muscle their way through the lead-out riders and gain an open line to the finish. Neither incident led to any official protest, however; in the Netherlands, the Amstel Gold is the only major one-day event in the calendar, competition is intense between the Dutch contingents, and such goings-on are commonplace.

Nonetheless, these incidents, and the close competition for Perrier World Cup points between competition leaders Moreno Argentin (Ariostea) and Gianni Bugno (Chateau d'Ax) of Italy and third-placed Belgian Rudy Dhaenens (PDM), brought the spring classics season to a dramatic close. After the photo finish camera revealed that Bugno finished 8th, Dhaenens 13th and Argentin 17th, the World Cup standings were: Argentin, 62 points; Bugno, 61 points; Dhaenens, 60 points!

The 249km Amstel Gold, raced in the hilly terrain of Limburg, which nestles between the Belgian and German borders of the southern region of the Netherlands, has always been hotly contested by the rival Dutch teams. The Dutch have won 14 out of 25 editions, and the winner of the other 11 – 1989's Belgian Eric Van Lancker of Panasonic, for instance – has usually come from a Dutch team. Ironically, Van der Poel is with a Belgian-based team, Weinmann, and it was the traditional 'war' between the members of the Dutch Panasonic and Buckler squads that helped pave the way for his long-awaited success. After a 1989 season that began badly because of over-racing the previous year, continued with a bout of bronchitis and – inevitably – poor form in the closing races of the season, Van der Poel embarked on 1990 determined to win a major classic. Despite fine form in the early classics, however – he was always in the prominent breaks and moves – he had so far fallen short of his goal. For Van der Poel, therefore, as for many other riders, the Amstel Gold was the last chance to salvage something from the spring campaign. 'I really wanted a win this spring. And yes, I have been in good form . . . and today, because of the battle between the Panasonics and Bucklers, I was hoping I could maybe get away in a break and stay away to the finish,' said Van der Poel later.

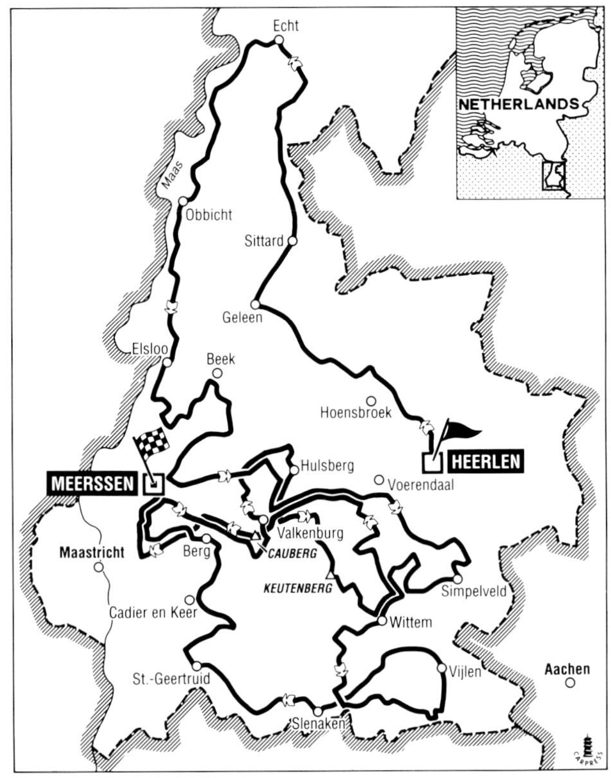

Amstel Gold, Holland: 249km

And he was indeed in an early break of about thirty-five riders that detached itself 30km after the start on a wet, windy Saturday in Heerlen. Among those with him were Argentin, Van Lancker, Frenchman Gilles Delion (Helvetia-La Suisse), Dutchman Steven Rooks (Panasonic) and American Andy Hampsten (7-Eleven). But such a large breakaway was difficult to sustain on the twisting route, and was duly caught after 65km.

The regroupment was the signal for a solo effort by Spaniard Marino Alonso, who was hoping to create a late opening for his Banesto team leaders and compatriots, Pedro Delgado and Miguel Indurain. At the top of the Schweiberg climb, at 149km, he was leading the lone chaser, Dane John Carlsen of Toshiba, by 40 seconds, with the Yugoslav Jure Pavlic (Carrera) and Frenchman Roland Le Clerc (Toshiba) at 1:10. At 10-second intervals behind them came Van der Poel – again showing good form – and an eight-man group including Indurain, trying to bridge the gap. The Buckler and Panasonic teams led the chase after the dangerous Indurain and Van der Poel, and the peloton came together again 30km before the first call at Meerssen, where the race set out on the final loop of 65km.

The crucial split came on the Keutenberg, at 210km. Throughout the run-up to the climb, the huge crowd lining the ancient Limburg roadway cheered for a Dutch victory, and the formidable Panasonic contingent looked very determined. The best plan for those expecting a Panasonic attack on the steep, narrow Keutenberg was to keep as good a position as possible up front. On the first stretch of the hill, it was Milan-San Remo winner Bugno who led the field, with Australian Phil Anderson (TVM). They were followed by two Panasonic riders,

Adrie Van der Poel steals victory on the line from Luc Roosen

Dutchmen Steven Rooks and Gert-Jan Theunisse, then 7-Eleven's Canadian rider Steve Bauer and his American team-mate, Ron Kiefel. Commenting later on his tactics Van der Poel said, 'I always try to start in front [in those situations]. Then I ride my own tempo. And then, if you lose five or six places by the top, you never let them get away far after the top; you can chase them back.'

As expected, 'Geronimo', as Theunisse is known, did produce his usual surge on the Keutenberg. And by the top, Van der Poel, Rooks, Dhaenens, Bugno, Indurain and Frenchman Ronan Pensec (Z) were right there with him. But Theunisse still had one more trick up his sleeve: soon after the summit, he shot up the road and bolted away. Only Pensec reacted, and the Z man and Theunisse were soon 45 seconds ahead. On the Elkengrade climb, with 30km to go, Pensec was clearly struggling to match the stylish attacking tempo of the Dutchman, and Theunisse set up another attack; but the little Frenchman fought back to his wheel three kilometres later.

With a lead of 1:05, 17km from the finish, it looked as though Theunisse and Pensec were racing towards a spectacular success. But a furious barrage of counterattacks now developed. The first to take up the chase were Buckler's Nijdam, Histor's Roosen, the PDM pair of Dhaenens and Irishman Martin Earley, plus Pensec's French team-mate Jérôme Simon, who was hoping to slow down the pursuit. These riders were soon joined by another twenty, including Van der Poel, and then – with 10km left – by another large group, creating a 40-man chase group.

The gap closed quickly, and the two fugitives finally conceded as the race entered its final two kilometres. A flurry of solo attacks followed; Belgian Michel Dernies of Weinmann was first, then Anderson, then Mexican Raul Alcala (PDM), and finally Roosen and his compatriot Jan Goessens, another Weinmann rider.

As the finish line approached it was Roosen, prematurely confident, who started to raise his arms aloft. Then a look of horror came over his face as he caught sight of the charging Van der Poel: having settled his pushing match with Jelle Nijdam 150 metres before the finish, Van der Poel still had enough speed to overtake Roosen before the line, while Nijdam came in third, just ahead of Goessens – who was sorry to lose, but happy that he lost to team-mate Van der Poel.

They say 'the show ain't over till the fat lady sings,' and in a Dutch classic, against Dutch riders, especially in a season strangely lacking in Dutch victories, Luc Roosen would have done well to remember it.

Four Days of Dunkirk: 1-6 May

Come the first week of May, Irishman Stephen Roche was in need of a big win. It wasn't so much that he wanted to add another title to his illustrious career tally, already glittering with his Tour of Italy and Tour de France wins and the world title; more that he needed to instil a proper sense of 'who's who' in his new team. Before the Four Days of Dunkirk in northern France, rumours of domestic troubles within the Irishman's Belgian Histor-Sigma team had been rife throughout the Continent. It seemed that not everyone in the team was happy with his 'protected' status as undisputed leader. And what was more, nasty rifts were starting to appear between the home-based Belgian contingent of Histor-Sigma and the French riders brought in by Roche. So, it was thought that a victory in this 36-year-old eight-stage race would quell the insurrection. If not, it would at least give Roche the authority to be team leader in fact as well as in name.

The Dunkirk Four Days, actually spanning six days, is billed as one of the top preparation races for the Tour of Italy. It has also, because of its notorious rain, wind and cobblestones, been dominated by Dutch and Belgian riders. Over the last thirty years the only exceptions to the rule have been French – Yves Hézard in 1972, Bernard Hinault in 1984 and Charly Mottet in 1989. Roche, preparing for his first 'injury-free' Tour de France since his 1987 victory, wanted to put Ireland's name up there too, and he did so with a display of courage and stoicism that will go down in Irish folklore. Roche did not win a single stage, but he certainly silenced his doubters.

After winning the leader's pink jersey on stage 2, Roche had little idea as to his fate on stage 3 from Saint Quentin to Armentières

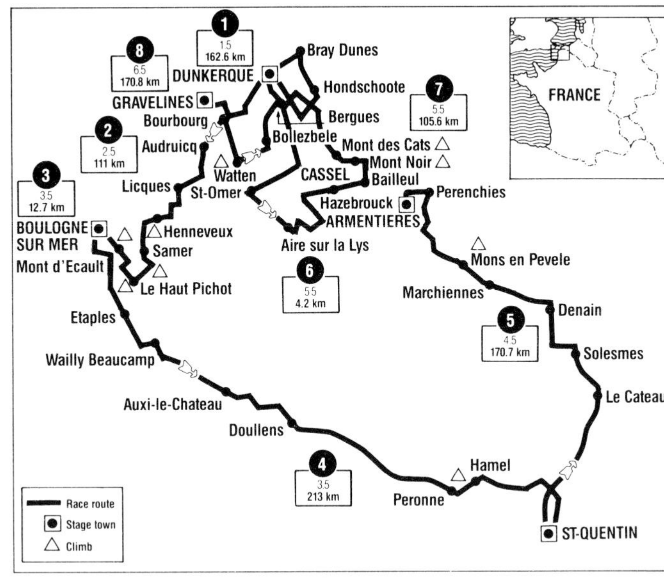

Four Days of Dunkirk, France: 950.6km

Belgium's Johan Museeuw (Lotto) won the opening stage, over 167km to the coastal town of Dunkirk. On the 112km second stage, from Dunkirk to Boulogne, Roche crashed after 72km, but stoically picked himself up and chased impressively to rejoin the peloton. Then, taking most of his rivals by surprise – after such a tiring chase, they had not expected him to attack – he bolted away. Only the Frenchman François Lemarchand (Z) was able to go with him, and they stayed away to the finish. For Roche, what mattered was not the stage win, it was the overall time gained on race favourites like Frenchman Thierry Marie (Castorama) and Dutchman Jelle Nijdam (Buckler). So he let Lemarchand take the stage, saving his energy for the afternoon's 12.7km time trial at Boulogne.

Predictably, Marie revealed his hand in this 'race of truth'. The nuggety blond Frenchman won with 0:16 to spare on his second-placed countryman and team-mate, Christophe Lavainne. But it was not nearly enough to topple Roche; finishing fifth at 0:46, the Histor leader easily accounted for Lemarchand's overnight lead of 0:03, as the Z rider taking 12th place at 1:05. So Roche took his place at the helm of the race, entering stage 4 with 0:16 on Lemarchand, second overall, and 2:08 on Thierry Marie.

By most reckonings, Roche now had the race sewn up. The only major hurdle remaining was Saturday morning's sixth stage, an uphill time trial over 4.2km to Mont Cassel, but it seemed highly improbable that Roche would let his lead slip from his grasp over such a short distance. Roche himself, however, refused to tempt providence by predicting a win; after stage 4, won by the Dutch Panasonic rider Jean-Paul Van Poppel in a bunch sprint, Roche was wary: 'We are not 100 per cent, there is always some risk of something happening,' he said.

It was on stage 5 that it did. Still sore after his stage 2 crash, Roche fell heavily on the first of eight cobbled sectors in the 171km leg from Saint Quentin to Armentières. Bleeding profusely from a gash in his right

Despite crashing heavily on the first sector of cobblestones (stage 3) – and losing one litre of blood – Roche still plucked up a winner's smile when greeted afterwards by his friend and team director, Patrick Valcke

elbow, he leapt back onto his bike without a moment's hesitation, sensing that the field would break out in a series of attacks, endangering his overall lead. Facing a deficit of 1:10, Roche and his team-mates embarked on a 20km team-time-trail-style chase.

Covered in blood, dust and sweat, Roche finally rejoined the main group; but almost immediately, and in quick succession, all his team-mates were dropped because of either punctures or crashes. Forced to chase down all the breaks himself, as Lemarchand's Z riders attempted to take control of the race, Roche was in a terrible state by the time the Armentières finish line passed under his wheels. In hospital overnight for observation, it was revealed that he had lost a litre of blood; nevertheless, by finishing 37 seconds behind a victorious Nijdam, the Dubliner was still holding on to his lead.

Displaying his legendary will-power, Roche rejected advice to abandon. Scarred, bruised, and more desperately weak with every kilometre, he never faltered in his refusal to be beaten. Marie's last assault on Roche's lead failed on the normally hard, fast, and partially cobbled seventh-stage circuit race at Mont Cassel; he reduced his deficit on Roche by a meagre 0:11, Lemarchand taking third place at 0:04. It was little wonder, when the eighth stage finished safely in a bunch sprint won by Van Poppel, the victorious Roche declared: 'After what I've learned here at Dunkirk, nobody will be able to make me believe that cycle racing is less dangerous than car racing.'

It was a hard-fought victory for Roche. Sadly, the win did not lead to the triumphant summer everyone expected

Tour de Trump: 3-13 May

With great poise and tremendous power, Raúl Alcalá of Mexico took a convincing victory in the second Tour de Trump. The prestigious American race, eleven days and 1800km long, ended in a crowd-packed Copley Square in Boston, Massachusetts, with the 26-year-old PDM star holding a 43-second advantage over the excellent Norwegian rider, Atle Kvalsvoll of Z, followed by Alcalá's Dutch team-mate Eric Breukink in third place at 1:44. But it was a 19-year-old Soviet amateur, Vladislav Bobrik, who caused the Mexican his biggest problems by clinging tenaciously to a race lead established by an opportunistic break on the third day. It was not until the penultimate stage that the young Russian finally surrendered to a stream of wicked attacks made by Alcalá and his team.

Alcalá first took the lead in a tricky 5km prologue time trial at Wilmington, Delaware, 7 seconds faster than any of the other 132 starters. His 46.75 kph average speed was quite remarkable on a course that contained a dozen turns and two demanding climbs: the short, cobblestoned Monkey Hill after two kilometres and a 500m drag to the finish. While Alcalá enjoyed a perfect ride, the prologue favourite Viatcheslav Ekimov of Panasonic-Sportlife – the multi-world-record-holder – crashed on the second corner when the tyre rolled from his front wheel. He continued on a spare bike, to finish 32 seconds slower than Alcalá. The Panasonic team's woes continued when its next starter, and the 1989 Trump runner-up, Dutch rider Henk Lubberding, arrived 45 seconds late for his start. As a result he was caught by his minute man, Bobrik, whose time of 6:36 was eventually 11th best of the night.

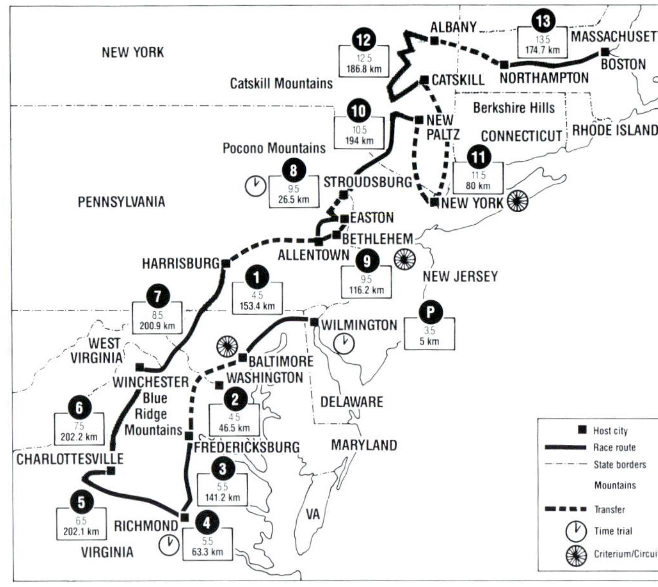

Tour de Trump, USA: 1800km

After the Ekimov and Lubberding fiascos, tension was mounting in the big crowd, especially when Canadian Steve Bauer of 7-Eleven came to the line two minutes after Bobrik. The Canadian's pugnacious style was suited to the twisty course, and he recorded 6:32.95 – two tenths of a second-faster than the previous fastest time, set by his English team-mate Sean Yates. Then, unexpectedly, American Steve Speaks of Team Crest bulleted across the line in 6:32.75. But as the television cameras gathered around Speaks, Alcalá was already

Raúl Alcalá of Mexico started the race as he intended to continue, by winning the difficult prologue time trial at Wilmington, Delaware

Vladislav Bobrik broke clear on the finishing circuit at Richmond, Virginia to win stage 3 and take the race lead

on the starting ramp. And 6 minutes 25 seconds later all the attention had shifted to the happy Mexican.

There were few surprises in next morning's opening road stage across the green countryside of Delaware and Maryland. PDM and Panasonic completely controlled the pace, and the stage ended in a mass sprint in Baltimore, where Panasonic's Olympic champion, Olaf Ludwig of East Germany, scored the sixth victory of his first pro season. At the end of the long, tiring day, Ludwig again proved the king of the sprinters in a wet, 1-hour, 47km circuit race beside Baltimore's Inner Harbor. The 10-second victory bonus put Ludwig into the hot-pink jersey as race leader, while Bauer's 6-second reward for second place pulled him into third place overall, 1 second behind Alcalá.

These small time differences didn't count for much the next morning, though, when Ludwig unexpectedly gave up his leader's jersey to the youthful Bobrik. The young Russian hadn't been considered a danger when he escaped in an early break on the 141km stage with American amateur Mike McCarthy of Subaru-Montgomery and the modest Belgian pro, Thierry Bock of Lotto. Behind them, the riders started to chase the break, when the gap was small, but when the other teams didn't help, Peter Post told his men to desist. Within 10km, a 1-minute gap grew to 3 minutes; within another 30km it had topped 12 minutes. The 7-Eleven *directeur sportif* Jim Ochowicz had regarded it as Panasonic's responsibility to chase, and by the time Sean Yates began to chase, quickly joined by four other 7-Eleven riders there was only an hour of the stage remaining – clearly not enough time to close the enormous gap. Bobrik dropped his two companions on the hilly, finishing circuit in Richmond, where a massive crowd saw him take the stage win by 42 seconds from McCarthy and Bock, 3:02 ahead of the peloton led by Michel Zanoli of Holland (Coors Light).

That evening's long 63.3km team time trial did not count towards individual classification – except for bonuses to the winners – although times did count towards team classification. The young Soviets made a strong bid for their second victory of the day, completing the first of their two 31.7km laps in an astonishing 37:05. However, in the second lap they faded to fifth best, 1:38 behind stage winners 7-Eleven. The other teams' strengths were confirmed when PDM came in second, ahead of Panasonic, with Greg LeMond's Z team fourth.

The 201km fifth stage revealed that Alcalá and Kvalsvoll were the strongest individuals in this increasingly difficult race – a revelation provided by Wintergreen Mountain, a challenging 5km climb that ended with a 400m stretch at a steady 15 per cent gradient. At its summit, 68km from the finish, Alcalá and Kvalsvoll had closed to 1 minute on a three-man break that had been more than 4 minutes clear at the foot of the climb. They gobbled up the three leaders, of whom only American amateur Nate Reiss (Subaru-Montgomery) was able to hold the tremendous pace set by Alcalá along the Blue Ridge Parkway, 1000 metres above the savagely beautiful, wooded hills of Virginia. After the climb, a chase group of thirty-two riders regrouped – including Bobrik. As the battle raged along the ridge, the gap between the leaders and the chase hovered around 1 minute. Behind them, the main field of seventy riders was dropping further and further behind; they would eventually concede more than 10 minutes.

Alcalá continued to do 90 per cent of the work, to push the break's lead to 1:42, with 23km of rolling

The Tour de Trump peloton rolls through the Virginia farmland on its way to the Blue Ridge Mountains

Frenchman Pascal Poisson of Z won the sixth stage ahead of his breakaway companion Paul McCormack of Ireland (left)

backroads still to go. It looked as though the determined Mexican was going to recapture most of the 3 minutes conceded to Bobrik the previous day; but strong chasing efforts were being made by Ekimov (on behalf of his former amateur club-mate, Bobrik) and by the 7-Eleven trio of Bauer and Americans Andy Hampsten and Ron Kiefel. On reaching a 2km finishing loop in the college town of Charlottesville, the gap was down to 15 seconds, but still Alcalá kept on the pressure. He even led out the final sprint – only to be dismayed to see first Kvalsvoll pass him, and then Reiss, who sprinted away to the stage win.

There was a similarity about the next two stages, which took the race north, out of Virginia, through Maryland and into Pennsylvania. Each was about 200km in length; each saw early aggression that stretched the resources of the young Soviet team (the 'seven little Ekimovs', as Hampsten dubbed them); and each ended in wins for riders well behind on overall time. The sixth stage, into Winchester, Virginia, was won by the Frenchman Pascal Poisson (Z), who easily outsprinted Irish amateur Paul McCormack of Crest, with American pro Todd Gogulski (Coors Light) in third.

The attacks were more serious on the seventh stage, to Harrisburg, the capital of Pennsylvania, including a fifteen-man move that contained Kvalsvoll, Ekimov and Speaks. Also in the group was Andy Bishop, an American who raced for PDM in the first two years of his pro career and was riding as a free agent for the California-based Spago team. Bishop was eager to get back racing for a European squad; and he realised that a stage win in this race would show off his abilities to an international audience. So, when he saw an opportunity to break clear of the front group, just before they were caught by the pack, Bishop put in a strong attack. There were still 119km to race, but with a billowing tail wind, and mostly descending roads to the finish, he knew there was a good chance of success. Riding superbly, the Arizona racer had gained 9 minutes halfway through his break, and held on to 3:39 at Harrisburg to score an impressive victory – which earned him a place on the 7-Eleven team for the Giro d'Italia and the Tour de France.

At Harrisburg, Bobrik described his leader's pink jersey as 'a coat of armour', weighing him down; and next day, during two stages in Pennsylvania's Lehigh Valley, it did indeed prove a burden, and his overall lead was cut to 1:37 by Alcalá. In the morning time trial, not only did Alcalá beat Bobrik by 1:06, he also defeated runner-up Kvalsvoll by 26 seconds, completing the 26.5km test at an average speed of almost 50kph. It was a dangerous course, as third-placed Steve Bauer found when he burst a tyre on a railway crossing, crashed, and lost any chance he had of winning the race. With no wind, and warm, hazy sunshine, conditions were perfect. It was ironic that out-of-condition LeMond's lowly position made him one of the early starters, and that his time of 35:11 remained the best for more than an hour. The first rider to go faster was 18-year-old American amateur Bobby Julich, 39 seconds faster than the world champion. It wasn't until Ekimov came hurtling home with 33:17 that Julich's time was beaten. Breukink finished with 33:05; and then the 28-year-old Kvalsvoll smoothly pedalled in with an astonishing 32:29.

Bauer's crash probably cost him a full minute, and his 2-minute man, Alcalá, was soon breathing down his neck. The Mexican swept past Bauer about 10km from the finish, descended into Easton 30 seconds ahead of his rival to cross the line in 32:03! Bobrik came in with 33:19 – fifth on the stage.

In that afternoon's 116km circuit race, Bobrik's suit of armour showed a few more chinks, but he clung tenaciously to his lead, though it looked in danger several times, particularly when he punctured on the second lap – when Ekimov's Panasonic team helped him by slowing down the peloton. Then, on the last of the three laps, cheered on by thousands of students on the final 3km climb through the Lehigh University campus, Alcalá and Kvalsvoll overhauled an earlier break and succeeded in splitting the pack into two groups.

Alcalá made another attack up the straight, wide Hickory Hill. Frenchman Henri Abadie, covering for team-mate Kvalsvoll, went with the Mexican, while Kvalsvoll, in the lime green jersey, bridged, with Ekimov and Bobrik on his wheel, along with Belgian Peter De Clercq (Lotto), Julich and French amateur Bruno Huger. These eight riders joined forces momentarily, but as the climb steepened Alcalá made another surge, and only Kvalsvoll could go with him. When the pair immediately gained 15 seconds, this looked like being the move that would finally bury Bobrik; but four official motorcycles had been trapped between the groups, and they aided the five chasers in catching the two leaders. After a long, fast descent into Allentown, sixty riders regrouped. In the 1km dash to the line, the indomitable Ludwig forced his way through to take his third stage win of the race.

Everything seemed set for Alcalá to ride into the pink jersey on the long, hilly 10th stage through the Pocono and Catskill mountains. The weather was appropriately challenging, with heavy rain and a strong following wind, and the course was extremely difficult, with incessant climbs on narrow, rustic backroads. Bobrik was tired, and Alcalá was feeling stronger than ever. However, a classic battle plan by Alcalá's PDM squad fell apart at the strategic moment. Three PDM riders – Belgian Rudy Dhaenens and Jos Van Aert and Nico Verhoeven of Holland – set the pace in an early attack. After 45km, they and seven others were 4:05 ahead, which forced the Soviets to initiate what looked like being a marathon pursuit. Bobrik's men chipped the lead to 2:19 on entering Port Jervis, where the riders had to cross a slippery, open, steel-deck bridge. While the momentum of the first riders was enough for them to keep their balance, four others in the break fell, with Abadie, Lubberding and Italian Max Sciandri (Carrera) all being hospitalized. Behind them, the peloton slowed and took to the boarded pavements, and the break, now down to six men, began to move away again. The gap stretched to 3:45 at 100km, when a chase group headed by Dutchman Johan Lammerts (Z) and Ekimov took shape. On the next climb, which ascended in steep, erratic grades, Alcalá and Kvalsvoll joined the two chasers just as the rain started to tumble again. Just over the top, Alcalá's foursome was caught by Breukink and Russian Vassil Zhdanov of Alfa Lum. As in the previous day's circuit race, Bobrik had been dropped on a climb,

A solo stage win for Andy Bishop at Harrisburg earned him a spot on the 7-Eleven team for the Giro d'Italia and the Tour de France

Hampsten, Kvalsvoll and Clark Sheehan on the Devil's Kitchen, the toughest climb on the Tour de Trump and closely watched by thousands of fans

but this time he didn't have Ekimov at his side. Within 10km the six chasers had closed to within 1:50 of the six leaders, while Bobrik's group was a further 1:15 seconds back. This was the signal for the three PDM riders in the break to stop working, in anticipation of the Alcalá-Breukink group catching them. However, when the two front groups merged, the gap had closed to only 31 seconds . . . and the PDM plan was soon dead.

The pace immediately slowed, and within 5km about sixty riders had regrouped. It was time for a respite in this destructive stage (fourteen riders would quit by the end of the day), and there was no response from the pack when four riders drifted off at the front. The new break comprised Kiefel, Lammerts, De Clercq and Marc Van Orsouw of Holland (PDM), while Zanoli jumped across the gap before it grew too big. Riding through thick mist on the climbs, and splashing through rivers of water on the backroads' many dips, the peloton lost interest in the break, and at the foot of Mohonk Mountain, 20km from the finish, it was 4:50 back. Zanoli was surprisingly strong on the climb, and when Kiefel made a darting attack at the summit, the Coors Light rider was the only one to respond. Down the wet, curving, main road descent, Zanoli risked everything to catch Kiefel, knowing that he could win the sprint once they reached the short, downhill finish straight in the New Paltz College campus. And he did.

Meanwhile, Alcalá and Kvalsvoll again went on the warpath, and drew away from fourteen others on Mohonk. An unofficial time check put the race's top two climbers 30 seconds clear at the summit; but when they came into the finish 2:58 behind Zanoli, their advantage over the Bobrik group was only 10 seconds. The Russian had lived to fight another day.

After almost a week of long road races, not much was expected from the 11th stage: an eight-lap, 80km circuit race in Manhattan's Central Park. There was a glitzy opening, when two of the featured stars, LeMond and the 1989 race winner, Norwegian Dag-Otto Lauritzen of 7-Eleven, attacked. After them went hometown hero McCarthy – who lives a block away and has been racing in the park since he was thirteen. 'I went up to the break,' reported McCarthy, 'and went straight through it. And then Bauer and some others came up to me.' So within half a lap of the twisting, rolling 10km Central Park circuit, McCarthy and Bauer had established a clear break with Matt Eaton (AC-Pinarello) and two amateurs, Michel Lafis of Sweden and Ed Kaczmarczyk, an immigrant Pole racing for the Canadian national team. They gained a maximum lead of 3:39, temporarily lifting Bauer into third overall, but as the bell sounded, the gap had been reduced to 2:46. Four kilometres from home, Kaczmarczyk jumped and was followed by Lafis. 'It was a pathetic attack,' said Bauer, 'but McCarthy and Eaton both sat on my wheel.' The result of the pros' stalemate was an easy stage win for Kaczmarczyk, who rode away from Lafis just before the downhill finish. It had been a tougher stage than expected, and a haggard-looking Bobrik declared, 'There's no such thing as an easy day in this race.'

The pressures and demands of being race leader were clearly weighing on Bobrik as he lined up next day with the other ninety-seven survivors in the small Hudson Valley town of Catskill. His biggest concern was the Devil's Kitchen, the Tour de Trump's toughest climb that would be tackled 30km into the 187km 12th stage. Rising at gradients of up to 20 per cent, the main part of

After the leaders had gained 30 minutes on the pack, American James Urbonas broke clear to win stage 12 in Albany, New York

the hill is only 3km long, but besides the steepness the climb negotiates a narrow, potholed backroad that's closed by snow in the winter. Its notoriety is such that thousands of fans had turned up, leaving their vehicles lining the early part of the ascent – a scene reminiscent of the Tour de France.

The pace on the climb was set by Hampsten, Kvalsvoll, Alcalá and AC-Pinarello's Clark Sheehan. Bobrik wasn't able to follow. He topped the 580m high climb in a small group, 40 seconds after mountain leader Kvalsvoll had sprinted hard to take the prime from Ekimov, Hampsten and Alcalá. The climb had split the race into several parts, and a few kilometres later a Bauer-led chase group was only 40 seconds down on the nineteen leaders, while Bobrik's group was at 1:05. The Bauer group caught the leaders 20km after the climb, by which point Bobrik's group was 2:40 back. Eventually, after the break had covered 47km in one hour, the exhausted Soviet riders sat up, thus conceding the race to Alcalá. At the finish in Albany, three hours later, Bobrik's pack was more than 32 minutes behind . . .

The 12th stage was won by Spago's James Urbonas, who broke clear in the final kilometres, with Speaks dashing in for second place after an attack in the streets of Albany. By now Alcalá was firmly ensconced in the leader's jersey, ahead of Kvalsvoll and Breukink; and the final stage – which gave Zanoli his second stage win, in a sprint from Ludwig and American Davis Phinney of 7-Eleven – provided Alcalá with a rain-sodden victory procession all the way to Boston.

After the finish in Boston, a joyful Alcalá asserts the superiority of himself and his PDM team-mates

Tour de Romandie: 8-13 May

Charly Mottet's claim to be a serious contender for the Tour of Italy was finally validated by the French RMO rider's victory in the Tour de Romandie in Switzerland. This traditional curtain-raiser to the Giro witnessed Mottet's first real demonstration of strength in the 1990 season: apart from his second place in the penultimate stage of Paris-Nice, he had been absent from the limelight all spring. But, as was the case with several aspirants to the Tours of Italy and France, it was a planned absence, aimed at allowing him to build up his reserves and peak at the right moment. For Mottet, the first Frenchman to win here since Bernard Hinault in 1980, the Tour de Romandie was the cue to resume business as usual.

The Tour of Romandie's not-too-exhausting balance of time trials, flat stages and one or two testing mountain legs – together with a handsome purse – add up to a comfortable race to ride, and a prestigious race to win. In its forty-four years, it has always drawn an ambitious field and has an impressive list of winners, amongst them Gino Bartali (1949), Eddy Merckx (1968), Bernard Thévenet (1972), Giuseppe Saronni (1979), Bernard

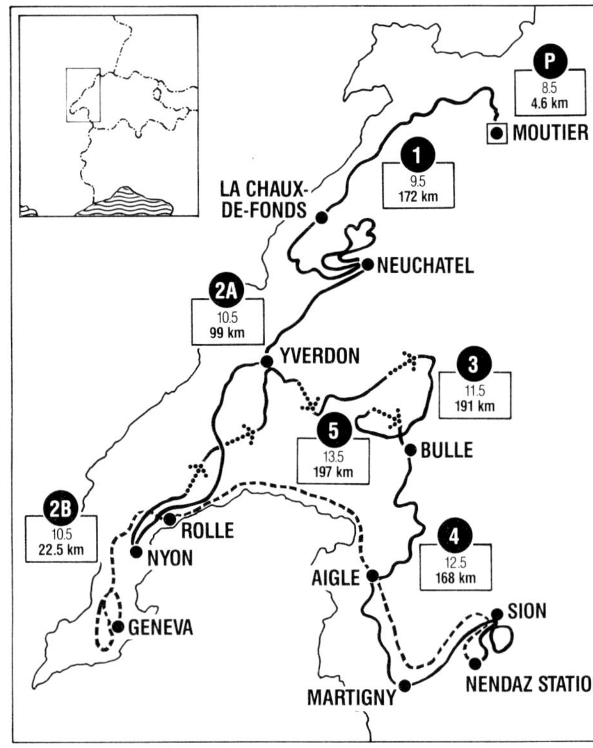

Tour de Romandie, Switzerland: 854km

His win in Romandie reinforced Charly Mottet's hopes for a good performance in the Giro d'Italia

Hinault (1980) and Claude Criquielion (1986). The most impressive winner of all is Ireland's Stephen Roche, with a record three wins, in 1983, 1984 and 1987.

As well as Mottet, among the main attractions this year were his French rivals Laurent Fignon (Castorama) and Jean-Claude Leclercq (Helvetia-La Suisse); Scotland's Robert Millar (Z); the Netherlands' Gert-Jan Theunisse (Panasonic) and Adrie Van der Poel (Weinmann); Belgium's Luc Roosen (Histor); and the defending champion, Australia's Phil Anderson (TVM).

Preparation for the Tour of Italy was the main emphasis for most riders. For teams like TVM, there was the pressure to earn vital FICP points before the Tour de France organizers made their post-Giro selection of sixteen teams. Other riders, like Millar, needed to do well here since their personal programmes focused on week-long events like the Dauphiné Libéré and Midi Libre, so they would be missing the Giro. All of these factors made for some competitive racing.

Nevertheless, after he won the opening prologue, it was evident that Mottet was going to be the man to watch. Like everyone else, Mottet knew that Fignon, who would in other circumstances have been a hot favourite, had only just recovered from a bout of bronchitis and would not risk his Giro hopes here; nor was he unduly worried when, on stage 1, the leader's green jersey went to Australian Micheal Wilson (Helvetia-La Suisse) – there was still one more time trial and a mountain stage ahead. Like Mottet, Wilson was a rider who had started the season lacking condition but Wilson – fourth in last year's Grand Prix des Nations and third the year before – had spent a difficult spring trying to convince his *directeur sportif*, Paul Köchli, that

Wilson (left) and Järmann made the early running, Järmann winning the first stage and Wilson claiming the leader's green jersey

it was all part of the plan, Köchli sceptically inclining to the view that he had been lazy over the winter.

When Wilson took second place and the green jersey in the first stage, via a two-man break with the Swiss Rolf Järmann (Frank), who had been prominent in the spring classics, he looked to be proving the critics wrong. But he had only 20 seconds on Mottet overall, and when Mottet won the second sector of stage 2, a 22km time trial at Nyon, taking back 11 seconds of Wilson's lead, the tall, dark-haired Tasmanian's chances of holding on to his jersey started to look slim. Wilson hung on through stage 3, won by Belgian sprinter, Michel Dernies (Weinmann), but Mottet delivered the *coup de grâce* on stage 4.

This was the biggest mountain leg of the race, and when Mottet went on the attack with Millar, Mexico's Miguel Arroyo (Z), Roosen, and Switzerland's Fabian Fuchs (Frank), Wilson – an able climber when finely tuned – missed the move. His subsequent efforts to chase were neutralised by the defensive tactics of Mottet's RMO compatriots Eric Caritoux, Thierry Claveyrolat, Jean-Claude Bagot and Christophe Manin, and a sorry day's racing for Wilson – he finished the day 2:41 down on Mottet and in fourth place overall – became the cornerstone of Mottet's victory. Happy to secure overall leadership, Mottet took a step back from the business of stage winning, and since Arroyo and Fuchs had been dropped it was left to pony-tailed Robert Millar to take the stage from Roosen.

For the fifth and final stage, the climbers conceded centre stage to the sprinters. And, as has become almost a tradition, it was the Swiss Panasonic rider, big, moustachioed Urs Freuler, who took victory in the stage. The top order stayed as at the end of the previous stage: Mottet, Millar, Roosen, Wilson; and almost before the finish they were all looking ahead – to Italy, or the Dauphiné, or Midi Libre . . . but ultimately, to the Tour de France.

Robert Millar was Mottet's closest rival at Romandie, finishing 2:00 behind the Frenchman. Pictured here in the prologue, Millar made his strongest showing in the fourth and final stage

Vuelta a España: 24 April-15 May

Twenty-eight-year-old Italian Marco Giovanetti of the Spanish Seur team confounded all the tipsters – and surpassed even his own expectations – when he won the Spanish national tour, the Vuelta a España, continuing Italy's dream run of success in 1990. Rising from virtual obscurity in his sixth year as a professional, Giovanetti must qualify as the most unlikely winner for many a year. He was ranked 98th on the world FICP rankings before the Vuelta; he had not won a major race since his stage win in the 1987 Tour of Switzerland; and with the apparent handicap of an 80kg body weight, the odds seemed heavily stacked against him. Besides, it is legendary that for a foreigner to win the Vuelta is as hard as for a rich man to enter the Kingdom of Heaven – failed *coups* by foreign riders litter the annals of this most insular of national tours. One only has to recall the loss of the *amarillo* jersey by Scotland's Robert Millar in 1985. As the race drew to a close, Millar looked certain to win – until, that is, a break including Spaniard Pedro Delgado rode away and, as Millar was only allowed to learn when it was too late, gained an unbeatable advantage over the Scot. Millar was unable, both then and the following year, to break through an implacable wall of Spanish hostility. The roll call of foreign winners testifies to the calibre required. The twenty-one foreigners who have managed to win the Vuelta include

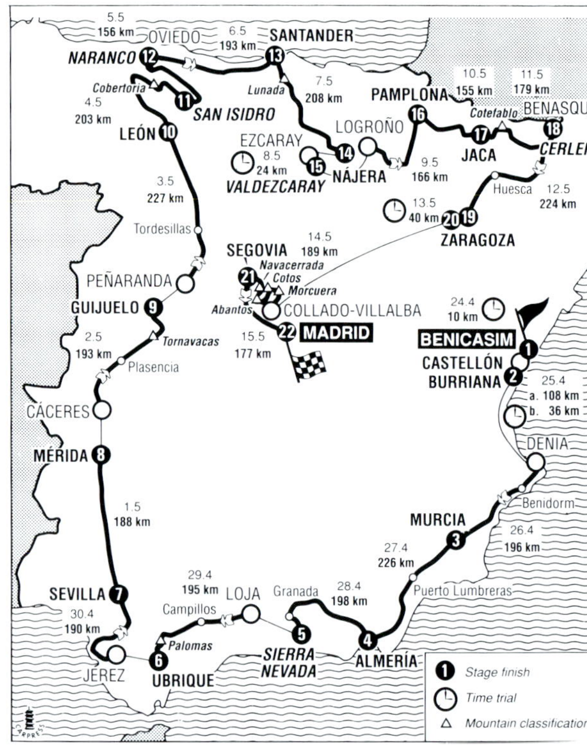

Vuelta a España: 3680km

Delgado stuck to his plans to use the Vuelta as preparation for the Tour de France

Marco Giovanetti doggedly defended his yellow jersey for ten days

Jacques Anquetil (1963), Eddy Merckx (1973), Freddy Maertens (1977), Bernard Hinault (1983), Luis Herrera (1987) and Sean Kelly (1988). Hinault called it his 'hardest ever Tour to win'.

When the 1990 edition wheeled away on 24 April, the Spanish contenders included 1989 winner Delgado; his Banesto team-mate and Paris-Nice winner Miguel Indurain; and ONCE's Anselmo Fuerte and Marino Lejarreta. Foreign aspirants were Colombia's Fabio Parra (Kelme) and Luis Herrera (Café de Colombia); East Germany's Uwe Ampler (PDM); Switzerland's Toni Rominger (Chateau d'Ax); the Soviet Union's Ivan Ivanov(Alfa Lum); and Frenchman Jean-François Bernard (Toshiba). It quickly became apparent, however, that not all of them were up to the unique rigours of the Vuelta. It might not be the most prestigious of the three major national tours, but the Vuelta is the first and the fastest: day after day, attack after attack, the peloton assumes the form of a speeding pace-line, with not a trace of the processional parades that characterise the French and Italian tours.

Herrera arrived on the starting line overweight and out of condition, and his visible lack of interest in the race never altered. Bernard, who had showed promise in the spring with his Col d'Eze time trial win in Paris-Nice and the marathon break in Liège-Bastogne-Liège, reserved his energies for stage wins, liked his stage 15 triumph in the time trial to Valdezcaray. Lejarreta had an injured foot, and – not wishing to prejudice his chances in Italy and France – kept his notorious assaults in check. Rominger, the great Swiss hope supposing his hay fever held off, couldn't find the form that would have put him in contention. And then, when it came to the anticipated climax in the Pyrenees on stage 18, and the penultimate mountain leg on stage 21, Delgado, Fuerte and Indurain all failed to produce any kind of confrontation.

An erratic Jean-François Bernard scored a surprisingly emphatic time trial win at Valdezcaray

This all played into Giovanetti's hand very nicely. So, too, did the fact that he was riding for a Spanish team, Seur, and began the Vuelta with the intention of riding for his team leader and 1986 winner, Alvaro Pino. But a barrage of injuries from an earlier crash, and a dose of knee tendinitis, saw off the veteran Spanish stalwart on the mountainous 21st stage. And by then, Giovanetti was clearly on a winning streak. To give credit where it is due, the lanky Italian raced far above himself. When he took the *amarillo* jersey from the Spaniard Julian Gorospe (Banesto) on stage 11, however, his ultimate victory still seemed unthinkable. 'It will take a miracle for me to keep the lead even after the time trial at Valdezcaray [stage 15],' he said, after becoming the fourth and final overall leader.

Beginning with a three-man team time trial over 11.5km, the Vuelta's first leader was dark horse Pello Ruíz Cabestany of ONCE. However, his stage win with fellow Spaniards and team-mates Fuerte and Melcho Mauri resembled a prologue in its formality, and it was not until stage two that individual road racing talents became evident. And the man with the early form was the Soviet sensation, Viktor Klimov (Alfa Lum). On the second sector of stage two, the 25-year-old neo-pro carried off the yellow jersey after placing third in a winning four-man break, which finished an amazing 8:06 clear of the peloton. The Vuelta had its first Soviet leader! Early in the race though it was, such a commanding lead still struck fear into every aspiring Vuelta champion. Throughout the race entourage, profile books, event programmes and old magazines were being scoured for information about this boyish-looking Russian. All anyone knew was that he had been a member of the winning Soviet 100km team time trial squad in the 1985 world titles...

Klimov spent the next four days in yellow, surviving not only the second stage time trial, in which his Alfa Lum team finished ninth to Lotus at 0:40, but also stage 3, which saw Belgian expatriate Nico Emonds of Teka win by 0:53 in a solo break (although Emonds later failed the mandatory dope test and had his winning laurels taken away). It was to his credit that Klimov didn't succumb where everyone expected, on the 198km fifth stage which was the Vuelta's first true test. On the 2400m Sierra Nevada, the finish scene – after Frenchman Patrice Esnault's (BH) 2:05 victory over Colombian Martin Farfán (Kelme) – was like a field hospital. After struggling to the crest of the finishing 28km climb, exhausted riders were pried off their bikes

Siesta time for Gerhard Zadrobilek

and hauled away by helpers. Many needed oxygen, particularly the Colombians, who had 12 riders amongst the first 30 to finish. But Klimov, hanging on to his lead with a 45th place at 8:28, had once again confounded the tipsters.

Klimov eventually lost his yellow jersey on stage 6, when Gorospe finally asserted the Banesto intent, no doubt as a decoy for either Delgado's or Indurain's planned final attack. The Spaniard was the instigator of a nineteen-man break which, while splitting up for the stage finale, managed to discard the main group, containing a tired Klimov. The loyal Banesto rider didn't expect to keep his jersey until the finish at Madrid. 'Pedro and Miguel shouldn't think about playing my card here. I am not a good enough climber . . .'

Five stages later, with the Vuelta heading towards the nationalistic hotbed of the Basque country, Giovanetti walked into the limelight. His twelfth place on the 203km eleventh stage from Leon to Estación Invernal de San Isidro was enough to push Gorospe back into fourth place overall at 2:40. This was a tough stage, finishing with a 20km climb. As he had himself affirmed, Gorospe is not a great climber, and after five exhausting stages in the lead, this crucial stage proved too much. He finished 37th, at 4:08 behind the Spanish stage winner, Carlos Hernández (Lotus) while, as expected, most of the heavyweights were up with Hernández: Rominger(3rd at 0:42), Indurain (4th at 0:46), Fuerte (5th at 0:50), Pino (7th at 0:50) and Parrá (8th at 0:50). Some of the disappointments were Ivanov (24th at 2:27), Herrera (46th at 5:12) and Lejarreta (69th at 13:42).

The following days focused on the build up to stage 15, the mountain time trial which Giovanetti feared would be his downfall. Along the way, victories went to Colombia's Alberto Camargo (Café de Colombia) on stage 12; on stage 13 a defiant Emonds expunged the disgrace of the earlier doping scandal; and the hard work of West Germany's Bernd Gröne (Stuttgart) was rewarded on stage 14. Come the Valdezcaray stage, one notable absentee was Klimov, who was now suffering the consequences of his previous exhausting efforts. But these events were eclipsed when the early, fine weather turned to heavy fog, and continuous rain and high winds swept the course of the mountainous, 24.1km time trial

Martín Farfán and Fabio Parra

to Valdezcaray. The Frenchman Bernard was the star of the day, winning by 1:03 from the Russian Vladimir Poulnikov (Alfa Lum), 1:03 from Frenchman Philippe Louviot (Toshiba) and 3:01 from East Germany's Ampler (PDM). But Giovanetti, finishing 31st at 5:10, still defied reason. His lead was intact by 1:31 – Fuerte, third placed overnight but second by the stage finish, could only make up 0:27. Now in third place was Ruíz Cabestany, at 1:32, and Delgado was fourth at 2:00. Other overall placings were: Ivanov, 6th at 2:29; Parrá, 7th at 2:35; and Indurain, 8th at 2:53.

Giovanetti's survival in stage 18 was as much due to his tactical sense and courage as it was to the obvious inability of Delgado, Fuerte or Ruíz Cabestany to pull off a timesaving attack. On the 178km race from Jaca to Estación de Cerler in the Pyrenees, only Farfân and team-mate Parrá attempted a break. They broke away together on the finishing 16km ascent, but only made 1:00 on Giovanetti. The surprising Italian took 8th place and finished with every favourite except Indurain, whose selfless efforts to tempo for 9th placed Delgado saw him drop off to finish at 1:50. By the finale in Madrid, Giovannetti would have come to regard the time trials, rather than his climbing prowess, as the source of his win, and in many ways he was right: he held on against the odds at Valdezcaray, following up after Estación de Cerler with an unexpected fifth place in the stage 20 time trial at Zaragoza, finishing 1:08 behind Ruíz Cabestany. This stage win gave Ruíz Cabestany second place overall – at a threatening 0:24 deficit – but it was only a temporary success. The menu of five major mountain passes – in the 188km twenty-first stage to Delgado's home town, Segovia – sapped every ounce of his pedal power. With 10km to go, he was left 1:52 adrift of the favourites, who were only 0:04 short of catching the victorious Frenchman Denis Roux (Toshiba). It was a battle no one anticipated – certainly not the stars fighting it out at the front-line. Finally, there was stage 22's 177km parade to Madrid, and the climactic explosion into the traditional bunch sprint – which saw East German Uwe Raab (PDM) triumphant for the third time in twenty-two days. The Vuelta had ended, and Giovanetti had made his name. And when, three weeks later, he placed third in the Tour of Italy, he made sure that his name would not be forgotten that easily.

Uwe Raab clinched the blue jersey points title with a final stage win over Malcolm Elliott in Madrid

Dauphiné Libéré: 28 May–4 June

Normally upstaged by the Giro d'Italia which is held at the same time, the 1990 Critérium du Dauphiné Libéré more than matched its longer Italian counterpart, both in the quality of its field and its racing. Of those riders who had pretensions to winning the Tour de France, only American Greg LeMond of Z, Frenchman Laurent Fignon of Castorama, and the 1989 Dauphiné winner Charly Mottet (RMO) had travelled to Italy. Competing in the French race were Irish stars Stephen Roche (Histor-Sigma) and Sean Kelly (PDM); American hope Andy Hampsten (7-Eleven); Switzerland's Toni Rominger (Chateau d'Ax); Colombians Fabio Parra (Kelme) and Luis Herrera (Café de Colombia); Belgium's Claude Criquielion (Lotto); French riders Thierry Claveyrolat (RMO), Jean-François Bernard (Toshiba) and Luc Leblanc (Castorama), and Britain's on-form climber Robert Millar (Z). What attracted them were the nine days of competition and the feast of climbing that awaited them in the French Alps, which would provide ideal preparation for the Tour. For others – notably the Colombian teams Café de Colombia and Postobon – the race provided a last chance of impressing the Tour de France organisers, and perhaps gaining a 'wild card' selection for the Tour.

The Dauphiné resulted in a battle between two climbers, Claveyrolat and Millar, both 31 years of age. After the two crucial mountain legs, Millar was just 9 seconds down on his French rival – a lead that the Scot was confident of overcoming in the eighth and final stage, a 37.8km time trial around the beautiful Lake of Annecy. Discussing their rivalry, Millar said, 'Thierry and I have ridden together long enough to know each other's strengths and weaknesses by heart. He was better than me in the mountains, but I knew that in a time trial, I would take up to two minutes from him. That's the game . . .'

It was to the event's credit that the final verdict was in doubt until the final stage. And although the race started not far from Annecy, at the similar lakeside town of Aix-les-Bains, the early stages favoured the riders emerging from the classics. Indeed, the very first stage was taken by that star of the West German classics, Rolf Gölz (Buckler), who was one of forty riders who emerged at the front of the race after the third-category Col du Chat climb in the final 20km. Gölz won the stage over the classy Belgian Sammie Moreels (Lotto), who was making a comeback to racing after suffering a broken leg at the Tour of the Americas three months earlier. Gölz enjoyed a three-day reign at the top of the standings, but any hopes he had of retaining the blue-banded yellow jersey of race leadership were mercilessly dispelled on stage 4 – a flat, 183km run from Vals-les-Bains to the ancient papal city of Avignon. Gölz's mistake was to ignore a series of attacks launched at the feeding station by Roche's Histor-Sigma team-mates, Frenchmen Laurent Biondi and Francis Moreau. Most of the other race favourites joined the move, but the inattentive Gölz and his Buckler colleagues were left behind when the pack was split by a sideways blast from the powerful Mistral wind in the Rhône Valley. Roche commented: 'I have a good team. When I see too many leaders not

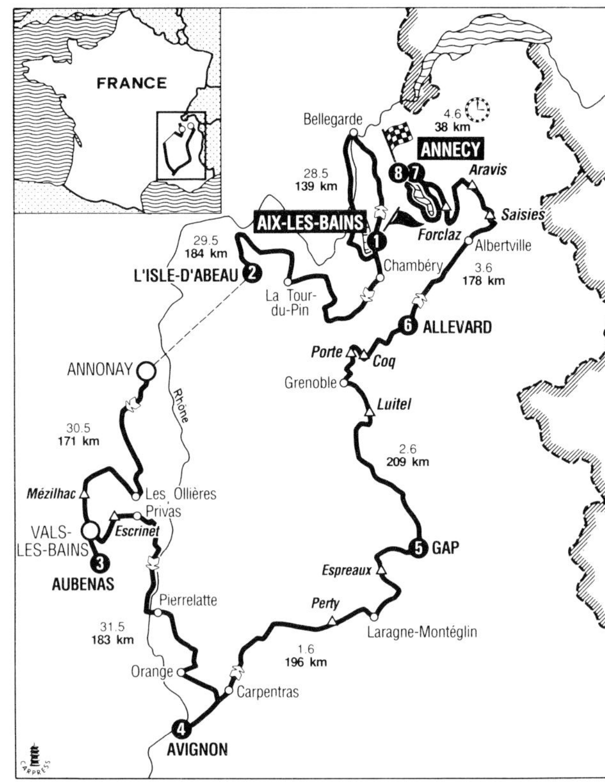

Dauphiné Libéré, France: 1298km

doing enough work, they are always ready to race.'

Eager to help Roche and his team in setting the pace of the front group was Rominger, winner of the third stage and handily placed in second overall. And after Castorama's Frédéric Moncassin won the stage in Avignon, just as he'd won the second stage two days before, it was Rominger who donned the leader's jersey. The elegant Swiss rider, still searching for the form that gave him a second Tirreno-Adriatico victory in March, was favoured to defend his leadership into the Alps. But like Gölz, Rominger suffered an unexpected reversal the next day.

This time, it wasn't a concerted group effort that deprived the leader of the jersey, but a 60km solo break on the hilly backroads of Provence, bravely made by French hope Luc Leblanc. He arrived in Gap, at the doorstep of the Alps, with a winning margin of 1:41, which he hoped would be enough to take him through to final victory. However, Leblanc had yet to prove his climbing ability in the high mountains – and the days ahead would test even the strongest climbers to the limit. The first day in the Alps was a 209km stage from Gap to Allevard-les-Bains, comprising a daunting litany of five mountain climbs – including the first-category climbs of the Col de Luitel, Col de Porte and Col du Coq.

As can often happen in these mountains to the west and north west of Grenoble, fog and rain awaited the field, heightening the fear of crashes on the narrow, twisting descents. The inexperienced 23-year-old from Brittany was let down by his nerves and left isolated by his team, in a concerted attack launched by Millar's Z team. By the end of the day, Leblanc was more than 10 minutes behind the leaders, and left with only memories of what might have been.

Striking north from Gap, the peloton huddled together in their rain jackets during the initial climb of the Col Bayard and the subsequent undulations of the broad Route Napoléon. After this initial 'warm-up', the Z riders began their attacks on Leblanc's lead, headed by the Norwegian Atle Kvalsvoll. Beneath the dripping trees, on the steep and narrow Luitel, Kvalsvoll began a menacing, lone break that caused the peloton to explode. By the summit, a chase group had emerged, with Millar calmly following the pace set by Histor's Roche, 7-Eleven's Hampsten, RMO's Claveyrolat and three Colombian riders, the Kelme pair Parra and Martín Farfãn, and Alvaro Mejia of Postobon. Local rider Claveyrolat – who finished third in the 1989 Dauphiné, and was leading the Grenoble-based RMO team in the absence of Charly Mottet – split things up even further on the Col de Porte. Only Millar, Parra and Farfãn could reply to Claveyrolat's accelerations, and they joined up with Kvalsvoll before tackling the shorter, but steeper, Col du Coq. With his job done, the Norwegian dropped back. Millar and Claveyrolat kept on the pressure, and also distanced the two Colombians. Parra was only slightly behind the two leaders as they negotiated a stretch of unpaved road at the 1370m summit; but the Kelme leader crashed twice on the treacherous descent, and not even the presence of team-mate Farfãn could help the stony-faced Parra close the ever-widening gap.

There were more descents and climbs in the remaining 40km, but these only allowed Mejia and Rominger to catch Parra, while Farfãn fell back, and was also passed by the Roche-Hampsten duo. At the uphill finish in Allevard, Claveyrolat dashed away to take the stage win, by 10 seconds over Millar. Rominger came in alone, at 2:43, followed by Mejia (at 3:46), Parra (3:54), Roche (6:35) and Hampsten. Leblanc rolled into Allevard in 21st place, 11:29 down. Claveyrolat was radiant when he pulled on the yellow jersey – trading it for the jersey as best climber – but the little Frenchman knew that he would have to extend his overall 5 second lead on Millar before the concluding time trial. The only chance of achieving this would come on the 15 per cent Col de la Forclaz, just before the finish of the 177km seventh and penultimate stage into Annecy. After the day's first two category 1 climbs, a lead group of thirty-six riders allowed Bernard, who was out of contention, and Roche's Belgian team-mate, Luc Roosen, to escape; but the more important battle was played out behind them.

Attacking on the Forclaz, 'as if the summit were the finish line', Claveyrolat played his final card. Millar, however, was fully prepared for the onslaught, and stuck like glue to the RMO rider's wheel. Claveyrolat *did* take the 4-second bonus for third place in Annecy, minutes behind stage-winner Roosen and Bernard, to increase his overall margin to 9 seconds. But he knew that this wasn't going to be enough to fend off Millar in the time trial, and indeed after only 12km of the 37.8km test, Millar's lead was already 50 seconds, and the Scot was able to cruise to a 1:44 advantage over his only rival by the end of the rolling, lakeside course.

Millar finished a commendable 12th in the time trial, 1:45 behind the unexpected winner, Mejia. The Postobon rider produced an outstanding time of 47:04 that elevated him into third place in the final standings, winning the stage by 30 seconds over the Lotto rider Johan Bruyneel of Belgium, with 7-Eleven's Sean Yates of Britain in third place (at 1:00), followed by Belgian Edwig Van Hooydonck of Buckler (1:06) and Roche (1:18). Besides giving him overall third spot, Mejia's performance clinched his Postobon team's wildcard slot for the Tour de France.

For Millar, this gratifying win was perhaps his most important since taking the Tour of Catalonia in 1985. His eleven years of professional racing included second places in the Giro d'Italia, the Tour of Spain, the Tour of Switzerland . . . and the Dauphiné. Earlier in the season, he finished second to Mottet in the Tour de Romandie. Millar agreed: 'It is certainly the most important win of my career. I'm part of a French team, and the Dauphiné is a major race on the French calendar.' Among those celebrating his victory was the team's *patron*, Roger Zannier, whose huge investment in a cycling team was finally starting to pay big dividends. And with the Tour de France only a few weeks distant, Millar's good form was a tremendous boost to the Z team's morale as they prepared for the greatest race of all.

The Dauphiné Libéré did not see the best of Roche. However, he salvaged some success with his fifth place in the final 37.8km time trial at Annecy

Colombia's Fabio Parra was a sorry victim of the treacherous descent of the Col du Coq on stage 6, the fifth of five major climbs that day. He crashed twice!

Claveyrolat (in yellow) needed more than nine seconds' advantage going into the final time trial. Yet, on stage 7 – the second last day – every acceleration he made on the climbs was matched by Millar

Come the final day's time trial at Annecy, Millar knew he would beat Claveyrolat, and in fact turned a nine-second deficit into a 1:35 overall lead

Giro d'Italia: 18 May-6 June

In a wave of fervent nationalism, Italy's cycling fans – the *tifosi* – watched delightedly as their new, home-grown hero, Gianni Bugno of Chateau d'Ax, swept to a faultless Giro d'Italia victory. The 26-year-old from Milan wore the pink jersey of leadership for nineteen straight days, after winning it in the opening-stage time trial. In the process, he earned enough FICP points to make him the world's number one ranked professional.

18 May, stage 1 time trial: Bari, 13km
An indication of which riders are going to shine in a major tour usually comes from the prologue. But the 1990 Giro was a few days shorter than its maximum sanctioned length, and so the organizers took the opportunity to start the race with a time trial, 5km longer than the usual prologue distance. The course was completely flat, following a slightly curving course besides the Adriatic Sea. The extra kilometres in this 'prologue' test eventually favoured the riders on form. First-year pro and reigning world amateur road champion Joachim Halupczok of Poland (Diana-Colnago) showed his talents to record a fine 15:41, Australian Stephen Hodge (ONCE) set a startling 15:31, and former Tour de France prologue winner, Frenchman Thierry Marie of Castorama, came home with 15:22. His time remained the fastest until Bugno blasted home in 15:19 – an indication of things to come.

19 May, stage 2: Bari-Sala Consilina, 239km
After the longer than usual 'prologue', the 198 starters set off from Bari next morning on a longer than usual first road stage, across the peninsula to Sala Consilina. The stage was too long to expect much action over fairly easy terrain – but with time bonuses to go for at the InterGiro sprint after 62km and at the finish, some sparks would fly. With 6, 4 and 2 seconds available at the InterGiro – a stage within a stage that has a separate General Classification and £65,000 ($125,000) in prizes – Marie had a chance of taking over the pink jersey from Bugno. But the French rider could clinch only

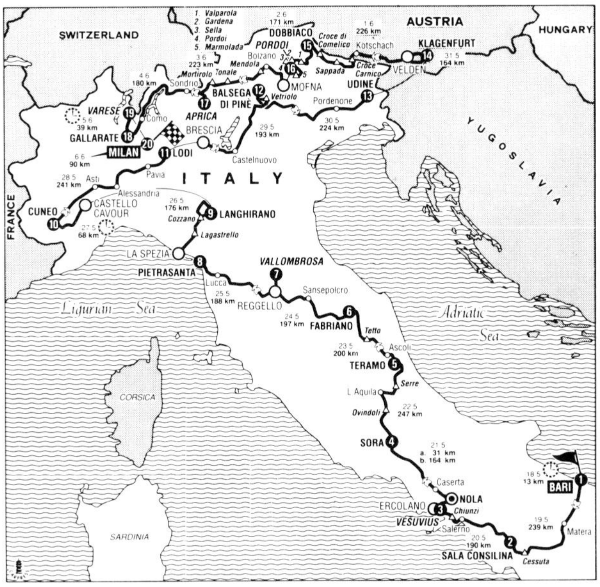

Giro d'Italia: 3464km

third place, which left him one second short of his goal. Marie's team leader, Laurent Fignon, was also keen to make up lost time – and an ideal opportunity was presented by a 100m climb over the final 1.8km to the finish line. Fignon did indeed make a furious attack, matched by his French rival Charly Mottet of RMO; but the Italian uphill sprint expert Giovanni Fidanza, Bugno's Chateau d'Ax team-mate, moved faster than either to win the stage. However, Fignon's 8-second bonus lifted him to sixth overall, while the 4 seconds earned by Mottet for third place also boosted his confidence after a poor time trial performance at Bari.

Gianni Bugno, Gert-Jan Theunisse of Panasonic and Marino Lejarreta of ONCE

20 May, stage 3: Sala Consilina-Vesuvius, 190km
Besides seeking bonuses, Fignon and Mottet were perhaps also flexing their climbing muscles for the third stage's mountain-top finish on Mount Vesuvius, the active volcano that dominates the Bay of Naples. The field stayed together until the day's first climb was reached, the 600m high Valico di Chiunzi, where Spaniard Eduardo Chozas (ONCE) began the break that would earn him the stage win and lift him to second place overall 50km later.

The split peloton partially regrouped on the 30km of flat roads before tackling Vesuvius, a climb which proved ideal for Bugno's big-gear climbing style. One by one he left behind the 15 riders with him, though the pink jersey was still 26 seconds behind Chozas at the finish. Bugno's impressive effort gave him a 43-second cushion over Chozas overall. Daniel Steiger of Switzerland (Frank-Toyo) moved into third place, with Fignon climbing to fourth, though he was now 1:08 down on the leader.

21 May, stage 4: Ercolano-Sora, 195km
There were no changes to the overall standings on the fourth day, which was split into two: a 31km sprint through the outskirts of Naples to the commercial centre

at Nola, followed by a fairly flat 164km to Sora. The Italian sprinter Stefano Allocchio (Italbonifica) took the first part in a mass sprint, just ahead of Chateau d'Ax's East German hope, Jan Schur; and Australian Phil Anderson (TVM) won a well-earned stage victory at the end of the day, when one of his many attacks left him clear with French rider Christophe Lavainne of Castorama.

22 May, stage 5: Sora-Teramo, 232km
The fifth stage should have been the longest of the race, but landslides on the day's scheduled course over the Vado di Sole climb forced the organizers to reroute on a less difficult course, 15km shorter. The changes (and an unfortunate crash in a tunnel) allowed an early break of twelve riders to remain clear until the finish – with Italian Fabrizio Convalle of the Amore & Vita team jumping ahead to win the stage in the last kilometre. The crash came when the pack was descending from the replacement climb. Fignon was sent flying on to his back, while Bugno's Italian team-mate Valerio Tebaldi fractured a bone in his pelvis. Fignon, who was heavily bruised and grazed, had to chase for 20km with his team to rejoin the peloton.

23 May, stage 6: Teramo-Fabriano, 200km
On the sixth stage, the break began just 40km in. The seven leaders gained enough time to stay away over the Sasso Tetto – one of the steepest climbs in the race, with a gradient of 14 per cent during its final six kilometres – and continued together to the final climb, just 3.5km from the Fabriano finish. Here, four of them were

Phil Anderson won the afternoon stage into Sora ahead of Christophe Lavainne, an achievement which heralded the Australian's best ever performance in the Italian Tour

A moment of panic for Laurent Fignon after the tunnel crash that wrecked his season

absorbed back into the peloton, while the aggressive Anderson sprinted away with his Italian companions, Massimo Ghirotto of Carrera and Luca Gelfi of Del Tongo. Anderson had taken all three mountain sprints to gain the leading climber's green jersey, but the Australian didn't have enough power left to resist Gelfi in the slightly uphill sprint to the line, and the Italian won the stage.

24 May, stage 7: Fabriano-Vallombrosa, 197km
Next day, Bugno again split the pack on the Giro's second mountain-top finish, at Vallombrosa, just east of Florence. Rising in steep steps, with no respite because of the narrow, twisting back-roads, this climb again suited Bugno, who won the stage on his own. Fignon was greatly troubled by his painful back injuries, and arrived 1:18 down, to drop out of the top ten.

25 May, stage 8: Vallombrosa-Pietrasanta, 188km
On this wet stage to the Mediterranean coast at Marina di Pietrasanta, virtually the whole pack arrived together. The speedy Allocchio took his second stage win, ahead of his compatriots Mario Cipollini (Del Tongo) and Guido Bontempi (Carrera).

26 May, stage 19: La Spezia-Langhirano, 176km
Overnight, the sultry, humid weather turned even nastier, and the 188 survivors had to don rain jackets for the four difficult climbs in the Appennines. The race started climbing almost from the start at La Spezia, a town where Fignon last year won a stage, wearing the pink jersey. His memories were to be more bitter this year.

The bedraggled pack reached the foot of the Lagastrello Pass, 35km into the stage, at Tavenelle, where the narrow road lifted the riders 750m into the clouds, in just 11km. Fignon – whose doctor had said he needed four days of complete rest – topped the mountain in the back group, 5:15 behind the leaders. But at the next village, Rigoso, Fignon finally had to call it a day; he braked to a halt and climbed into his number two team car.

Meanwhile, the battle for the pink jersey was finally evolving. A group of five riders escaped on the next climb, the much shorter Ticchiano Pass: two Soviet riders, Dmitri Konyshev and Vladimir Pulnikov (both of Alfa Lum), Anderson (determined to defend his lead in the InterGiro competition), the enterprising Italian Claudio Chiappucci (Carrera), and the opportunistic Chozas.

Over the 15 per cent climb to Corzano, and into the stage finish town of Langhirano, the five leaders gained over 4 minutes, before setting out on a 66km finishing loop. This put Chozas into the overall lead by 2 minutes, and forced Bugno and three team-mates in his group to start a laborious chase through the rain to close the gap. They managed to get within the crucial 2 minutes before the last climb, the Valico di Fragno. There the Alfa Lum riders started attacking, and Pulnikov broke clear on the fast, swishing descent to become the first ever rider from the Soviet Union (he was born in Kiev) to win a stage of the Giro d'Italia. The 24-year-old arrived 1:39 before Konyshev outsprinted Anderson, Chiappucci and Chozas for second place; only 47 seconds later, the Italian Massimiliano Lelli (Ariostea) and Spain's Marino Lejarreta (ONCE) led in Bugno's group of 22.

27 May, stage 10: Castello Cavour-Cúneo (time trial), 68km

So, going into the time trial, seven riders were still within 2 minutes of overall leader Bugno. Chozas had moved up to third place, while overnight runner-up Steiger had dropped to 24th. With Fignon out, the focus switched to Mottet as Bugno's likely challenger. But on this stage the challenge came from elsewhere.

Except for a 5.2km climb through the Barolo vineyards, and a twisting 4.1km descent, the course

Allan Peiper rode the race of his life to win the 14th stage to Klagenfurt in Austria, but was quick to acknowledge the assistance of his co-escapee, Pascal Poisson

was mostly straight and flat. Bugno, for one, had no hesitation in choosing two disc wheels to go with his Moser-style time trial bike. The Chateau d'Ax leader raced through the first check point, at 27km, with a lead of 24 seconds on the previous fastest, stage 6 winner Gelfi – a 24-year-old third-year pro from Bergamo, who before his Fabriano win had never won a pro race, and who wasn't even mentioned in a list of 74 names selected by the daily *Tuttosport* as riders to watch. Before Gelfi arrived in the pre-Alpine city of Cúneo, on an overcast afternoon, the fastest time had been set by stage favourite Lech Piasecki of Poland (Diana-Colnago), whose 1:32:43 improved on the previous best of Marie by almost 1 minute. So there was some incredulity when the unheralded Gelfi sprinted across the line in 1:31:46, to take his second stage of this Giro.

Earlier in the day, American Greg LeMond (Z) had heartened his supporters by arriving in Cúneo with a good time of 1:33:52. It was finally the 20th fastest, even though LeMond hadn't been among the 60 fastest at the InterGiro check point at 41.5km. The Tour of Spain winner, Marco Giovannetti of Seur, also rode strongly, and finished in 1:33:31 – 5 seconds slower than Anderson, but good enough to lift the 11th-placed rider into a temporary overall lead. Of the next nine finishers, Mottet was best, with 1:34:14 – but this was much slower than expected for a man regarded as one of the world's strongest time triallists, and it left the French star 1 second short of Giovannetti on overall time.

Meanwhile, Bugno had been eating up ground with his slowly turning 55 x 12 gear. He passed and dropped Chozas for 3 minutes, but lost time on Gelfi over the final 25km, and came through Cúneo's impressively ornate Piazza Galimberti into the finish straight 6 seconds too late to win the stage. But his 1:31:52 was good enough to increase his overall lead to a monumental 4 minutes!

28 May, stage 11: Cúneo-Lodi, 241km

The next stage was both the longest and the flattest, and it ended in a chaotic mass sprint in the narrow streets of Lodi, just south of Milan. The Ariostea team controlled the fast run-in to propel Italian Adriano Baffi to the first Giro stage win of his career, and his 26th victory in all. A rejuvenated Anderson took advantage of the Ariostea lead-out to grab second place, and thus took the cyclamen-coloured jersey as the points leader.

29 May, stage 12: Brescia-Balsega di Pinè, 193km

Starting out from the city of Brescia the next morning, there was much speculation as to whether Mottet and the other climbers could open up the race again. The route to Balsega di Pinè included three climbs: the Vigolo Vattare and the Vetriolo, both in the last 60km, followed by a gradual 12km ascent to the finish line.

Castorama's Gérard Rué went 50 seconds clear on the first climb, and the attack became even more interesting when Chozas joined the French rider on the sharp descent. This pair started the climb to Vetriolo with a lead of 1:05 on the Z team's French rider Eric Boyer, and of 1:25 on the lead group.

Greg LeMond shrugged off his early season apathy in this 139km breakaway with Bruno Leali. Even though they were caught and paid dearly for their efforts the following day, the break was evidence of LeMond's renewed determination

Now Mottet began his attacks, to which only Bugno could reply. By the time they reached the 1200m summit, Mottet and Bugno had caught Rué, who had been dropped for 10 seconds by Chozas and Boyer. They all regrouped before the climb to Balsega di Pinè, where four men went clear. One of these, Boyer, made a strong counterattack when he saw the group closing and it was enough to take the Frenchman to a solo stage win, 33 seconds ahead of the indomitable Bugno. With eight stages left, Bugno looked to be on his way to a clear victory.

30 May, stage 13: Balsega di Pinè-Udine, 224km
At this point half-way through the Giro, the one remaining question was: could Bugno dominate the climbers in the high mountains of northern Italy as he had in the low mountains of the south? No challenges were expected on the preceding flat stages because, as 7-Eleven's Andy Bishop pointed out, 'This is the most controlled race I've ever ridden.'

That control came from eleven Italian teams that formed half the field and had strongly mutual interests, while at least eight other squads wanted to keep the pack together to favour their field sprinters. The Panasonic-Sportlife team tried to set up Dutch rider Jean-Paul Van Poppel for a win, in an attempt to salvage something from the Giro after his compatriot Steven Rooks's crashes and the withdrawal of Swiss sprinter Urs Freuler. However, Van Poppel couldn't follow his lead-out men, Harry Rozendal of Holland and Australian Allan Peiper, and the stage was taken by Cipollini from the chunky Russian Djamolidin Abdujaparov of Alfa Lum. Van Poppel came in only ninth, a position which didn't please the newly arrived Panasonic team manager Peter Post. He wanted a more aggressive performance in the next stage, that would cover three laps of a rolling circuit around the Wörther See, in Austria.

31 May, stage 14: Klagenfurt, 164km
Post's words obviously had an effect. A few kilometres into the final lap, Peiper made a strong attack, and he was joined by the French rider Pascal Poisson of Z. Over the remaining 49km, the Australian-French tandem kept at bay a 14-man chase group, that closed from 1:23 (with 40km remaining) to 0.09 (entering the final 3km). The two leaders kept up their pace and fought out a vigorous sprint that eventually went to the delighted Peiper.

1 June, stage 15: Velden-Dobbiaco, 226km
After being upstaged at Klagenfurt, the sprinters would have to wait another three days for their next chance. Three mountain stages lay ahead, starting with four medium-sized mountain passes in the second half of the stage to Dobbiaco. Leaving Velden in Austria, the pace was unusually brisk during the opening flat kilometres, and riders who paused for impromptu rest stops had a hard time chasing back to the peloton. One of these was Greg LeMond. On his return to the pack, 63km

The stage to Passo Pordoi, which takes in five mountain passes, is the most difficult and prestigious of the Giro, and it gave Bugno the opportunity to demonstrate his completeness as a rider and his right to be regarded as a great champion. Mottet, who had struggled to stay with him, managed to sprint away at the finish to win the stage

out, LeMond launched an attack. He was joined by former Italian champion Bruno Leali of Jolly, and on flat valley roads before the first climb they established a lead of 10:45.

On the 10km long, category 1 climb to the Plöcken Pass they lost a minute of their advantage – but with LeMond riding impressively, the gap increased to more than 12 minutes after they descended for 18km to the feed zone. LeMond led Leali over the short Sella Valcalda climb, with their lead still 12 minutes, but with more than 80km left to race. After a fast, curving descent, the course climbed for the following 20km, culminating in the Cima Sappada. Here, Bugno emphasized his authority by splitting the peloton with a relentless display of climbing speed. No one could match his pace, and he crossed the Sappada crest 5:05 behind the two breakaways, while Italian Franco Chioccioli (Del Tongo) and Mottet did their best to stay within range.

On the subsequent descent, half the field regrouped, to start the final climb 4 minutes behind LeMond and Leali. The Monte Croce di Comelico doesn't have steep gradients, so the chasers were able to work a paceline on the smoothly surfaced road. With the gap below 2 minutes, a counterattack was made by Chioccioli, the Venezuelan Leonardo Sierra of Selle Italia, and Spaniard Jon Unzaga of Seur, along with Eric Boyer, the stage 12 winner. The four counterattackers caught and passed LeMond and Leali 5km from the top; and their 139km escapade was over. The battle for stage victory now centred on the four new leaders, and on three men who took up the chase: Chozas, Ghirotto and Soviet rider Piotr Ugrumov (Alfa Lum).

These seven riders regrouped on the descent, and a sprint finish looked probable, but Boyer surprised the others with an attack 500m from the line to win his second stage easily. It had been a difficult race, but would prove to be mild compared to the destructive terrain awaiting them next day. With seven significant climbs, totalling more than 4,000m of altitude gain in 171km of racing, stage 16 was expected to be one of attrition rather than attack.

2 June, stage 16: Dobbiaco-Pordoi, 171km

The day began slowly, and after rolling steadily up most of the 17km long Valparola climb out of Cortina d'Ampezzo, a break was made by Gis-Benotto's Maurizio Vandelli of Italy and the Swiss Urs Zimmermann of 7-Eleven. They reached the cool, exposed 2300m pass 45 seconds ahead of the peloton, and on the spiralling descent they were chased by a group of nine that included Chozas, mountains leader Chiappucci and the talented Konyshev. Riding in bright sunshine, the two leaders were a minute clear over the Gardena Pass, where the race encountered heavy snow last year. But Zimmermann faltered on the following Sella Pass, midway through the stage, and the 25-year-old Vandelli continued alone to top this climb with a 1:15 lead over the chasers.

On reaching the first slopes of the Pordoi Pass, a solo chase was launched by Konyshev. By the time he reached the crowd-packed summit, the Soviet rider had gained a minute on his companions, but was still 1:15 behind Vandelli. Bugno's group, 3 minutes down on Vandelli, had been reduced to thirty riders – and there were still 60km left, including the fearsome 14km Marmolada climb and the final 12km ascent to the Pordoi finish.

On the long, sometimes dangerous two-part descent – where a weary Zimmermann crashed out of the race –

Chioccioli and Giovannetti on the Pordoi Pass

Mottet delightedly wins the Pordoi stage from Bugno

Konyshev caught Vandelli. They climbed the Marmolada together, bravely overcoming the frequent 13 per cent gradients, but at the summit were only 35 seconds ahead of Bugno and Mottet, who had ridden away from the rest. Behind them came another pair, Chioccioli and Giovannetti, while the rest of the field was scattered over 30 minutes. Konyshev and Vandelli were passed by both chasing duos as they headed into the final, curving ascent. Throughout the final 10km, Bugno set the pace without looking around – he knew that this Giro d'Italia would be his. Even so, Mottet upset the thousands of screaming Bugno fans by sprinting away at the finish to win this prestigious stage, and move into second place overall. Previous runner-up Giovannetti came in with Chioccioli, 2:16 later, while the courageous Vandelli, after 125km in the lead, came in fifth, at 3:38.

3 June, stage 17: Moena-Aprica, 223km
Everyone was clearly very tired; and the stage from Moena to Aprica, with another 4,500m of climbing, proved to be the slowest of the race. The peloton rode in procession over the first two climbs; and the first real attack, by a group of fourteen, didn't come until 110km from the finish. This group – which included the race's most aggressive rider, Italian Stefano Giuliani (Jolly), Bugno's room-mate Alberto Volpi and the promising Sierra – gained a minute by the top of the gentle Tonale Pass. They continued to gain time over a lethargic pack down the ensuing valley descent, which preceded one of the toughest climbs of the Giro: the Mortirolo Pass, which climbs 950m in 13km, in a succession of tight switchbacks.

As soon as the climb began, 52km from the finish, Sierra sprinted away from the lead group. This talented 21-year-old topped the climb 1:05 ahead of Volpi and Ghirotto, and 2:10 ahead of the remainder of the original break. Three times on the awesome descent – which drops through 1300m in only 12.8km – Sierra flirted with danger on the sharp turns. He once hit the kerb, but stayed upright, and reached the Valtellina valley with a 1:12 gap on the two chasers and 3:45 on the Bugno group.

There were still 25km left, including a final 11km climb to the finish at the ski resort of Aprica. But Sierra continued to show outstanding form, and he won by 52 seconds over Volpi, becoming the first Venezuelan rider to win a stage of a major European tour. In taking fourth place, Bugno displaced Phil Anderson from the points jersey he'd worn for a week, although the Australian was hopeful that he could regain it next day.

4 June, stage 18: Aprica-Gallarate, 180km
Despite Anderson's hopes, this stage predictably ended in a pack sprint at Gallarate, only a few kilometres from Bugno's home. Anderson did his best with limited team support, and although he was boxed in after negotiating five turns in the last 2km, he came through to take fourth place behind Baffi, Cipollini and Abdujaparov.

Cipollini protested, claiming that Baffi had used unfair tactics. 'Baffi's a bandit,' he exclaimed. But the result remained. It was Baffi's second stage win of the Giro, and his seventh victory of the season. Anderson *did* win

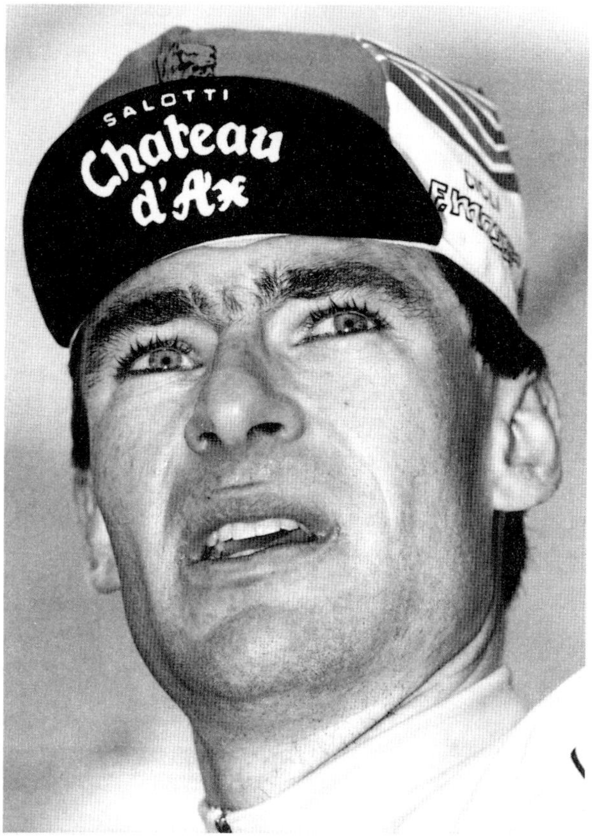

Gianni Bugno seemed to grow in stature and authority with every passing day

Even shrouded in cloud, Val Gardena provides the perfect setting for the Giro

back the points jersey, with a 12-point lead over Bugno; but that was small insurance against the next day's time trial, in which the winner would collect 37 points if he were fastest at the InterGiro (33.3km) and at the finish (39km). Bugno was indeed to prove the fastest at both points, in his most impressive performance of the race.

5 June, stage 19: Gallarate-Varese (time trial), 39km

Held in an almost continuous rain storm, and ending with a climb of 425m into the clouds above Varese, the time trial was intensely demanding. And it was here that Bugno put the finishing touches to his impressive race. The Chateau d'Ax rider swept through 2:20 faster than his rival Mottet to establish his final winning margin of 6:33 over the French star. Giovanetti came in third overall, at 9:01.

6 June, stage 20: Milan, 90km

By the final stage, a 90km circuit race around the Parco Sempione in Milan, Bugno was so far ahead of Mottet that the Italian could have been lapped on the 5km circuit, and he would still have won the Giro. Not since Eddy Merckx overcame Felice Gimondi by 7:42 in 1973 had anyone won the Tour of Italy by such a margin, or led the race from its opening to the finish. The *tifosi* had found their new hero.

With Bugno's lead by now unassailable, promising young climber Leonardo Sierra took the opportunity to establish himself as a star of the future by winning the difficult stage to Aprica

LeMond continued to use his new drop-in handlebars during the Giro, the aerodynamic advantage of which can be seen here on the stage to Dobbiaco

Milk Race: 27 May-9 June

Though the record books show an Australian at the top of the overall classification of the 1990 Milk Race, many of his fans considered the victory of Shane Sutton (Banana-Falcon) as good as a British win. When he first arrived in the UK in 1984 he was best known as the little brother of Gary, World Amateur Points Champion in 1980, but when the wins started coming Shane quickly established a reputation as a plucky all-rounder. Initially the wild man of British cycling, his long hair and moustache setting him apart from his better-groomed colleagues, he has become the unofficial *patron* of the small, self-contained Pommy peloton.

In criterium races round tight town centre circuits he could do no wrong, winning the 1985 Kellogg's City Centre series at a time when criterium racing was the number one discipline for UK riders. Despite his wiry, almost frail physique, few could match Sutton's nerve in the sprints, and his sunny disposition brightened the dullest of days. Out on the open road he was equally competitive, finishing third overall in the 1986 Milk Race, and playing a part in team-mate Malcolm Elliott's win the following year. In 1988 Sutton teamed up with his old friend Keith Lambert and the two of them, with Lambert as manager and Sutton as the captain on the road, set about building up a top UK-based team. Two years later, the Banana-Falcon team were dominating the domestic scene in a manner reminiscent of the ANC-Halfords team of 1986-7; after a promising early season with successful performances in the Tour of the Americas and minor races in Spain and Italy, the team returned to Britain and cleaned up in the pre-Milk Race criteriums and road races. In the weeks leading up to the Milk Race Sutton was going well, but a niggling knee problem and the success of younger team-mates like Dave Rayner and Rob Holden kept him out of the headlines. 'At thirty-two, you're not looking for miracles any more,' he had said the previous year, 'you're just looking to get a good team around you, and I think I can be a big influence as a leader rather than a winner.'

Although Tom Bamford chased hard to get back after being delayed by a puncture and faulty wheel on the stage to Hull, tardy team support made a hard job hopeless

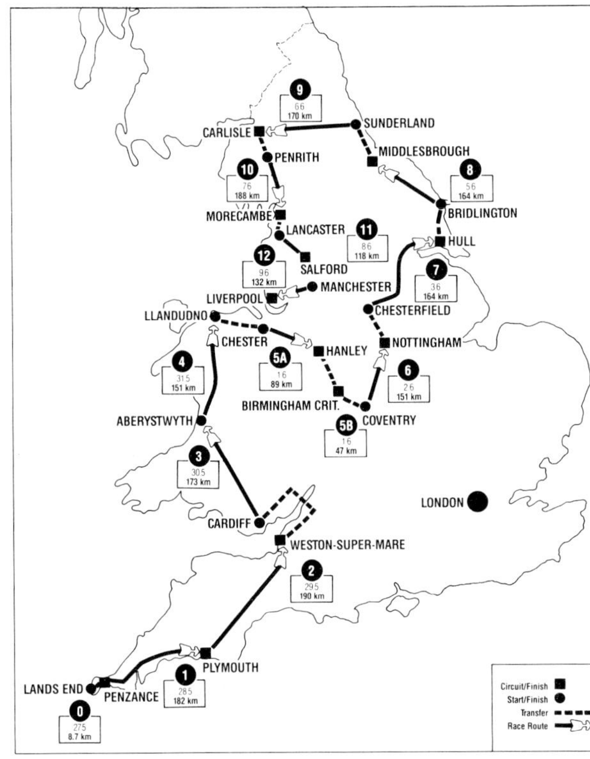

Milk Race, Britain: 1920km

Sutton certainly didn't seem to be riding as a winner on the second stage of the race, when he struck out with more than 160km to go on the long haul across the West Country to Weston-super-Mare. His team-mate Chris Walker had won the yellow jersey on the first stage from Land's End to Plymouth, and this was a textbook move to divert attention from the race leader and force rival teams to chase a potentially threatening breakaway. It worked perfectly; Sutton and his breakaway companion, Pavel Padrnos of Czechoslovakia, were caught with just over three kilometres to go, and Walker, having sheltered all day behind the wheels of the opposition, retained his yellow jersey. Sutton failed to win the stage, and his efforts were expected to have put him out of contention: '. . . people said that was the end of me in the bike race – "he'll be legless tomorrow!" ' said Sutton later. But his long break had taken less out of him than people supposed, and he used his unexpected energy to devastating effect the following day.

The stage between Cardiff and Aberystwyth is a frequent feature of the Milk Race, and is always good for a shake-up in the field. Run in the opposite direction in 1986 it witnessed Joey McLoughlin demolish the opposition with a courageous lone break through the narrow Welsh lanes and go on to win the race; in 1988, Soviet climber Ivan Ivanov took the race lead on the road to Aberystwyth on a day which ended the hopes of a number of leading contenders. This year it was Sutton's turn to crush the competition on the two stone anvils of the 174km stage 3 route, the Devil's Staircase and Gammalt climbs. After the opposition had been softened

Jan Bogaert's extensive experience of Continental criterium racing stood him in good stead for the many bunch sprints, of which he took five. Here he wins a stage in Birmingham

up by a number of attacks from the Banana-Falcon riders, Sutton jumped on the pedals just after the halfway mark and went clear in the company of Ben Luckwell (Ever Ready-Halfords). Luckwell, a first year professional not noted as a climber, was also suffering from back trouble, and though he hung on gamely until the foot of the Devil's Staircase he was powerless to stop Sutton's victory charge. Only New Zealander Tom Bamford realised the danger, crossing the four-minute gap and joining Sutton with 24km to go. Victory, and the yellow jersey, went to Sutton, with a 35 second advantage over Bamford and Sutton's team-mate Rob Holden third overall at 2:40. In the space of three days, the Banana-Falcon team had taken a firm grasp of the overall lead, put three other riders (Holden, Walker and Chris Lillywhite) in the top ten overall, and gone into the lead in the team competition.

Once safely in the yellow jersey, Shane Sutton and his Banana-Falcon team-mates let the opposition make the racing, contenting themselves with chasing down dangerous breaks

As the remaining nine stages took the race further north, Sutton and his 'boys' neutralised the opposition, chasing down dangerous breaks and dragging the race back together after hilly sections. Sutton's closest challenger, the unfortunate Tom Bamford, lost 28 minutes on the seventh stage to Hull, when a puncture and faulty wheel left him trailing hopelessly behind the bunch as it sped towards a £2000 prime halfway along the 164km route. That day's stage was won by East German Frank Augustin in one of the many bunch sprints which, on five occasions during the two-week race, were won by Belgian professional Jan Bogaert (La William). Overall, this was a race dominated by the professionals, outnumbered by amateur squads though they were; apart from the Hot Spot Sprints, won by UK amateur rider Simeon Hempsall, by the time the race had completed the twelfth and final stage to Liverpool – also won by Bogaert – the professional teams had collected all the major classifications.

Shane Sutton sprints to victory, and the yellow jersey, at Aberystwyth

CoreStates Championship: 17 June

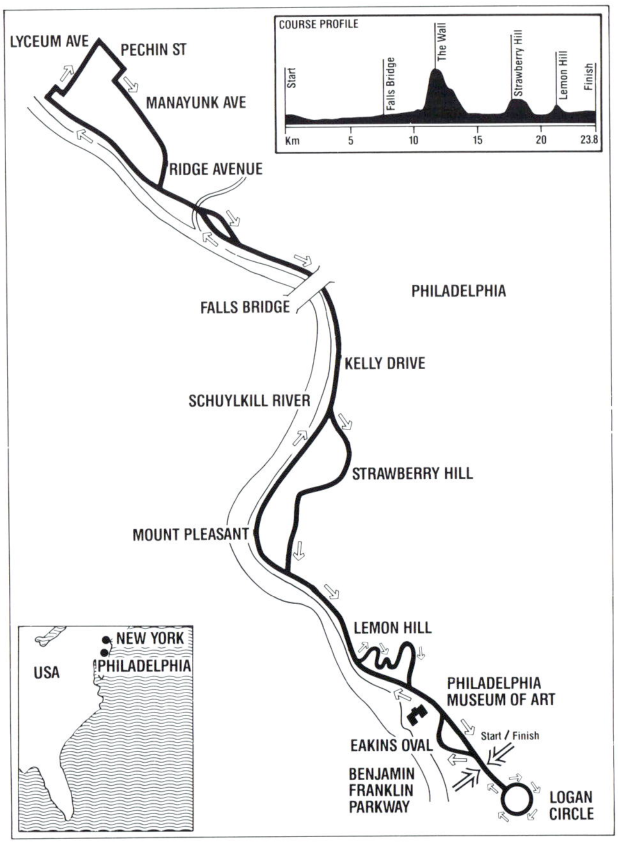

Core States Championship, Philadelphia: 250km

There was a look of irrepressible happiness on the dusky, dust-streaked face of Paolo Cimini when he realised he'd won the richest one-day race in the world – the sixth annual CoreStates Championship in Philadelphia. Enough to make anyone look happy, but Cimini's joy was not just at the prospect of the $25,000 first prize – his victory also proved that he had at last triumphed in a year-long struggle with an intestinal infection.

Cimini, an Italian with the Gis-Benotto team, who was one of the world's fastest prior to his illness, proved unstoppable when he unleashed his final kick to overcome two other latecomers, Frenchman Laurent Jalabert of Toshiba and third-placed American Kurt Stockton of American Commerce. The 250km race had been a destructive, six-hour battle between the event's two strongest teams, Coors Light and 7-Eleven, but in the end they raced each other into exhaustion, and were not amongst the contenders at the finish.

The sun was shining when the 92 starters set out down Philadelphia's Benjamin Franklin Parkway on what for many of them was the longest race of the year. The first attack came when Steve Speaks of Crest, the top American at the Tour de Trump, stormed up the main climb – the infamous Manayunk Wall – on the first lap of the course's principal 23.7km circuit. Only one rider, Irishman Alan McCormack of Coors Light, followed. As the temperature rose, and the lap times started to drop, the two leaders began to look capable of maintaining their break all the way to the finish: after 112km, they were 7:05 ahead. However, their inevitable fatigue caused them to be caught after more than 160km at the front.

The next significant break comprised nine riders: Americans Alexi Grewal and David Farmer, Italian Roberto Gaggioli, Dutchman Michel Zanoli, all of Coors Light; American James Urbonas of AC-Pinarello; and 7-Eleven's Americans Norman Alvis and Davis Phinney. Although Coors Light appeared to be in a position of strength, its four front-runners were in danger of giving rival sprinter Phinney an armchair ride to the finish.

Into the ninth lap, with 55km of racing still remaining, the nine leaders had a 0:29 advantage. And then a series of attacks split the front group, leaving only Grewal, Farmer, Alvis and Urbonas ahead. The gap between this new four-man break and the pack increased to 0:34, and then dropped to 0:23 as American Andy Bishop of 7-Eleven spearheaded a chase with the Stuttgart and AC-Pinarello teams. Italian Angelo Canzonieri – Cimini's Gis-Benotto team-mate – then made a spectacular

The Philadelphia Museum of Art formed an impressive backdrop for the 92 starters in the sixth annual CoreStates Championship

American Steve Speaks was first to the top of the Manayunk Wall seven times in his 149km break with Irishman Alan McCormack

bridging effort to catch the leaders, and with the Italian's added pulling power, their lead increased to 0:48, 32km from the finish.

The gap was reduced to 0:29 as the five leaders began the final haul up the Manayunk Wall. Sensing that he was having an inspired day, 1984 Olympic champion Grewal stretched his legs on the climb; only the courageous Urbonas and classy Canzonieri could get up to him, leaving Alvis and Farmer to drop back to the main group. But Alvis was soon helping Bishop with the chase, and the gap continued to reduce. Bishop launched a counterattack, followed by Americans Kenny Adams (American Commerce) and Gary Mulder (Spago), and with 8km remaining they had closed to 0:07.

On the first of the three 2.5km finishing circuits, the two trios came together, but a 12-strong chase pack was only six seconds behind as the race started the penultimate lap. Past the Philadelphia Museum of Art on the Parkway, the chasers closed, and Mulder made a solo attack. He was soon joined by 11 others, but his acceleration *did* succeed in shaking off four dangerous sprinters – Farmer, Gaggioli, Phinney and Dutchman Ad Wijnands (Stuttgart) – while Alvis was dropped completely. The Coors Light stranglehold on the race had suddenly been loosened: Grewal was now their only man amongst the 12 leaders. As for 7-Eleven, they still had Bishop and American John Tomac in front, but they were both tired from pulling back the earlier breaks. Even so, Bishop did try a solo, just after hearing the bell for the final, three-minute lap. But he was kept close company by a still-hopeful Grewal and Spago's American Oliver Starr . . . and then by the other nine.

With Starr, Mulder and Urbonas in the winning split, Spago coach Mike Neel again seemed to have worked his magic; but their numerical superiority didn't count for much on this completely flat finish: none of them can sprint. However, there *were* some sprinters in the group – notably the lone Jalabert, Cimini (with his team-mate Canzonieri) and Stockton (with support from his American team-mate Kenny Adams). As they rounded Logan Circle for the final time, with about 800 metres to go, Mulder again tried a solo. Grewal chased and caught him; they were quickly brought back; and the sprint was under way.

Never had the Philadelphia crowds seen so many riders come together for the final sprint. With about 300m to go, Jalabert (who had finished second in the points competition of the Tour of Spain) committed himself. 'I didn't think anyone would beat me,' commented the French second-year professional later. However, he hadn't reckoned with Cimini, who was still sitting snugly in Canzonieri's slipstream. With 150m left to go Jalabert opened up a four- to five-length lead, but then Cimini catapulted from behind Canzonieri and flew past Jalabert as they entered the final 50m. After a last thrust to the line, Cimini raised his arms to celebrate his upset victory. The Gis-Benotto rider was back, all right, in a finale as dramatic as you could wish for the rebirth of a star.

Italian Paolo Cimini (right) made a late charge to win from Frenchman Laurent Jalabert (left) and the lunging Kurt Stockton, whose third place earned him the US Pro Championship title

Tour of Switzerland: 13-22 June

Any fears that Irishman Sean Kelly might start the Tour de France in indifferent form were speedily dispelled when the 34-year-old PDM rider won the 10-day Tour of Switzerland in magnificent style. Kelly took the yellow leader's jersey on stage 4, defending it flawlessly against stiff opposition from Tour de France aspirants Robert Millar from Scotland (Z) and the American Andy Hampsten (7-Eleven), and keeping it right up until the 11th and final stage at Zurich. Kelly had previously won the event in 1983, beating Peter Winnen of the Netherlands, but his return to winning form this year was all the more impressive as it was only one month since he had been able to resume training after a broken collar bone forced a six-week lay-off.

It was also a good race for Millar and Hampsten. Millar finished second overall at 0:41, a result which – together with his Dauphiné Libéré win – confirmed his status as a top ten Tour favourite; and Hampsten finished third at 1:04, a performance whose highlight was a stage win on the biggest mountain leg of the race. For American Greg LeMond (Z), whose Tour de France hopes still looked doubtful in spite of better form in the Giro d'Italia, the Tour of Switzerland was an opportunity to respond to his critics, and he rose reassuringly to the challenge; his tenth place overall at 5:54 was his best result all year. Significantly, his best day in the event was the hardest – the 195km seventh stage to San Bernardino, in which he finished ninth at 1:56.

It was clear from the start that Kelly was at the very least going to pull off a confidence-boosting result. His campaign kicked off on stage 1 when he hopped into the

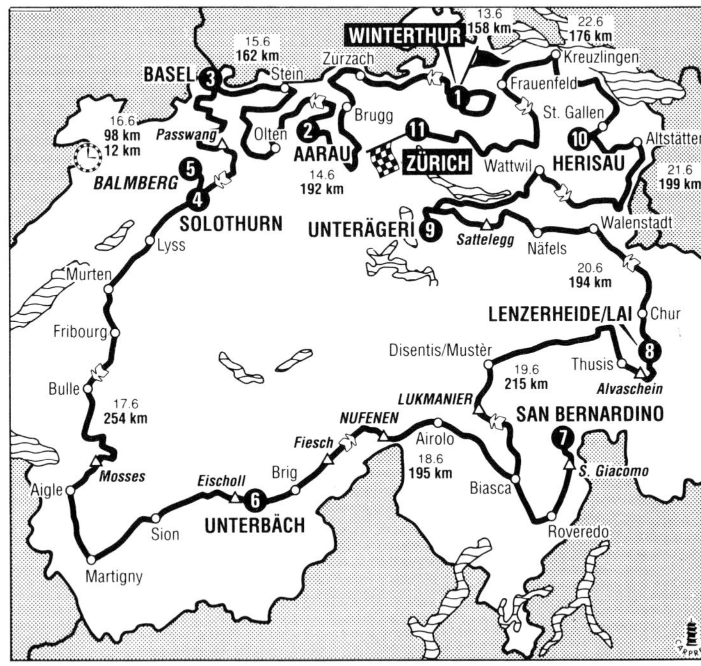

Tour of Switzerland: 1855km

winning five-man break after 42km, taking with him New Zealand's Nathan Dahlberg (7-Eleven), Italy's Roberto Pagnin (Malvor), Switzerland's Stefan Joho (Ariostea) and Dutchman Theo De Rooy (Panasonic). The break had no trouble staying away to the finish, with Kelly second to a surprised Dahlberg – although, because of the intermediate sprint time bonuses characteristic of this Tour, Joho became the race leader.

In the second and third stages, it was East Germany's Olaf Ludwig (Panasonic) and Belgium's Luc Roosen (Histor) who controlled affairs. Ludwig clinched his ninth win of the season on stage 2: Roosen, who had made it clear to his team director that he would not work for the sole interests of Stephen Roche in the Tour de France and had as a result been dropped from their team for the Tour, won stage 3, further fuelling doubts about the wisdom of his exclusion and adding impetus to his declared intention of shopping around for a new backer . . .

Kelly, however, had no team troubles – in fact, PDM were working better than ever. Kelly's authority asserted itself when he won stage 4 in a bunch sprint from Joho and Pagnin, and PDM's Eric Breukink of Holland won the fifth stage – a 12km time trial. Other PDM riders in the top ten were Mexican Raul Alcala (fourth at 2:30), Kelly (seventh at 0:12) and his compatriot Martin Earley (ninth at 0:37). By the end of stage 6, in which Kelly finished second in the bunch sprint to Belgium's Thierry Bock (Lotto-Superclub), the Irishman had an overall lead of 1:13. This was a good lead, and Kelly could not disguise his optimism. 'Honestly, I could get into trouble. But, at the worst, if I do not win this race, it will be one of my team-mates,' he said, referring to the good overall placings of Alcala and Breukink, fourth at 1:20 and seventh at 2:05 respectively.

It was clear from the very start what Sean Kelly's intentions were

It was anticipated that Millar (fifth at 1:21) and Hampsten (sixth at 1:44) would try to topple King Kelly on the seventh, 195km stage from Unterbach to the mountain top at San Bernardino, and so it came about. Kelly and his team-mates were riding at the front of a star-studded twenty-man lead group which had formed after 120km when the race passed the 2480m summit of the Col du Nufenen. The moment came five kilometres up the 15km final ascent. It was Hampsten, hoping for a third Tour of Switzerland, who launched the attack and, not surprisingly, Millar jumped away in pursuit. Before long, the duo had a 0:45 lead: exhausted by their efforts to control the race and the sharp attacks, the PDMs fell back – all, that is, but a determined Kelly, who dug deep into his pride to give chase. With him went the Swiss Daniel Steiger (Frank) and Dutchman Eddy Bouwmans (Panasonic), and this three-man pursuit saved Kelly's neck.

Millar and Hampsten quickly disposed of Steiger's presence in the top order, but were unable to bridge their respective 0:41 and 1:04 deficits over the following days: their weaponry was spent on that crucial seventh leg, about which Kelly coyly confessed two days later: 'I really suffered there, which was a fact I didn't want getting around . . .' The eighth stage went to the Swiss Rolf Järmann (Frank), stage 9 to Moreno Argentin of Italy (Ariostea), stage 10 to East Germany's Uwe Ampler (PDM). The final stage to Zurich was won by the Dane Kim Andersen (Z); but when it was all over there was one fact that everyone knew: Sean Kelly, the King, was unquestionably back.

After he missed six weeks' racing because of a fractured collarbone sustained in the Tour of Flanders, victory in the Tour of Switzerland heralded a welcome return to form for Kelly

Robert Millar was one of the prime catalysts in the Tour of Switzerland

Tour de France: 30 June-22 July

In a Tour de France that opened with four dark horses taking a remarkable 10-minute lead, it took a superb Greg LeMond to unlock the key to the yellow jersey – and then only 24 hours before the finish in Paris. Starting with a handicap of 10:35 on stage 1 breakaways Steve Bauer of Canada (7-Eleven), Claudio Chiappucci of Italy (Carrera), Frans Maassen of Holland (Buckler) and Frenchman Ronan Pensec (Z), the Tour favourites had a hard time making up their deficit. First Bauer, then Pensec and eventually Chiappucci held the race lead . . . and the plucky Italian's persistence almost earned him the biggest upset victory since the Tour was first held in 1903. Brilliant riding by Mexican Raul Alcalá (PDM) and the Spanish stars Pedro Delgado and Miguel Indurain of Banesto and Marino Lejarreta of ONCE only dented the big lead held by Chiappucci. And two time trial wins for Dutchman Eric Breukink (PDM) still left him 13 seconds short of Chiappucci at the end. But steady time trial performances and outstanding rides in the toughest mountain stages finally allowed the Z team's American star LeMond to join Philippe Thys of Belgium and Louison Bobet of France as a three-time Tour de France winner.

30 June, prologue: Futuroscope, 6.3km
Whenever Eddy Merckx wanted to impose his authority on a Tour de France, he would race to his limit in the

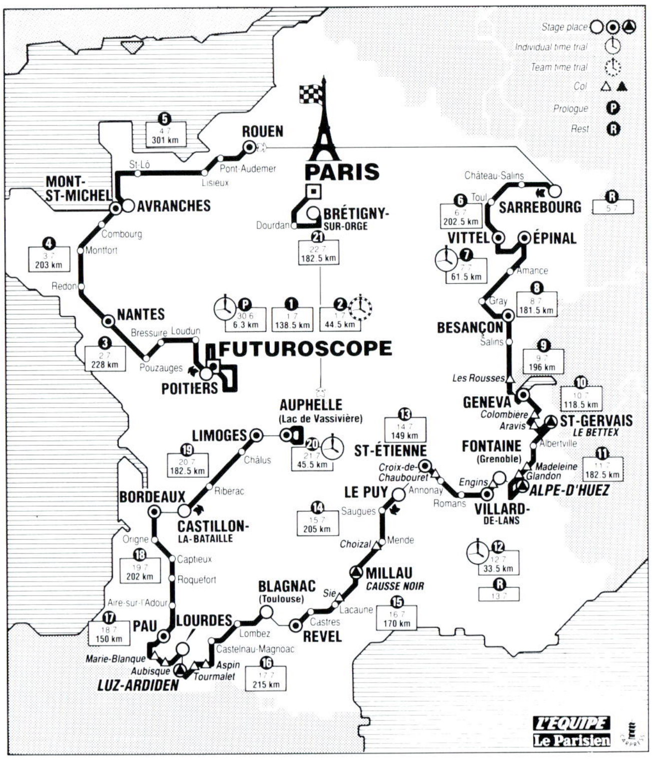

Tour de France: 3043.8km

The stage one escape led by Bauer gained so much time that two other members of the break – Chiappucci and Pensec (behind Chiappucci) followed him into the lead as the race unfolded. But it was Maassen (in blue) who took the stage victory at Futuroscope

prologue and destroy the morale of his opponents before the race had really started. Such was the thinking of LeMond, too, when he went into the prologue time trial of the 1990 Tour. And although LeMond – wearing the yellow jersey as the defending champion – was beaten into second place by French short-distance specialist Thierry Marie of Castorama, he left behind all of his anticipated rivals, except for Alcalá. Alcalá surprised most observers when he raced the prologue circuit at Futuroscope in 7:53.19 – the fastest at that point, and almost 6 seconds faster than the previously best time set by French specialist Francis Moreau of Histor-Sigma. 'I'm not a specialist of prologues,' commented Alcalá, whose smooth, powerful style suited the flatter, less windy sections of the course around the geometric, glass-and-concrete edifices of the Futuroscope theme park. The more heavily-built Marie fared better than Alcalá in the wind, and he hurtled around the final turns to stop the clock at 7:49. Like most of the favoured men, Marie used clip-on tri-bars; after finishing, he said: 'If I'd had only normal bars, I wouldn't have won today.'

There were still twenty-three remaining starters, including most of the race favourites, but none of them came close to Marie's time – except for the last starter, LeMond. Armed with a brand new pair of tri-bars called Extreme, LeMond startled most of the critics by recording 7:53.19. This was 5/100ths of a second faster than Alcalá's time, and gave the world champion an excellent second place. The best of the other favourites were Irish riders Stephen Roche (Histor) and Sean Kelly (PDM), and Laurent Fignon of France (Castorama), who all conceded a quarter-minute to LeMond and Alcalá. A little further back came Delgado, who arrived on time for his prologue start this year but was 20 seconds slower than LeMond. Chateau d'Ax's Giro d'Italia winner, Italian Gianni Bugno, conceded 21 seconds; and Charly Mottet of France (RMO), 23 seconds.

1 July, stage 1: Futuroscope circuit, 138.5km

By finishing with a four-man breakaway group on the first road race stage, Bauer stole an amazing 10-minute lead on all the pre-race favourites. The breakaway by Bauer, Chiappucci, Maassen and Pensec started as a low-scale attack, and ended as a move that would influence the race all the way to Paris. 'It's great to have the yellow jersey again,' said Bauer, who also led the Tour de France on the opening day in 1988. Race followers were left wondering how Bauer and his three companions were able to gain so much time on an innocuous-looking stage that traversed the windswept wheat and sunflower fields of Poitou. 'Chiappucci started the break, and I followed him,' explained Bauer. 'We were only going for the two king of the mountain sprints. But when the bunch didn't chase, we all started riding harder.' They had 45 seconds lead when they crossed the first hill at 24km, but the gap was then closed to just 16 seconds and it appeared that their early move was destined to fail. Then the four riders increased their tempo . . . and when they turned right, into the wind, after 43km, their lead was 2:05. A reaction was expected from the peloton. Instead, the wind seemed to stop the pack in its tracks, and the lead

The peloton, reluctant to chase hard because of the afternoon's team time trial, wound its way serenely through Poitou and unwittingly allowed the Bauer breakaway too much leeway

had reached 11:10 when the breakaways headed back toward the finish on the circular route. The pack was slowed momentarily by demonstrating agricultural workers – but the break was already 10 minutes ahead at that point. Bauer, Chiappucci, Maassen and Pensec worked in perfect synchronisation, knowing that opposing teams would be reluctant to chase because of the afternoon's team time trial. The onus to chase was really on the Castorama team of yellow jersey Marie, but his team leader Fignon seemed happy to let the break develop. The only tactical moves at this point were made by Z *directeur sportif* Roger Legeay (who told Pensec that 10 minutes' lead was sufficient, and that he should stop working), and PDM manager Jan Gisbers (who ordered his team to start the chase with 50km to go).

The gap was soon cut by 40 seconds, as the race sped north, past sandstone castles and fields of orange marigolds. But then Gisbers reluctantly told PDM to stop chasing. 'None of the other teams would work with us,' he said later, 'so I told my riders to stop.' As a result, the gap started to grow again . . . and the pack passed the 10km-to-go banner 13 minutes behind the four leaders! A belated chase closed the gap to 10:35 by the finish, where Maassen easily won the uphill sprint from Pensec, Chiappucci and Bauer. But it was Bauer who took the yellow jersey – by only 2 seconds over Maassen.

The Panasonic team's jubilation at their victory in the team time trial helped compensate for the absence of Gert-Jan Theunisse, their great hope for the Tour until he was suspended for positive dope controls

1 July, stage 2: Futuroscope team time trial, 44.5km

After the dreaded team time trial stage was over, great attention was given to the fine sixth place of 7-Eleven – which allowed Bauer to extend his overall lead by 8 seconds over Maassen. But perhaps the more significant result was the near-victory of PDM in this 44.5km test, which pushed Alcalá into fifth place overall, 9:47 behind Bauer; and, more importantly, moved the Mexican well ahead of the other favourites – by 0:33 on Roche, 0:41 on Fignon; 0:46 on Lemond, and more than two minutes on Delgado and Bugno. The team trial was won by the Dutch squad Panasonic-Sportlife, beating rival PDM by 7 seconds – a win that brought tears of happiness to the eyes of its veteran team coach, Peter Post. Equally pleased was 7-Eleven manager Jim Ochowicz. 'That's the best we've ever done,' he crowed, when it was confirmed that Bauer had retained the yellow jersey.

On a twisting, turning course that headed through the narrow streets of seven villages in the first 20km, it was difficult for any team to focus entirely on speed. By the 20.3km check, the 7-Eleven team was timed through at 23:57, only 10th best, 24 seconds behind Panasonic and 6 seconds behind Maassen's Buckler formation. At that point, Bauer temporarily lost the yellow jersey. Despite some raggedness in the last four kilometres, the American team finished with a time of 54:12 – the fastest at that point. There was a long wait to see if the team's strong comeback was enough – and indeed it was. Buckler came home in 54:20, having lost 14 seconds to 7-Eleven in the second half. The American team's time was also good enough to beat Z, though LeMond was impressively strong. Panasonic then came in with its 50kph effort of 53:24, powered by the East German Olaf Ludwig. Neither Roche's Histor team (53:46.47) nor Lejarreta's ONCE (53:46.47) was able to match the Dutch team's effort, while Fignon's Castorama squad slowed to fifth place (15 seconds faster than 7-Eleven). This left only the final starter, PDM, with its two East German powerhouses Uwe Ampler and Uwe Raab, and such fine time triallists as Alcalá, Breukink and Kelly. But at 20.3km, its deficit was 16 seconds – which seemed too much to take back. The PDM riders slowly pulled back time. 'I thought we were going to win,' Alcalá said later, 'but Breukink wasn't good, and we had to wait for him in the last four kilometres.' Despite slowing for Breukink – who was suffering with a stomach virus – PDM failed to beat Panasonic by only 7 seconds.

2 July, stage 3: Poitiers-Nantes, 233km

World Cup leader Moreno Argentin of Italy (Ariostea), riding his first Tour de France at the age of twenty-nine, was an impressive winner of the third stage. Riding with the assurance that had won him a similar victory in the ninth stage of the Tour of Switzerland two weeks earlier, Argentin's 52km solo allowed him to finish 2:29 before the other 196 riders.

Meanwhile, Bauer began this day of strong winds and tiresome rain showers in great style. Only 5km out of

Poitiers, and blown along by a strong south-westerly wind, he and fifteen others broke clear from the pack. Also in the front group were a commanding looking LeMond, and an aggressive Roche. The 16-strong break was soon caught by the main part of the peloton, but the pursuit had left forty riders behind, including Maassen, Delgado and Fignon. Fignon had punctured, and several of his team-mates stayed with him to help him chase. Even so, it wasn't until 28km had been covered in the first half-hour of racing that the back group closed its 30-second deficit. Calm was temporarily restored . . . and extended when the race was officially neutralised for 16km so that it could bypass two political demonstrations by agricultural workers.

Within 40 minutes of the race restart, and with rain falling, the day's second serious breakaway was launched by Sören Lilholt of Denmark (Histor). Eleven others eventually caught him, including Frenchman Jean-François Bernard of Toshiba, and Russian rider Dmitri Konyshev of Alfa Lum. The twelve leaders were held on a 30-second leash for the next 24km before the pack closed in on them. Shortly afterwards, with the rain starting again, Argentin made his well-timed charge to victory. The Ariostea leader quickly gained ground, and he was already 1:51 ahead of the pack when a crash disrupted the chase at Clisson, 39km from Nantes. A dozen riders, including the unfortunate Fignon, crashed on a rain-slick turn.

Argentin's lead increased to 4.02 before a counterattack was finally launched, 20km from the line. Prominent in this group were four sprinters, Belgians Eric Vanderaerden of Buckler, Eddy Planckaert of Panasonic and Johan Museeuw of Lotto, and the Italian Adriano Baffi, of Argentin's Ariostea team. But they couldn't coordinate their efforts, and the peloton swept them up 2km from the finish. Then, with one kilometre left, local man Christophe Lavainne of Castorama bolted out of the bunch to cross the line with hands aloft, thinking he'd won the stage. His mistake – Argentin had arrived 2:29 earlier – typified the miscalculations and mishaps befalling Fignon and his Castorama team.

A relaxed Argentin enjoying the taste of victory at Nantes; unfortunately, a crash on the wet stage to Rouen two days later forced him out of the race overnight with inflamed knee ligaments

Laurent Fignon, forgetting for a minute his dislike of photographers, explaining to Denys Clement of l'Equipe *how he came to be delayed by a crash in front of him on the run-in to Mont St Michel . . .*

. . . whilst a delighted Steve Bauer, in yellow for the third day, posed in front of the magnificent Benedictine abbey

3 July, stage 4: Nantes-Mont St Michel, 203km

The fourth stage, which ended at the foot of Normandy's touristic jewel, Mont St Michel, was won in a tumultuous sprint by 24-year-old Museeuw. Museeuw edged out Carrera's Guido Bontempi of Italy, points leader Ludwig, and American Davis Phinney of 7-Eleven in excellent form. Maassen was caught out by the ultra-rapid finishing pace, while Bauer again finished in the front group of fifty riders to extend his overall lead to 30 seconds over Pensec. The stage result might well have been different if Ludwig hadn't made his major effort 500m too early. He and the other expected sprint protagonists, Vanderaerden, Raab and Phinney, mistook the finish; they sprinted when they saw a large crowd gathered on a stand beside the big red Coca-Cola truck that is normally parked close to the finish. 'We all sprinted at the Coke truck,' admitted Phinney, 'and then cursed when we saw the real finish another 500 metres away.' As they eased back, another finishing specialist, Dutch rider Jelle Nijdam (Buckler), jumped away. But he faded with 200m still to go, and Museeuw came flying past him to win from the fast-finishing Bontempi.

More drama was being played out behind them, with several race favourites, including Fignon, Delgado, Bugno and American Andy Hampsten of 7-Eleven, all chasing to catch the leaders, after being blocked by a crash about 14km from Mont St Michel. It wasn't a serious crash, but happened on a sharp right turn, where barriers and hay bales restricted the width of the roadway. Caught up in the 'traffic jam' was 7-Eleven's Ron Kiefel of the USA. 'Fignon was in the group with me,' Kiefel said later. 'Some of his teammates waited back and then they went so hard that they split the group . . . but Fignon was in the back part.' Delgado, Bugno and Hampsten also had some team-mates with them, and they managed to bridge up to the second of the three parts into which the peloton had split. They would lose 21 seconds by the finish, while Fignon would lose 44 seconds to a front group that included Bauer and LeMond.

This often slow-moving stage across the undulations of Brittany only really came to life in the final 55km, when a brave solo attack was made by the former Danish champion Lilholt. He gained a maximum of 54 seconds, but then Ludwig's Panasonic team set a tremendous pace that brought him to heel, 15km before reaching Mont St Michel.

4 July, stage 5: Avranches-Rouen, 301km

This marathon fifth stage across the hills and valleys of Normandy, the longest of the race, was won by Dutch long-distance specialist Gerrit Solleveld of Buckler; but of more interest was the retirement from the race of two expected challengers, Tour of Spain winner Marco Giovannetti of Italy (Seur) . . . and Fignon. The victim of a crash on stage 3 and suffering from a bruised calf, Fignon had still not fully recovered from the effects of a pelvis injury incurred when he fell in the Tour of Italy. Now, with his morale at a low ebb after losing 44 seconds on stage 4, Fignon climbed off at the first feed zone, after 125km of racing. Giovannetti, suffering from diarrhoea, followed Fignon into retirement at the second feed, 72km from the finish.

With its length, eight time-bonus sprints and eight hill climbs, this was bound to be a difficult stage, even without the almost incessant rain. There was a particularly nervous opening, with Dutchman Henri Manders of Helvetia-La Suisse twice making attacks – the second one took him away from the pack as they crested the climb away from the English Channel coast at Granville. With the route now heading almost due east and with the wind at their backs, six others soon joined Manders, including Norwegian Dag-Otto Lauritzen of 7-Eleven. At first, the acceleration split the peloton into three echelons; but there were still 265km to go and when it became clear that bad weather had set in for the day, the chase slowed and riders started calling for their rain jackets. As the leaders turned onto a narrow, winding byway, the gap opened to 5:41 within 10km. This was a fine move by 7-Eleven, because Lauritzen was the best placed of the break, and he could legitimately follow the others in defence of Bauer's yellow jersey. For the next hour, on a twisting road made more difficult by the rain, the gap slowly decreased. But the increased tempo saw several riders dropped, while others crashed. It was during this difficult period that Fignon dropped to the back of the line . . . and on reaching the feed zone at Villers Bocage, ended his Tour de France. The break was caught a few kilometres later.

There was 97km still to go when Solleveld attacked from a small break, and quickly gained time on a long descent from Lisieux. And when the 29-year-old Buckler rider moved to a maximum lead of 9:30, 33km from the finish, Bauer's 7-Eleven took up the chase. By the finish, Solleveld was 4:27 ahead of Musseuw, who slipped away with Belgian Etienne De Wilde of Histor in the final kilometre, while Ludwig took the field sprint three seconds later. Solleveld consequently moved up to fifth place overall, 7:26 behind Bauer. Bauer himself rarely left the head of the pack throughout this long, rainy day, and even picked up another time bonus to increase his overall lead to 34 seconds over second-placed Pensec.

Equally pleased with the state of the race, despite being involved in a crash caused by the Alfa Lum team car, was a confident LeMond, who was lying poised in 23rd place overall, 10:41 behind the Canadian. About 10km out of Rouen, LeMond had even attacked with Pensec in an attempt to catapult his French team-mate into the yellow jersey – but the fast-moving peloton soon swept them up on the straight, wide roads leading to the finish. Also out of luck was LeMond's Scottish team-mate Robert Millar, who was involved in a pile-up 43km from Rouen, and lost almost five minutes on the leaders.

Only a Dutchman could enjoy such rain! Gerrit Solleveld was one of the few riders to prosper in the appalling conditions on stage five to Rouen

A cold headwind slowed the peloton to walking pace as it passed through the rolling countryside near Sarrebourg on stage 6

6 July, stage 6: Sarrebourg-Vittel, 202.5km
It was not until 42km before the end of the sixth stage, just after turning left at the village of Coussey, that seven riders clipped clear of the peloton to make the first real attack of the day – although the pace had been high for an hour, ever since Bugno accelerated strongly at the feed zone. More importantly, among the seven riders in the break were three favourites: LeMond, Mottet and Dutchman Steven Rooks of Panasonic. The move was started by Mottet, with his RMO team-mate, Belgian Michel Vermote, and they both worked hard to establish their escape. But as Mottet admitted later, 'We needed a Roche, a Bugno or an Alcalá with us to make the move really stick.' Roche was well aware of this: 'I tried to get across to the break,' he said, 'but I couldn't do it on my own, in the wind. So I waited for the group to come up. It would have been a very important break . . .'

The attack split the pack into two, and caused problems for LeMond's team-mate Pensec, who was the victim of one of two crashes right before the acceleration. Pensec managed to reach the back part of the peloton just as the front part caught the break – but it needed some energetic work from some of his Z team-mates before Pensec closed the 24-second gap that had opened up. In the relative calm that followed the two crashes, the attack and the chase, the aggressive Dane Jesper Skibby (TVM) counterattacked with Italian sprinter Giovanni Fidanza (Chateau d'Ax) and Panasonic domestique Guy Nulens of Belgium. They opened up a 25-second gap before three others took up the chase: Nijdam, soviet rider Viatcheslav Ekimov of Panasonic and Museeuw. They bridged to the leaders with 18km still to go. These reinforcements, with Museeuw working especially hard, enabled the six leaders to move 50 seconds clear – and then came the fight for the day's honours.

First Nijdam jumped to a 10-second lead with Nulens, and Skibby towed up the others, with 3km to go. On the long downhill into town, Ekimov tried his luck in an attack with Fidanza, moving to a 100m lead on the twisting run-in, which was still wet from earlier rain showers. The leaders continued to battle for victory in the curving streets of Vittel, and the two leaders were caught just as they began the 400m uphill haul to the line. This development worked well for Nijdam – the winner of two stages at the 1989 Tour – who used his tactical savvy to take the eventual sprint from Skibby and Museeuw, with the peloton only 8 seconds behind.

7 July, stage 7: Vittel-Epinal (time trial), 61.5km)
In its preview of the time trial stage from Vittel to Epinal, one newspaper used the headline: 'Superman against the rest', in reference to LeMond's chances. The only discussion, according to the papers, was by how much 'LeMonster' would beat Bauer and the rest. Race followers listening attentively to Radio Tour assumed that the stage was going as expected when the American's first time split was given: 'At kilometre 20, the time for number one, Greg LeMond, is 24:45, the best time so far. The previous fastest time was 24.57 by number 25, Miguel Indurain.'

Indurain had completed his time trial on dry roads much earlier on this cold, humid, overcast day in the hilly Vosges countryside, and he'd taken the stage lead with a time of 1:18.29 – 23 seconds faster than Bugno and 41 seconds faster than Delgado. However, LeMond was still the favourite to win. LeMond rode the difficult opening 20km at more than 48kph, and all the signs indicated that he would continue to go faster than those before him. But a few minutes later, Radio Tour reported: 'New best time by number 32, Eric Breukink, 24:39.' Breukink's time remained unbeaten by riders like Roche, Ekimov and Kelly. And then came this message from the crackling radio: 'Time for number 31, Raul Alcalá . . . 24:00.' You could almost feel the shock wave of stunned silence that swept through the race entourage.

Most of those hearing the 20km time split presumed that Alcalá had started too fast, and that he would pay for his imprudence later in the long stage. But it soon became clear that Alcalá wasn't going to slow down. Over the middle section of the course – which included three more climbs, and a narrow backroad descent – he was still gaining time. 'At halfway,' the Mexican later

Raúl Alcalá was in a benevolent mood the morning after his scintillating time trial win at Epinal

revealed, 'I was told that I was one and a half minutes ahead of the others. I knew then that I had the stage won, and I didn't have to take any risks after that.'

Alcalá's 41km split showed him in the lead with 50:51, followed by Indurain at 1:22, Bugno at 1:33, Breukink at 1:39 . . . and LeMond, only ninth fastest, at 2:00. The world champion explained: 'I was riding at only 80 per cent up the hills – maybe I took it too easy. And once you've lost time in a time trial, you can't make it up again.' LeMond did ride strongly over the next 10km, which climbed the two steepest hills on the course, and he took back time on Indurain, Bugno and Delgado. But the American again conceded a few seconds to Alcalá. Then, on the final section, both Alcalá and LeMond had to be extra cautious on the steep descent into Epinal, which ended with seven tight turns, including two with adverse cambers. LeMond was running 3 seconds faster than Alcalá over these last kilometres, but both of them lost about 15 seconds to Bugno, Indurain and Delgado, all of whom had descended when the roads were dry. Alcalá finally arrived with a time of 1.17.05, still 1.24 ahead of Indurain, in second place . . . and 2:11 over LeMond, in fifth. Almost as big a surprise as Alcalá's upset victory was the performance of Pensec, who was only 15 seconds slower than team-mate LeMond. The effort left the French rider completely exhausted, but it nearly earned him the yellow jersey. He halved his 34 second deficit on Bauer, while Chiappucci conceded only 6 seconds to the race leader.

Among the many other unexpected results of the time trial were the poor finish of Breukink, who dropped to 12th place, 2:40 down on Alcalá; and the disastrous finish of Roche, who was a second ahead of LeMond at the 41km split – and then bonked. The Irish star lost 3 minutes and almost fifty places over the final 20km.

8 July, stage 8: Epinal-Besançon, 181.5km

The stage started out from Epinal in a drizzle, but this didn't discourage a barrage of attacks that had the 7-Eleven team on red alert. The turning-point in the race pattern was a crash on a stretch of greasy cobblestones in the town of Fontenay-le-Château, after 32km. No one was seriously hurt, but the crash calmed down the aggressors; and when Vermote jumped away on his own just after Fontenay, there was no immediate chase. By the feed zone in Lavoncourt, halfway through the stage, his lead was 11:30. 'I really needed 14 or 15 minutes if I was going to stay away till the end,' said a disappointed Vermote after the finish. He was caught 30km from Besançon . . . when a final series of attacks resulted in a historic victory for Olaf Ludwig.

Winning stages is old hat for Ludwig – in amateur events such as the Peace Race. But until the Berlin Wall came down this splendid East German athlete was not free to turn professional. So, his win in the eighth stage at Besançon allowed Ludwig to become the first cyclist from an East European country to win a stage of the Tour de France. What was most surprising about his success was that this king of sprinters, who was dominating the green jersey points competition, didn't win his stage in a field sprint. Instead, he was one of thirteen men who escaped from the pack with 9km still to go.

The move was started by local rider Pascal Lance of Toshiba and five others. Two kilometres later Ludwig came charging across the 200m gap with the rest of the winning break. Nearing the finish, Italian Massimo Ghirotto of Carrera was the first to take advantage of the complicated run-in. But he was quickly caught. At 1km to go, Ghirotto again accelerated, and Kiefel followed. But the 7-Eleven rider knew that such a move was doomed; Ludwig had his team-mate, Belgian Eric Van Lancker, to help him contain the opposition. A final attack came from Frenchman Bruno Cornillet of Z, but his effort 400m from the line was soon scotched by Ludwig's acceleration. Kiefel went with Ludwig, but the East German had the sprint won with 20m still to go, while Museeuw came through for second place.

Olaf Ludwig's seemingly effortless victory at Besançon, the last sprinter's finish before the Alps, consolidated his claim to the green jersey

9 July, stage 9: Besançon-Geneva, 196km

With the Tour scheduled to enter the French Alps the next day, not much was expected from the ninth stage from Besançon to Geneva. Nonetheless, the stage was exceptionally fast: an average speed of 41.102kph on a route that crossed one second- and two third-category climbs in the Jura mountains. One reason for the speed was the motivation of the Swiss riders to win in their city of Geneva, but the stage winner turned out to be Massimo Ghirotto, the 29-year-old Carrera rider who'd tried hard to win the previous day. The fast pace over the hilly course was too much for many, and fifty-three riders arrived in Geneva 6 minutes or more behind, with green jersey Ludwig more than 14 minutes in arrears.

No break gained more than 30 seconds in the opening two hours. Then an attack on a long, gradual climb took seven riders clear, including Spaniard Eduardo Chozas of ONCE. They were joined 10km later by thirteen others: Ghirotto was one . . . and fourth-placed Maassen was another. His presence in front forced the 7-Eleven team into a 15km chase to close the 35-second gap. But just before the regroupment, Chozas jumped clear on a long descent into the mountain town of Morez, and was joined by Ghirotto in the narrow main street just before they began climbing the second-category Côte des Rousses. Their 40-second lead was cut to 20 seconds by the summit after Bugno had set the tempo with LeMond, but the gap quickly widened to 54 seconds on the plateau following the climb.

The two leaders were chased by a group of seven – including the Swiss Toni Rominger (Chateau d'Ax) and the Danish champion Brian Holm (Histor). By the start of the fast, swishing 16km descent of the Col de la Faucille, the gaps were 0:52 to the chase group, and 1:42 to the pack. With 15km left, the two leaders were still 1:30 clear, but the peloton was now only 20 seconds further back. Sensing a chance of a stage win, Lavainne now jumped across to the chase group, and then jumped again, hoping to close the 1-minute gap to Chozas and Ghirotto. It was a brave effort by the Frenchman, but as the course turned back toward the lake, he was faced by a strong headwind, and although he had the two leaders in

His face a mask of desperation, Steve Bauer approaches Le Bettex knowing his eight days in the yellow jersey are at an end

his sights with 4km still to race, Lavainne couldn't quite close those final 200 metres.

Ghirotto accelerated with 500m left to win the stage from Chozas, with Lavainne at 16 seconds. The main group sprinted in 37 seconds behind, with a late attack by Maassen allowing him to pick up 10 seconds and move into third place, 1:06 behind Bauer. Defending his yellow jersey for the eighth day, Bauer commented, 'I'm not letting the pressure get to me. I know that everyone is saying that I could lose the jersey in the mountains tomorrow, but I'm just taking it one day at a time.'

10 July, stage 10: Geneva-St Gervais (Le Bettex), 118.5km

As expected, the first mountain stage of the Tour made some significant changes in the overall standings, with Delgado, LeMond and Bugno all showing that they were indeed in contention. But it was Pensec who finally displaced Bauer from the yellow jersey. Celebrating his 27th birthday, Pensec finished only 16th on the tenth stage, but the 1:38 he gained on Bauer easily moved him into the overall lead. Bauer lost contact with the principal group 4.5km from the finish, just after a fierce acceleration by the Z team's climbing specialist, Robert Millar. Pensec, with his eyes on the yellow jersey, even followed an attack by Delgado, but when Delgado went ahead with fellow Spaniard Lejarreta to gain 19 seconds over the other race favourites, Pensec dropped back to the group that was led in by LeMond. In the overall standings, Bauer, who finished 50th on the stage, was also overtaken by Chiappucci. The Italian finished in the same group as Pensec, 2:29 behind the day's winner, Thierry Claveyrolat of RMO.

After a solo break of 66km, this veteran French climber arrived at the finish almost two minutes clear of his team leader, Mottet, and PDM's Ampler, who both emerged from a chase group that had formed on flatter roads 15km earlier. To win the first Tour de France bouquet of his long career, Claveyrolat chose to break clear of the pack near the foot of the Tour's first major climb, the 1500m high Col de la Colombière, 37km into the stage. 'A Colombian [Omar Hernandez of Postobon] attacked and I went after him,' said Claveyrolat. 'I was only intending to go for the climber's points, but I saw that a stage win was possible when I was on my own at the top.' Claveyrolat built up a 3-minute lead before the last of the three climbs. Behind him, Roche made a surprise, but futile, attack on the Colombière, and Bauer showed signs of his vulnerability when he crossed the summit 35 seconds after the LeMond group.

The 7-Eleven baton had now passed to team-mate Hampsten, and at the bottom of the final climb, Bauer told Hampsten to go on with the leaders, as no one could have helped the Canadian at that point. And so the yellow jersey passed on to Pensec. Asked about his having to play second fiddle to new race leader and team-mate Pensec, LeMond replied, 'Pensec's riding really well at the moment, and he deserves to get the jersey. I'm not sweating about it as I'm free to go with any breaks.' LeMond was a little disappointed, however, to lose time to Delgado. He explained: 'I always have problems on the first day in the mountains, especially short ones like this. I don't like all the surging that happens.'

Thierry Claveyrolat's indomitable performance on l'Alpe d'Huez surpassed his stage win the previous day and helped the little Grenoblois earn his climber's jersey

11 July, stage 11: St. Gervais – l'Alpe d'Huez, 182.5km

At l'Alpe d'Huez, the hallowed mountain climb where a quarter of a million pilgrims of the velo congregate each year, the unheralded Pensec extended his lead to 1:28 over second-placed Chiappucci, while LeMond moved into third place, 9:04 behind, followed by three other race favourites: Breukink, Bugno and Delgado. The biggest losers on this magnificent stage were Alcalá, who lost 5 minutes and dropped to eighth place overall; Kelly and Roche, who lost respectively 7 and 24 minutes; and former race leader Bauer, who struggled to the finish 21 minutes behind Pensec.

Bugno and LeMond were happy to let Delgado tow them up l'Alpe d'Huez, but the Spaniard's unassisted efforts caused him to blow up three kilometres from the summit

Involving almost 5000m of climbing, the stage was probably the toughest of the whole Tour. After the peloton had raced 45km in the first hour, mostly down the spectacular Arly Gorge, Delgado started his challenge by sending team rider Juan Martinez-Oliver off the front. He gained almost three minutes before starting the fearsome Col de la Madeleine, where several riders were immediately dropped, including Toshiba leader Bernard, who abandoned. Out front, Martinez-Oliver was caught halfway up the 25km climb by a front group of about fifty riders. Claveyrolat, the previous day's winner, sprinted clear in the final kilometre to take the mountain points, followed by another Delgado delegate, Indurain. At the 1800m summit, 88km into the stage, Claveyrolat was 7 seconds ahead of Indurain; 10 seconds ahead of the now 33-strong lead group; and 2:34 ahead of a small group containing Roche and Bauer.

Indurain passed Claveyrolat on the long, fast descent, and reached the feed zone in the valley 35 seconds ahead of the mountains leader, and 1:02 ahead of the chase group. The pack slowed as riders collected their food bags – and LeMond fell. While holding his bars with one hand, his front wheel hit a pothole and he crashed to the ground, taking an elderly woman spectator along with him. 'I fell on my left hand,' LeMond reported later. 'The middle finger was bent out at an angle. I had to pull it straight, and push it back into its socket.' Luckily, he still had six of his Z team-mates with him in the group, and two of them dropped back to help him regain the 45 seconds he'd lost.

Meanwhile, Claveyrolat caught Indurain on the first slopes of the savagely steep Col du Glandon, and their lead increased to 3 minutes by the time they were halfway up the unremitting 18km ascent. Then the

RMO climber rid himself of his Spanish companion; he reached the top 1:22 ahead of Indurain and 3:35 up on the lead group. Halfway down the ensuing descent, Delgado attacked on a steep (12 per cent), 1km uphill that bypasses a massive rock fall, and only LeMond and Bugno were strong enough to go with him. Ahead, Indurain – who'd been joined by Chozas at the start of the descent – awaited his team leader. And when the three counterattackers joined him, they were 40 seconds ahead; after sweeping up Chozas and Claveyrolat, the gap was 1 minute. Indurain did most of the work to pull the six leaders 2:30 ahead when they arrived at the foot of l'Alpe d'Huez.

As soon as the 21-turn climb began, the overworked Indurain dropped back (and would lose 12 minutes by the top), and Delgado made an impressive surge. Chozas was dropped, and Claveyrolat followed him a few moments later. It appeared that Delgado, LeMond and Bugno were on their way to regaining up to 5 minutes on the race leaders . . . but it also became clear that the break was operating on only one cylinder. LeMond was

Sean Kelly found himself completely unable to find the form of his 1989 Tour, a broken collarbone in April having prevented any serious preparation for the race

As always, it was l'Alpe d'Huez which produced the most enthusiastic crowds; here Dag-Otto Lauritzen is apparently hemmed in on the last kilometres of this popular stage

riding conservatively to defend Pensec's yellow jersey; and Bugno was reluctant to ride hard, saying later that he was more interested in the stage win. Delgado started to weaken . . . and was dropped by the other two, 3km from the finish.

In the meantime, Claveyrolat rejoined the break; Delgado's Colombian team-mate Abelardo Rondon almost bridged before joining forces with his dropped leader; and Breukink jumped across to the leaders when the gap was down to a minute. Claveyrolat dropped back for a second time, but he managed to hang on to the wheel of the flying Colombian Fabio Parra of Kelme, who was able to cross to the leaders in the streets of l'Alpe d'Huez ski resort.

LeMond looked as though he would win the finishing sprint on the 300m, 8.4 per cent haul to the line. But after diving between Bugno and Breukink into the final 90° turn, he almost fell. 'I went to touch my brakes,' he said afterwards, 'but I couldn't use the front brake because of my injured finger. I had to use my back brake, and almost hit the barrier.' Despite this setback, LeMond's effort was too much for anyone to overcome . . . except Bugno. The Italian matched the world champion's speed, and sprinted by him to become the first Italian to win at l'Alpe d'Huez since the legendary Fausto Coppi in 1952. Behind the five leaders, Hampsten climbed well to catch and come in with Delgado, 40 seconds behind Bugno; while Pensec extended his overall lead by riding the whole of the 13km climb in the slipstream of team-mate Millar.

12 July, stage 12: Fontaine – Villard-de-Lans (time trial), 32.5km
The extreme emotions engendered by the Tour were never more real than in the moments following the 12th stage: a 33.5km uphill time trial. Pensec, the last man to ride by virtue of his overall leadership, had just finished his effort. He'd raced himself into the ground. But his best effort was not good enough. And after zipping a Z team jersey over his sweat-saturated yellow skinsuit on this hot, humid afternoon, Pensec sat on a folded tarpaulin behind the winner's podium, his body bent over and his head in his hands. His dream had been shattered.

No more than five metres away, up on the stage, Chiappucci had just donned the magic *maillot jaune*. As he waved to the crowd, and kissed the Crédit Lyonnais hostesses, a captivating grin lit up his tanned, round visage. His dream was just starting . . . this year's topsy-turvy Tour had taken yet another turn. Just when it seemed that the race had found its definitive character, it had changed again. The day before, Pensec was being hailed as the new French hope; but on this time trial from the outskirts of noisy Grenoble to the verdant pastures of the Vercors plateau he struggled to 49th place. Pensec lost almost 3 minutes to Chiappucci, who finished eighth and so became the first Italian to wear the yellow jersey since Francesco Moser, fifteen years before.

Ronan Pensec could not withstand the pressure of being the only Frenchman with a chance of winning the Tour, and his performance in the time trial to Villard-de-Lans disappointed all of France

Eric Breukink amazed everyone with his flawless time trial performance on stage 12 to Villard-de-Lans

The stage itself was won by Breukink, who finally put together a faultless performance and moved over LeMond into third place overall. Also increasing his chances of overall victory was Delgado, who almost repeated his victory in a similar stage in 1988. But a change of bikes in the last kilometre, and his choice of a rear disc instead of a spoked wheel, probably cost him the 30 seconds by which Breukink beat him.

LeMond, also using a rear disc, steadily lost time to his principal rivals, but energetically fought his way up the short, final hill to record the fifth best time, 0:56 slower than Breukink. Although LeMond was still 6 minutes behind team-mate Pensec on overall time, the American could at last plan his own race. He would have to pay close attention to Chiappucci, whose excellent seventh place – only 9 seconds slower than LeMond – had given him the yellow jersey. Among the other surprises were the third and fourth places of Indurain and Lejarreta respectively. Alcalá also returned to the list of contenders by taking 10th place, and moving up to sixth overall.

14 July, stage 13: Villard-de-Lans – St-Etienne, 149km
On as intense a stage as the Tour de France has seen in recent years, LeMond and Breukink regained almost 5 minutes of their 7-minute deficit on race leader Chiappucci. The Bastille Day stage was not long, but it was so full of action and dramatic twists that race followers were left bemused and dazzled. From start to finish, the attacks and counterattacks zoomed out like the fireworks that would conclude the celebrations on this French national holiday. The stage was finally won by Chozas, but it was an attack by LeMond 43km from the stage end that caused the Tour to take a dramatic new turning. On a short climb out of Aubenas, after Chiappucci and his Carrera team had been stretched to their limits in chasing a 30-man break that contained Pensec, LeMond made the move that blew the race apart. With the gap still at 10 seconds on six remaining

A rapid start down the limestone gorge out of Villard-de-Lans set the scene for an amazingly fast and dramatic stage 13

leaders, LeMond made a dramatic counterattack. Breukink went with him, but the exhausted Chiappucci couldn't follow, and Delgado was taken by surprise. Delgado's team-mate Indurain did catch the flying leaders, as did Hampsten a few moments later.

Riding strongly, LeMond and Breukink swept up the six riders ahead of them, and within 12km, by the foot of the difficult Croix de Chabouret climb, had gained 90 seconds over the Delgado-Chiappucci group. Then, with the tar melting from a burning sun, Delgado counterattacked with Bugno, Lejarreta and the young French rider Fabrice Philipot of Castorama. Yellow jersey Chiappucci had nothing left. He was even dropped by a second chase group, and rode most of the 12km climb on his own. Pensec, whose attack had opened the way for team-mate LeMond's startling move, was even further back.

Halfway up the climb, the Delgado-Bugno-Lejarreta group was still 75 seconds behind, and looked unlikely to make much more progress. But Indurain was ordered to wait for his team captain, and his extra firepower enabled the chasers to close to within 20 seconds by the 1200m summit. The pursuit continued on the descent into St Etienne between LeMond (followed by Breukink, Hampsten, Chozas and the Italian Ariostea rider, Roberto Conti) and Indurain (towing Delgado, Bugno and Lejarreta). LeMond increased his group's advantage to 30 seconds by the finish, where he waved the others through to contest the sprint – which was won by Chozas from Breukink.

Behind, the race had been split into ten separate groups, with Chiappucci coming in with the third (4:53 down) and Pensec with the sixth (at 7:47). Despite the hills and the intense heat – many riders were suffering from dehydration – the stage had been completed at a near-record speed of 44.655kph.

On the stage to St Etienne Breukink started to look like co-favourite for the Tour after forcing the breakaway with Greg LeMond that killed Chiappucci's chances

15 July, stage 14: Le Puy-Millau, 205km
During the decade that Marino Lejarreta has been competing in the major international tours, he has gained a reputation as a follower rather than an aggressor. But his steadily improving form in this race – after coming seventh at the Giro d'Italia – convinced the ONCE team's *directeur sportif*, Manuel Saiz, that the 33-year-old Lejarreta was capable of winning a stage of the Tour. He had spoken with Lejarreta for two hours on the rest day at Villard-de-Lans, to give him a more aggressive attitude, and the results of that talk became apparent on the 7.6km long, first-category climb to the Causse Noir that ended stage 14. After the remnants of an early break had been caught 3km into the narrow, winding ascent, and various other attacks had been neutralised, Lejarreta suddenly bolted away on his own, 2km from the top. Bugno took up the chase, with Indurain on his wheel, while LeMond, Delgado and Breukink seemed content to watch each other. At the line, Lejarreta was 24 seconds ahead of Indurain and Bugno, and 33 seconds ahead of Alcalá, who won the sprint for fourth place ahead of LeMond.

The time gained by Lejarreta was the principal change on overall classification, except for another 13 seconds conceded by Chiappucci and 1:31 lost by Pensec. This was far less than everyone expected, especially as the Banesto plan had been for Delgado to make a major assault on this stage. However, a major attack proved difficult on what proved to be another rapid stage that was completed half an hour ahead of schedule. It had seen attacks begin and collapse as frequently as the number of hills and valleys traversed on the 205km route from Le Puy.

The most impressive was the break made by RMO's Jean-Claude Bagot of France, who broke away from a front group of seventeen on a spectacular hairpin drop into the Tarn Gorge. Bagot gained 2 minutes along the scenic backroad beside the river, but with the pack closing in on his pursuers, as they began to close in on him, the race came together for the dramatic finale.

Out of the running for overall victory, Charly Mottet concentrated his energies on a stage win, and it paid off on the fifteenth stage to Revel

Two beaten men – Steve Bauer and Sean Kelly struggling forlornly up the Causse Noir on stage 14

16 July, stage 15: Millau-Revel, 170km
After dropping from contention in the Tour de France, RMO team leader Charly Mottet decided that he would probably never win the event. 'In the future,' he said, 'I'll focus on doing well in the classics, and winning stages at the Tour.' His new focus paid off on the 15th stage, where Mottet took the first Tour de France stage of his career. As the riders suffered in the continuing heat wave – LeMond's top team-mate, Millar, was forced to abandon with a stomach virus – Mottet constructed his win in opportunist style, starting on the long winding climb of the Col de Sie, 58km into the hilly 170km stage Mottet jumped across a 30-second gap to an earlier break, with Roche, Chozas and four others. And as befits a rider who started the Tour as the world's number two-ranked cyclist, Mottet won the stage by breaking clear from the 19-strong lead group and riding the final 31km on his own. He finished 2 minutes ahead of his former companions, headed by Italian Giuseppe Calcaterra of Chateau d'Ax, and almost 5 minutes ahead of the main field.

Of more concern to the race leaders was the presence in the breakaway of ONCE's Chozas. The 28-year-old Spaniard was lying in 11th place overall, 10:31 behind Chiappucci. So when, with only 58km remaining, his

Chiappucci was popular with the girls too . . .

Chiappucci was expected to lose the race lead to Greg LeMond on stage 16 to Luz Ardiden, but his unexpected attack halfway through the stage saved his yellow jersey by just five seconds. Here he is seen climbing the Col du Tourmalet flanked by Johan Bruyneel and Roberto Conti

group swept through Lacrouzette 8:12 before the pack, Chozas was up to third place overall. By the finish, Chozas retained only 2:17 of his gains, moving him into eighth place. However, the rapid chase on a hot, muggy afternoon was the last thing the field needed before the vital stage in the Pyrenees – now only 24 hours away.

17 July, stage 16: Blagnac – Luz-Ardiden, 215km
A super-confident LeMond came within an ace of sewing up his third Tour de France on the climb to Luz-Ardiden, the finishing point of stage 16. But the man who forced the American to play his strongest card was not, as expected, Delgado or Breukink, but Chiappucci, the under-rated race leader. Starting the day with a lead of 2:24 on LeMond, Chiappucci decided that attack was his best form of defence. The 27-year-old Italian surprised everyone by joining in the attack started by Swiss rider Jörg Müller (TVM) at the foot of the Col d'Aspin, 76km from the finish. 'I hadn't intended to attack,' said Chiappucci later. 'I was simply riding at the front, and went with Müller when he accelerated. But I realised that all the leaders would hesitate.' Four others joined the front group on the Aspin, which Chiappucci topped 34 seconds ahead of an uninterested main pack.

After catching Chiappucci on the descent of the Tourmalet, LeMond set a furious pace that only Lejarreta and Indurain could follow . . .

And after hurtling down the 13km descent to Ste Marie de Campan, the gap grew to 2:02. They now began climbing the Col du Tourmalet, the highest pass in this Tour, at over 2000m high.

Into the dusty modern ski resort of La Mongie, less than 5km from the summit, the Spaniard Miguel Martinez-Torres of ONCE was in the lead, 0:50 ahead of the small Chiappucci group – whose advantage over the pack was holding steady at 2:10. LeMond was starting to get nervous, and decided that unless he took action immediately, the Tour would be lost. So, on the stiffest part of the climb, with 37km to go, LeMond attacked once, twice, before drawing ahead with Indurain and Delgado. By the Tourmalet summit, he had closed to within 1:08 of Chiappucci, and opened up a 50-second gap on Breukink (who was being paced by Alcalá). LeMond kept up the pressure throughout the spectacular 20km descent, and caught Chiappucci's group just as they started the final climb to Luz-Ardiden. If he hadn't made his brave escape, the Italian would most likely have been back with Breukink at this point, 1:20 in arrears. But, with only 10km left to the finish, Chiappucci was still riding alongside the world champion. Complimenting him afterwards, LeMond said, 'Chiappucci was very strong when we caught him. But when he went to the front, I knew that he was faking me out, trying to make me think he was a lot stronger.'

LeMond didn't wait much longer to ascertain his rival's strength. With about 7km and 600m of climbing remaining, the American followed a strong surge by Parra, to which only Indurain and Lejarreta could respond. Meanwhile, Martinez-Torres had established a lead of 3:35, and seemed set for the stage win – which no doubt would have pleased the hundreds of thousands of Spanish fans massed all over the mountainside. But LeMond climbed the hill as if in a sprint, gaining time with every pedal stroke. Within 2km of his attack, LeMond (with Indurain and Lejarreta on his wheel) had closed to 2:05 on the leader – and he had gained 0:45 on Delgado and 1:03 on Chiappucci. The gaps continued to grow. LeMond soon passed a bemused Martinez-Torres, Lejarreta was dropped, and only Indurain, impressively strong, remained. A last timecheck put Chiappucci 2:15 behind LeMond. But as LeMond faded slightly in the last kilometre, and Indurain dashed ahead to score a well-merited stage victory, Chiappucci seemed to find his second wind. He sprinted through the final turn to cross the line 2:19 behind LeMond, saving the yellow jersey by 5 seconds. LeMond, who took 1:32 from Delgado and 4:16 from Breukink, observed: 'The Tour's not over until we reach the Champs Elysées, but I did the biggest part of the job today.'

. . . but then LeMond could only watch as Indurain left him for dead with 500 metres to go

18 July, stage 17: Lourdes-Pau, 150km

After his brilliant performance at Luz-Ardiden, LeMond said that he 'might take Chiappucci out' on the next day, the last mountain stage of the Tour – but the race turned out very differently from what he expected. Approaching the top of the Marie-Blanque climb, just after two thrusting attacks by Delgado had taken LeMond and the other race leaders a minute or so clear, the world champion's rear tyre exploded. LeMond had no team-mates with him, nor were there any support cars behind his group, due to the sudden acceleration by Delgado. LeMond later recalled his frustration, left standing at the side of the road: 'I looked left and right to see if there were any cyclists there to give me a wheel. What was the worst was not knowing whether Roger [Legeay, the Z team *directeur sportif*] was one, or even three minutes behind. I began thinking it was a stupid way to lose the Tour . . .' LeMond finally received a spare wheel, but after restarting, the wheel pulled over. He stopped again, and was given a spare bike, on which he crossed the 1000m summit of the Marie-Blanque, an enormous 1:27 behind the Delgado-Chiappucci group. Two of LeMond's French team-mates, Eric Boyer and Jérôme Simon, were now with him; and Legeay was arranging for two others, Frenchman Gilbert Duclos-Lassalle and Norwegian Atle Kvalsvoll – who were 7 minutes ahead in a breakaway group – to stop and wait.

Taking tremendous risks, LeMond raced down the steep, curving descent at 100kph, narrowing the gap to 0:56 by the bottom. The chase continued on a bumpy, rolling backroad. Ahead, Chiappucci had five of his Carrera team-mates to set the pace, but an incensed LeMond was gradually closing. The gap was down to 0:32 when Duclos-Lassalle and Kvalsvoll joined the Z trio; it finally closed after a chase lasting 21km.

Meanwhile, the battle for the stage win was being played out, 5 minutes ahead. From an original group of nineteen that had been allowed to break clear as soon as the flag dropped on leaving Lourdes, only thirteen were left in front after crossing the day's two main climbs, the Col d'Aubisque and the Marie-Blanque. It was from this group, 27km from the finish, that Lotto's Peter De Clercq of Belgium attacked. He was brought back by an alert Bauer, but the 7-Eleven rider couldn't respond when the other Belgian Lotto rider in the break, Johan Bruyneel, counterattacked on the next climb. He was quickly joined by Konyshev, and the two leaders took a 25-second lead before Bauer found his second wind, 5km from the finish. The Canadian chased alone, but was still 100m behind at the finish in Pau. Konyshev won the sprint to become the first Soviet cyclist to win a stage of the Tour. And more than 5 minutes later Indurain sprinted home, ahead of Chiappucci and LeMond, to earn a special $40,000 prize as the best-placed rider over the two stages in the Pyrenees. LeMond wasn't too upset about missing the bonus prize; he was just relieved that his puncture hadn't cost him the chance of winning his third Tour de France.

19 July, stage 18: Pau-Bordeaux, 202km

By now it had become clear that nothing could be predicted in this untraditional Tour de France. With the race back on the plains, stage 18 should have seen a long-awaited battle between the sprinters. Instead, Bugno, who had taken the toughest mountain stage at l'Alpe d'Huez nine days earlier, won his second success, this time in the flattest stage of the race.

Bugno's opportunity came when a split occurred in the 150-strong pack, 20km from Bordeaux. The pace had already been high for an hour, ever since Australian Phil Anderson of TVM made a solo attack, awakening everyone from their slumber on a day of 95° and high humidity. Anderson was caught 10km later by six riders, and the group gained a maximum advantage of 35 seconds before being reeled in by the fast-moving peloton, 29km from the finish. Then, as the stage traversed tiny backroads before entering the city, the pack split. All the favourites were in the lead group of nineteen, except Delgado, who had started the day in third place, only 7 seconds ahead of Breukink. The result was another superb pursuit match, this time between the stars at the front and Delgado and his team

At Pau Dmitri Konyshev became the first Soviet cyclist to win a stage of the Tour

Guido Bontempi rode like a man possessed to win a brilliant solo victory at Limoges. The former renowned sprinter said he could now retire 'a happy man'

behind. The gap between the two groups was 30 seconds when the nineteen turned left onto the Quai Brienne, alongside the River Garonne, 10km from the finish. At this moment, after a series of rapid attacks, Bugno went clear. He was chased by Breukink, who was closely followed by one of Bugno's Italian team-mates, Roberto Gusmeroli. They would stay away to the finish, where Bugno scored an easy sprint victory. Meanwhile, the others were caught by the Delgado-led pack 5km from the line, but they were still 18 seconds behind at the line – allowing Breukink to jump over Delgado into third place overall.

20 July, stage 19: Castillon-la-Bataille – Limoges, 182.5km

On a day when it finally became known that the 7-Eleven team was officially looking for a new main sponsor, one could sense the tone of frustration in the voice of team member Dag-Otto Lauritzen after missing a stage win at Limoges. Still gasping for air after taking second place in a long, uphill sprint from Belgian Peter Roes of Lotto, the 33-year-old Norwegian said, 'We were so strong, Steve [Bauer] and me . . . It's a pity we couldn't win the stage.'

The reason that Bauer and Lauritzen did not win was a rather extraordinary performance from Bontempi, who took the stage with a surprise solo attack. He made his move with 30km to go, just after Bauer had towed up four other riders to a fourteen-man break (containing Lauritzen) that had started to develop 40km earlier. 'It was too big a group to control every attack,' continued a breathless Lauritzen. 'Van der Poel attacked, then Bontempi countered. And I tried to join him up a hill. I got so close to him, only 50m behind. But I went into oxygen debt.'

Eight others came up to Lauritzen; but by now Bontempi was 1:20 clear, and he pushed this up to 1:40 on a fast descent into Aixe-sur-Vienne. There were still 11km to race, and it seemed possible that Bontempi would be caught on the ensuing climb.

'But the other guys seemed to be resigned that they were racing for second place,' Lauritzen lamented. Indeed, there was a lot of freewheeling and dummy attacks before Lauritzen and Roes drew clear on the 2km climb to the finish, where they arrived 1:28 behind an exultant Bontempi.

21 July, stage 20: Lac de Vassivière time trial, 45.5km

In the end, Chiappucci's tenuous, 5-second grip on the yellow jersey didn't last very long. Although the Italian made an energetic start to his time trial at Lac de Vassivière, it soon became clear that he was riding on courage rather than strength. After the first five, mainly downhill, kilometres of the penultimate stage, he was only 2 seconds slower than LeMond – who started 3 minutes in front of him. But then, climbing the first hill of an extremely hilly course, Chiappucci began to show signs of cracking. And by the first official time check, he was 11 seconds behind his American opponent. The yellow jersey had already changed hands.

The quality of Chiappucci's initial effort was shown by his having the fourth fastest time at this point – behind Breukink, Alcalá and LeMond. The PDM pair continued to battle out the stage win. From being 6 seconds behind, Alcalá was 1 second ahead of his team-mate at the halfway point. Breukink moved ahead again on a mostly downhill sweep to Nedde, 12km from the finish, to be 6 seconds ahead, and he sped through the finish in 1:02:40. Alcalá was 28 seconds slower. Breukink's performance, on an afternoon when the mercury again touched 95°, almost earned him second place overall, at Chiappucci's expense. After his good start, the Italian slid down the rankings: eighth at halfway (0:31 down on LeMond); 13th at the 33.4km check (where LeMond was 1:17 ahead); and 17th at the end, 2:21 behind LeMond and 3:18 after Breukink. The despondent Italian had saved his second place by just 13 seconds.

Before LeMond and the other principal players entered the arena, the 200,000 fans massed around the bucolic circuit had cheered their local favourite, Luc Leblanc of Castorama, to a fine 10th place (1:05:07), and had seen a back-to-form Lauritzen record 1:04:41 – the fastest for two hours, and good enough for seventh – before being beaten by Spaniard Pello Ruíz Cabestany of ONCE. Another surprise was that 33-year-old Lejarreta was the best of the Spanish riders: his 1:03:18, only 10 seconds slower than Alcalá, was 2 seconds faster than Indurain, and 1:43 better than Delgado.

22 July, stage 21: Bretigny-sur-Orge – Paris, 182.5km

With the top sprinters geared up for a prestige victory in Paris in front of 500,000 fans, Museeuw rocketed home to win by more than a bike length over Baffi and Ludwig – proving that his sprint win at Mont St Michel in the first week of the Tour was no fluke. 'Every lap around the circuit, I studied the finish,' reported a confident Museeuw. 'I decided that I had to be in front at the last corner.' His decision was based on the fact that, unusually, there was a strong easterly tail wind blowing up the Champs-Elysées, favouring a long sprint. Through the final kilometre, Museeuw followed his team-mate De Clercq, and Rooks, who was working for Ludwig. Across the Place de la Concorde, Museeuw held tightly to the third position until he burst past the two greyhounds around the right-hand curve into the 400m finishing straight. His early move seemed to catch

In the yellow jersey at last, a relieved Greg LeMond chats to Phil Liggett after the time trial at Lac de Vassivière

Johan Museeuw finally got the better of Olaf Ludwig at the prestigious Champs Elysées finish

A jubilant Greg LeMond celebrating his third Tour victory

the other sprinters by surprise, and when he started his sprint 350m from the finish, Museeuw was already several lengths clear – and that tail wind helped him maintain his trajectory all the way to the line.

Baffi, making his usual late burst, couldn't even draw level with Museeuw, although the squat Italian did pull convincingly away from Ludwig, whose third place clinched the green jersey for him. In fourth place came the persistent Soviet Djamolidin Abdujaparov of Alfa Lum, just ahead of a fast-finishing Phinney. The American's fifth place was a remarkable result for a rider who had been suffering from heat stroke three days before, and had had to hang on to British team-mate Sean Yates's jersey to get over some of the climbs! The 7-Eleven sprinter's good finish in Paris was made possible by a powerful lead-out from Yates, who earlier had been one of the strongest members in an interesting six-man break. The move, started by Thomas Wegmüller of Weinmann, included eighth-placed Alcalá – who was trying to win for his mother, visiting Europe for the first time. Alcalá carried the break 32 seconds clear on the third lap, but the gap was down to 8 seconds by the penultimate lap. The Panasonic and Lotto teams were now in full chase, and the scene was set for the only mass sprint of the Tour. One man not concerned with the sprint was the rider who crossed the line in 41st place, with his left arm raised in triumph. He was wearing a yellow jersey for the first time in this Tour – but it was the only time that mattered. Greg LeMond, without even winning a stage, had won his third Tour de France, 2:16 ahead of the unexpected Chiappucci, with Breukink another 13 seconds adrift, in third place.

The 156 Tour survivors greeted the sight of the Champs Elysées with relief

Wincanton Classic: 29 July

Brighton's seaside promenade on a searing hot July Sunday was the setting for yet another demonstration of Italy's cycling renaissance and the outstanding form of Gianni Bugno, leader of the Chateau d'Ax team. Bugno won the event by thirteen seconds from PDM's Sean Kelly of Ireland and Rudy Dhaenens of Belgium; he also, since the Wincanton Classic is the sixth round of the World Cup competition, gained enough points to give him the competition lead. After winning the competition opener, Milan-San Remo, and then the Giro d'Italia and two stages of the Tour de France, in which he finished seventh overall, Bugno's performance in this two-year-old British classic confirmed that he was on course to be considered cyclist of the year.

The consensus on the race itself was that this year's Wincanton Classic provided more testing racing than its Newcastle upon Tyne debut – four laps of a hilly 52km circuit which included the steep, narrow climb of Ditchling Beacon, followed by four 8km circuits in Brighton itself. From the rider's point of view, however, the most testing characteristic of the race was the traffic hazard; parked cars, and oncoming traffic stopped only briefly whilst the race passed, as well as riding on the left-hand side of the road, presented a formidable challenge to a peloton accustomed to the closed roads of Continental racing, and a number of near misses occurred as the pack swept round blind bends into the face of waiting traffic. And after the presentation, amidst a flurry of calls for roads to be completely closed in future editions, event organiser Alan Rushton of Sport for Television accepted that the complaints were fully justified: 'Unless we can get the roads fully blocked, as is the case on the Continent, I would rather not have a World Cup race,' he boldly asserted, after talking with Continental team personnel, local police authorities and various observers. The victorious Bugno tried diplomatically to avoid the traffic issue, but did comment when pressed that 'In England, the drivers are not used to bike racing. Instead of parking cars off the road, they left them on the road and it was dangerous for us,' he said. 'It would be better if the race was on a smaller circuit which could be closed off to traffic' – although most observers felt that for course difficulty and selectability the move from the shorter Newcastle circuit had been a sound one.

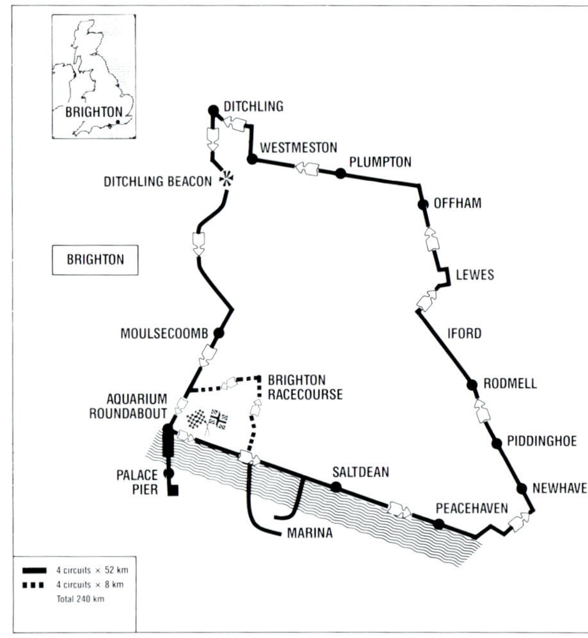

Wincanton Classic, England: 240km

The peloton snakes its way off Madeira Drive on the first lap

The only notable absentees from the field that lined up for the start were Tour de France champion American Greg LeMond (Z), whose scratching from the race was only confirmed the day before and attributed to a saddle sore sustained in the Tour; France's Laurent Fignon (Castorama), who was still recovering from the crash in the Tour which had caused his abandonment; and the reigning World Cup leader, Italian Moreno Argentin (Ariostea), also out for injury reasons. Bugno started the race ranked number one on FICP/Velo rankings but second on the World Cup.

The early racing was remarkable only for a nine-man break which attacked after 40km and stayed away until

The victorious Bugno

the final 32km, gaining a maximum lead of 8:30. Bugno's winning move came with six kilometres to go, from a lead group of seventeen including Kelly, Dhaenens, Italy's Claudio Chiappucci (Carrera), Scotland's Robert Millar (Z), France's Gilles Delion (Helvetia-La Suisse), Spain's Marino Lejarreta (ONCE) and Federico Echave (Clas), and Belgium's Marc Sergeant (Panasonic), Sammie Moreels (Lotto) and Dirk De Wolf (PDM). The final selection was made on the climb of Wilson Avenue. Bugno attacked, and Dhaenens, sensing the threat in Bugno's move, tried to follow; he was unable to match the Italian's strength, but the momentary uncertainty as to whether or not he could stay with him made Kelly hesitate, so the Irish star missed the move as well. 'I thought Rudy was going to follow, but he didn't. I might have been able to, but it was too late,' said Kelly later. Bugno passed the summit of Wilson Avenue alone, and went hurtling down the twisting descent to the coastal Madeira Drive and the finish line.

It had been a frustrating race for Sean Kelly, back in World Cup contention after he broke his collar bone in the Tour of Flanders only to lose his chance to the unsuccessful Dhaenens. But Dhaenens, cycling's perennial runner-up, commented in typically stoical fashion, 'There's still San Sebastian to go, and my form's still there.'

The Italian champion startled himself by his own fine form, so soon after the Tour de France and in such hot conditions. 'During the race I didn't feel all that well. At one point I even thought I would have to stop,' he said later. 'I was surprised that no-one chased me. But once I got away, it was easier than I thought. What kept me going was that it was a World Cup race and that I needed the points.' His win gave him what he needed; after the Wincanton Classic he led the World Cup with 86 points, with Dhaenens hanging on to his second place with 80 points, and the absent Argentin falling back to third place with 62 points.

Dhaenens, Chiappucci and Kelly contest the sprint for second place. Behind them are Michel Dernies (Weinmann) and Marc Sergeant

Kellogg's Tour of Britain: 31 July-5 August

It was expecting a lot of a weary European peloton that its riders should line up for 1093km of stage racing just one week after the end of the Tour de France; in fact, many sceptics had already decided that the fourth Kellogg's Tour of Britain would be nothing more than a promenade round the country by the 105 starters. But when the race finally came to a halt in Manchester, after setting off from the seaside resort of Brighton in south-east England six days earlier, the critics were redder in the face than the 66 pedalling survivors, because this year's edition was quite unlike its predecessors. Gone was the reluctance to race hard so soon after the Tour de France; gone were the unnecessarily long marathon stages which only discourage an already exhausted field; and gone, finally, was the delusion that the race was Britain's answer to the Tour de France.

The Kellogg's Tour of Britain has finally carved its own niche in the world of cycling. Whilst it is not a major event in the calendar for Tour de France winners, it does carry vital FICP points; it also provides those riders who failed to distinguish themselves in the Tour de France with an opportunity to redeem themselves.

This year, for the first time, a foreign rider won the race – Belgium's Michel Dernies of the Weinmann team. A stocky, sandy-haired 29-year-old, Dernies added a Continental flavour to a race which in previous years had seen Joey McLoughlin (1987), Malcolm Elliott (1988) and Robert Millar (1989) keep the honours at home. All three champions were back in 1990, but only Millar, the Scottish climbing specialist of the French Z team, constituted a serious threat to Dernies. From the time the duo made their winning two-man break on the hilly stage 3 to Sheffield, they were locked in a head-to-head confrontation which was finally decided only by a crash on the last two kilometres of the final stage.

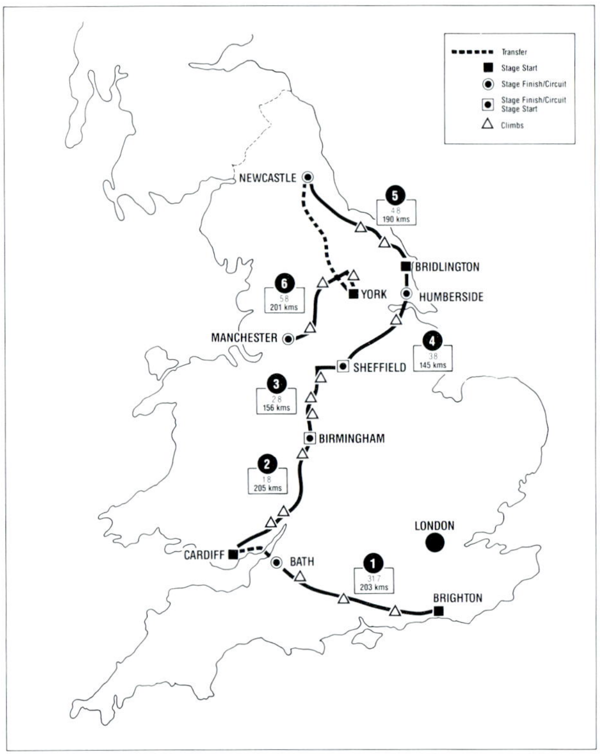

Kellogg's Tour of Britain: 1093km

The Kellogg's Tour racing for a TV Times sprint in Winchester on stage 1. The sprint competition was eventually won by Dave Mann (Airmarshall-Kirk)

One of the characteristics of this year's race was the hot and humid weather which tested every rider's mettle, especially those who had endured a scorching last ten days in the Tour de France. Riders began to feel the effects of the heat early on in the race, although the average speed did not show it.

Malcolm Elliott (Teka), wanting to shine in one of his few home-based events, encouraged hopes that he was on target for a second win by taking the first stage from Birmingham to Bath, but although his victory over Belgium's Sammie Moreels (Lotto-Superclub) and Frenchman Laurent Jalabert (Toshiba) put him into the yellow jersey, it turned out to be only a transient tenancy.

On stage 2, 198.4km from Cardiff to Birmingham, a seven-man break formed on the fast and tricky circuit finish at Birmingham and finished 16 seconds clear of the main field, containing Elliott. Up in the front group was Jalabert, only sixth to Italy's Andrea Tafi (Selle Italia) on the stage, but in the yellow jersey thanks to making up his pre-stage deficit of 4 seconds on Elliott.

But Jalabert too was not destined to wear yellow for more than a stage, losing his lead the following day on the third stage from Birmingham to Sheffield. It was a hilly leg, featuring some testing climbs in England's rugged Peak District. And with only 1:24 separating

Malcolm Elliott winning the first stage to Bath. Hidden behind him is Laurent Jalabert, who finished third

the first 73 riders overall, attacks were inevitable. Millar was not the first to go, but his escape, on a third category climb coming out of Matlock with 60km to go, was the most significant. The Matlock Saddlery, the third of five climbs for the day, saw Millar joined by Stuttgart's West German riders Josef Holzmann and Udo Bölts and Frenchmen Martial Gayant (Toshiba) and Gérard Rué (Castorama). Millar escaped alone; Dernies came into the picture when he caught the chase group before the first category Hathersage climb at 138.5km. It was here, under Millar's impetus, that the two got away, and by their arrival in Sheffield, with four 2.1km circuits to go, they had a lead of 1:47 on a ten-man chase group led by Italian Maurizio Fondriest (Del Tongo).

The scene was set for a clear-cut ending – two leaders with a 1:47 lead and only three stages to go – although there were still plenty of hills ahead. But at least the Tour now had a significant split in the overall order: by the day's end more than 28 minutes separated the top 73 riders. Initially, however, the stage ended in confusion; what happened was that the ten chasers arrived at the Sheffield circuit just as Dernies and Millar were completing their first lap. And when they heard the bell go for Dernies and Millar, denoting one lap to go, the entire group wound up its speed for what they all thought was the finishing sprint. Fondriest crossed the line first, thinking he was the winner, while Dernies and Millar both finished in the group, but with the Belgian just ahead. Who had won the stage? Who was now in the yellow jersey? The ensuing muddle was resolved when Dernies was awarded the stage and yellow jersey, with Millar – on equal overall time – given second place overall, as Dernies had fared better in the points competition. Fondriest, baffled and disappointed, was given third place on the stage and found himself third overall at 1:43.

For the remainder of the race, debate centred on expectations that Millar's fabled climbing prowess would win through. But realistically, the climbs on the Kellogg's Tour are not to be compared to the Alpine and Pyrenean passes where the Scot has made his name, and Dernies cut his teeth on the cobbled climbs of the Continental classics, which are just as testing as the steepest British ascents.

The 142km fourth stage from Sheffield to Hull was unlikely to see either rider change the status quo; its flat route was a sprinters' delight, and the bunch was expected to catch the escape group for a typical sprint finish. But the Danish duo of Sören Lilholt (Histor-Sigma) and Jesper Skibby (TVM) attacked before the first of four 2.4km finishing circuits. Lilholt finished triumphant in the ensuing sprint, 1:31 ahead of the peloton which saw Fondriest – in the green sprinter's points jersey – come in to take third place on the stage.

Fondriest's focus in the Tour was never in doubt. The 1988 world champion had missed the Tour of Italy through injury and, in view of the demands of the Giro d'Italia his team, Del Tongo, had opted out of the Tour de France. So the Kellogg's Tour and Wincanton Classic

Millar led Dernies into the final lap in Sheffield, though they were shortly to be swamped by Fondriest's group, which led to confusion over who had won. At the end of the day it was Michel Dernies who was in the yellow jersey

Westerdale Ford on stage 5 to Newcastle-upon-Tyne was expected to produce some excitement. The fallen riders are Andrea Tafi (Selle Italia) and Laurent Madouas (Z)

were his first real tests since the Spring classics against all-round European talent, and with the World Championships not long away, Fondriest had come to Britain with some hard racing in mind.

His sprinting prowess was in evidence again the next day, on the 180km fifth stage from Bridlington to Newcastle-upon-Tyne, as he took the sprint for fourth place, 19 seconds behind a break of three riders which got away with 60km to go. The men in this break were Dernies, Millar and the Italian neo-pro Gianluca Bortolami of Diana-Colnago. In a day already enlivened by two second category climbs, the sight of Dernies and Millar fighting to the finish drew a chorus of cheers from the thousands of spectators. They were still equal on overall time, and Millar tried desperately to beat Dernies by that elusive one second. But he didn't succeed, and on the uphill finish, Bortolami took advantage of the battle between Dernies and Millar to win the stage.

Stage 6 was certainly the toughest. As if the rigours of an early-dawn transfer from Newcastle to York weren't enough, the day continued with a 207km route taking in six climbs, and everyone really expected a race-winning attack from Millar. But for Millar, this stage through the Pennines from York to Manchester would go down as 'one of those days'. His misfortunes began with an early crash in which he hurt his hip. Having also to change bicycles, using the bike he had wanted to save for the descent to Manchester from the first category summit of Holme Moss at 162km, Millar was never able to recover his attacking form, and at the summit of the 20 per cent climb of Holme Moss, Rué was in front; Millar, fourth over the top, climbed well enough to secure him the lead in the King of the Mountains competition.

The rain and constant humidity made the final 45km tough going for the 19 breakaways who formed on the descent from Holme Moss. The group contained all the riders whose attacks, albeit unsuccessful, had enlivened the week's racing, including Dernies and Millar, of course, but also Fondriest, Rué, McLoughlin, Elliott, Jalabert, Ireland's Stephen Roche (Histor), Great Britain's Rob Holden (Banana-Falcon), Australia's Phil Anderson (TVM), and Spain's Federico Echave (Clas) – all intent on one last bid for success.

With Dernies and Millar on equal overall time, Millar only needed to finish ahead of Dernies to secure a second consecutive victory. However, going into the final right-hand corner, Millar fell again, taking with him Italy's Franco Chioccioli (Del Tongo) and Venezuela's Leonardo Sierra (Selle Italia) – and Michel Dernies. Unfortunately for Millar, Dernies was quicker to get back on his bike, and finished four seconds clear of the Scot on the stage.

The rest of the break behaved like a chorus line, with every rider trying to take one last bow: McLoughlin attacked, as did Rué and Anderson, but finally it was Fondriest who won the sprint from Anderson, finishing third overall and at the same time clinching his victory in the points category. Dernies, finishing 17th at 0:23, was soon taking his place on the winners' dais, with a bruised, cut and very disappointed Robert Millar second overall.

Rob Holden of Banana-Falcon leading Millar and Dernies towards the densely-packed summit of Holme Moss on the final stage to Manchester

After four years the Tour of Britain gets its first foreign winner

Clasico San Sebastian: 11 August

Miguel Indurain is a man who tries not to get involved in Basque nationalism, but as he comes from Pamplona in north-eastern Spain it takes very little for Basque cycling fans to adopt him as their own, and this proprietorial regard became irresistible when the strapping dark-haired Spaniard won the rich San Sebastian World Cup Classic.

The Banesto rider, still displaying the form which saw him finish 10th in the Tour de France a few weeks earlier, was certainly a worthwhile consolation prize for those fans who travelled to San Sebastian hoping for a win by Marino Lejarreta. As always, the Spanish ONCE rider was a favourite for the event: from its ten stagings he has won three – in 1981, 1982 and 1983, and his fifth place in the Tour de France surely justified his ambition to win a fourth San Sebastian in 1990.

Raced under a blanket of 31° heat San Sebastian – round seven of the World Cup – was enlivened by three attempted solo attacks, the most noteworthy of which was the five-kilometre break launched by American Ron Kiefel (7-Eleven) which immediately preceded the decisive action of the race.

Clasico San Sebastian, Spain: 244km

Lejarreta's attack on the Alto de Jaizkibel pulled Indurain clear, although Indurain later admitted that until the gradient eased he thought he was going to be dropped

The serious antics began on the first-category Pyrenean climb, Alto de Jaizkibel, 34km from the finish, and much to the satisfaction of the throng of flag-waving Basques it was Lejarreta who opened hostilities. After his ONCE team-mates had caught Kiefel, Lejarreta broke free from the regrouped peloton. It appeared to be *the* move: the summit was only eight kilometres away, followed by a similar descent, and it was all flat to the finish. All Lejarreta had to do was to secure enough lead on the climb to stay ahead of the inevitable chase on the flatter stretch to the finish, and with his confidence boosted by a win in the lead-up Tour of Burgos it was clear that the skinny black-haired Spaniard thought he could do it. The only problem was that Indurain thought he could too, being quick to follow Lejarreta's move – far quicker than several others, including West German Thomas Durst (Panasonic-Sportlife), Frenchman Gilles Delion (Helvetia-La Suisse), Norwegian Jaanus Kuum (Teka), France's Charly Mottet (RMO) and Italy's surprise Tour de France runner-up Claudio Chiappucci (Carrera). These riders tried to latch on to the speeding wheels of Lejarreta and Indurain but never succeeded: the Spanish duo's superior strength left the other five riders further and further behind as the climb proceeded, and they had to resign themselves to racing a moderate tempo, ready to join any future chase up to the summit. It was Lejarreta who set the attacking speed, Indurain – in a repeat of his winning antics in the Tour de France on the stage to Luz Ardiden – tucking into the Basque's slipstream, then attacking alone with two kilometres to go to the summit.

Behind, the World Cup contenders were making life exciting in the field: up there was the World Cup leader, Italian Gianni Bugno (Chateau d'Ax), and his Swiss team-mate Toni Rominger; defending World Cup champion Sean Kelly of Ireland (PDM) and his Belgian team-mate Rudy Dhaenens; Canada's Steve Bauer (7-Eleven) and Spain's Federico Echave (Clas).

The long, gradual descent into San Sebastian was tailor-made for Indurain's heavy build

At the summit, overlooking the blue wind-swept Atlantic, Indurain passed with 58 seconds on Lejarreta, who had been caught by a chase group including Chiappucci, Echave and Indurain's Banesto team-mate Jesús Rodriguez-Magro. One minute after them were more chasers – Kelly, Rominger and Switzerland's Pascal Richard (Helvetia-La Suisse).

The twisting descent, shaded by lush green forest, suited Indurain and his 80kg bodyweight very well. The Spaniard took every corner perfectly, with gravity as much as pedal power achieving the optimum speed. As the descent levelled out with 22km to go, his lead was 1:30. With 15km to go to San Sebastian, Indurain's lead had increased to 2:05 and his success looked assured, but the lure of World Cup points was enlivening the chasing group. This now numbered thirteen, the original chasing group – Kelly, Chiappucci, Lejarreta, Echave and Rodriguez-Magro – having been joined by Rominger, Delion, Bauer, Richard, Kuum, the French Toshiba riders Laurent Jalabert and Martial Gayant and Spain's Eduardo Ruíz (BH). Interestingly, Bugno and Dhaenens (joint second on the Cup ladder before the race), were not in the action. Neither was Greg LeMond (Z), although his position at the front before the climb indicated his world title training was on schedule.

Unfortunately, as Indurain hurtled towards the San Sebastian finish line, the chase behind was hindered, as so often this season, by hesitation within the group, although Kelly, Richard, Bauer and Echave were trying to stir things up a little. Even Lejarreta, sensing that a second place gained by an attack would be popular with his followers, tried twice to leave the group. But his rivals were merciless in pursuit, and he was chased down on both occasions. By the time the chase group finally split, under the pressure of Kelly, Jalabert and Rominger, Indurain was into the final kilometre.

Indurain's victory was safe and he eased up over the last four hundred metres, waving and grinning as much as every one of his adoptive countrymen. His advantage was two minutes and 24 seconds on the next rider, twenty-one-year-old Jalabert, who led out the sprint against Kelly and Rominger and beat them convincingly to the line in that order, with the rest of the chasers five seconds behind.

As for the World Cup rankings, San Sebastian left the top three unchanged. Bugno's 24th place earned him no World Cup points, whilst Dhaenens was cheered with his one point bonus for 20th place.

Indurain's by-now familiar victory salute delighted the Basque fans at the finish

Championship of Zürich: 19 August

In his last race as 1989 World Champion, American Greg LeMond of the Z team displayed magnificent form in Switzerland's Championship of Zürich, but he was just beaten by Frenchman Charly Mottet of RMO in an exciting and controversial finishing sprint.

Unlike recent courses for this Swiss classic – a giant opening loop, followed by two-and-a-half laps of a 50km finishing circuit – this year's 77th edition covered five laps of a 48km circuit. This made for a more demanding event, negotiating the difficult Regensberg and Stig climbs five times each, instead of three, as on the old route, and the modified course proved a great success.

185 riders lined up for the start, on a warm, sunny Sunday morning, and almost immediately there was a breakaway of 22 men. Away went such notables as Irishman Sean Kelly of PDM, Dutchman Adrie Van der Poel (Weinmann) and Gilles Delion (Helvetia-La Suisse) – but a fierce chase saw them reeled in before the first ascent to Regensberg, 20km into the lap. 5km later, on the Stig climb, another break formed, of nine men. Again, the PDM team was represented – by Dirk De Wolf of Belgium – while Mottet's RMO team put Eric Caritoux of France and Belgian Michel Vermote into the break, and the other escapers were Belgian Peter De Clercq (Lotto), West German Josef Holzmann (Stuttgart) and the Swiss riders Pascal Ducrot and Marco Diem of the Frank team and Guido Winterberg and Karl Kälin of Helvetia-La Suisse.

A lap later, the nine riders had built up a lead of 6:25, provoking a concerted chase by LeMond's Z team and the Chateau d'Ax squad of World Cup leader Gianni Bugno. The gap closed to about a minute, and on the third Regensberg climb the on-form Spaniard Eduardo Chozas of ONCE – marked by RMO's Mauro Ribeiro – jumped across to the leaders, while Kälin dropped back. The reinforced break, now numbering 10 riders, started to pull away again, but at the start of the fourth lap the chase was joined by the 7-Eleven team of 1989 winner Canadian Steve Bauer, and the peloton soon closed the gap. With riders' legs beginning to tire in the front group, Chozas went clear on the curving

The second main escape of the day was this nine-man break which formed after 25km and got up to 6:25 lead over the next 40km before the peloton started chasing

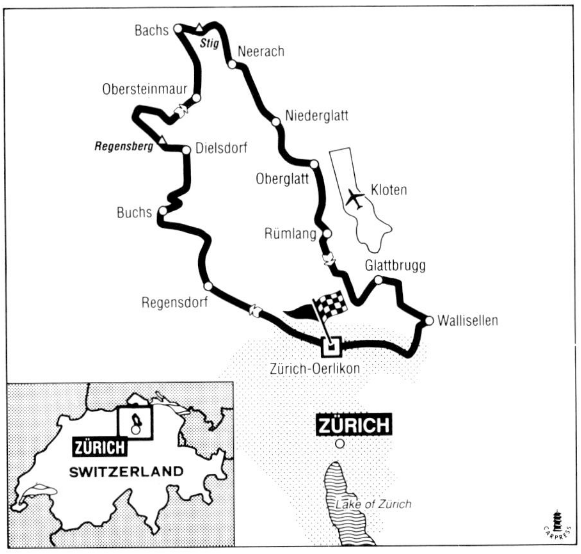

Championship of Zürich, Switzerland: 240km

Regensberg ascent, and only Ribeiro, De Wolf and De Clercq were able to stay with him.

But now, with 75km remaining, the favourites were starting to get anxious, and as the four leaders were about to be caught Miguel Indurain, the Spanish Banesto rider, made a strong counterattack on the straight, 600-metre-long Stig climb. The peloton exploded: with Indurain went LeMond, Mottet and Chiappucci (and his Carrera team-mate Massimo Ghirotto), as well as Belgian PDM rider Rudy Dhaenens, lying second in the World Cup competition (but no leader Bugno), the on-form Swiss rider Mauro Gianetti (Helvetia-La Suisse), Italian Roberto Conti (Ariostea), Belgian Johan Bruyneel (Lotto), Dutchman Eddy Bouwmans (Panasonic) and Venezuelan Leonardo Sierra (Selle Italia). By the end of the fourth lap, with 48km to go, the powerful 11-strong break had a 52-second advantage over the first group of chasers, which was being led by riders from the Chateau d'Ax and ONCE teams.

Out of the city and back into the patchwork of fields and wooded hills, the gap began to close. But no sooner had Bugno and Lejarreta jumped across to the leaders, at the picture postcard town of Buchs, with 37km remaining, than Chiappucci made a spectacular uphill attack; still climbing, the Italian was joined first by LeMond, then Mottet, whilst a splendid Lejarreta launched a successful solo pursuit.

Once together, the four leaders worked in perfect harmony to protect their advantage. Leading the chase was Bugno, along with Delion, the Ariostea riders Rolf Sörensen and Davide Cassani, a third Italian, Franco Ballerini (Del Tongo), the Spaniards Pedro Delgado (Banesto) and Iñaki Gaston (Clas), and Thomas Wegmüller (Weinmann) of Switzerland. Further back came a group that contained Kelly and team-mate De Wolf (but not Dhaenens), and 7-Eleven's Norwegian rider Dag-Otto Lauritzen. After the last two climbs, the gap between the break and the chasers hovered around one minute, and it remained that way until Lejarreta, Chiappucci, LeMond and Mottet began their final manoeuvring.

The four men began shaping up for the sprint more than a kilometre out from the finish, alongside Zürich's famous Oerlikon Velodrome. Mottet and Lejarreta accelerated on the right, while Chiappucci waited until the 300m mark before launching a wicked attack on the left. LeMond followed Chiappucci, and Mottet jumped after them. 'I knew that Greg was the strongest,' Mottet admitted later, 'so I followed him in the sprint.' Indeed, the American seemed to be headed for victory. Then, just as Mottet counterattacked, LeMond swerved, his bike clipping Chiappucci's, and he was several lengths down before starting to chase the Frenchman. Every stroke of his pedals brought him closer, but he was still half a wheel behind Mottet at the finish. Chiappucci was in third place, and Lejarreta fourth; almost a minute behind them, Bugno easily won the fifth-place sprint from Sörensen, thus consolidating his lead in the World Cup points.

LeMond was understandably disappointed about losing, especially in such a fashion, as he was eager to point out to the mob of surrounding reporters: 'It's been said, and written, that I'm not interested in anything except the Tour de France and the Worlds. That's untrue. The fact is that I can't allow myself to be on top form in April, as that's bad for the Tour de France. And don't ask me if I'd prefer to win here or at the Worlds. I'd rather win everywhere!'

Mottet let LeMond lead out the final sprint, and then counter attacked in the final metres to score a superb victory by half a wheel

LeMond after Mottet's triumph: 'Don't ask me if I'd prefer to win here or at the Worlds. I'd rather win everywhere!'

NORBA Series: 5 May–26 August

When Coors Light signed on as the title sponsor of America's premier off-road race circuit, which for three years had simply been called the NORBA National Points Series, the deal heralded a quantum leap for American mountain bike racing. Competition in this season-long series has always been intense, but the increased prize money, combined with the fact that the series now determined the selection of the US team for the World Mountain Bike Championships, have radically altered the character of the competition, and the quest for NORBA points turned each event into a battleground. About 60 pro-elite riders are committed to contesting the circuit, with each rider's best seven-out-of-eight results tabulated to find the overall winner, and since the final race carries double points and cannot be the throw-out race, it is of supreme importance.

The levels of talent and competitiveness in the Coors Light series were so high that the leader's jersey changed hands after every race until six events had been contested; it wasn't until Dave Wiens of Diamond Back won at both Park City, Utah and Winter Park, Colorado that any kind of winning streak was established. But Specialized's perennially consistent Ned Overend held on to the overall points leader's white jersey with a pair of top-three finishes in the same events, and went on to clinch the national championship with a win in the finals at Mammoth, California.

The Coors Light series represents each geographical sector of the USA, and the guaranteed purse at each stop is $7500. The points chase began on the steep, dry climbs of the Southern California mountains, with Don Myrah overcoming a challenge by Daryl Price to triumph at the Snow Summit ski area. Round two took the series to the steamy jungle-like trails of Flowery Branch, Georgia, where Max Jones rose to the top, and in the next event the sandy, roller-coaster paths of

Although not eligible for the overall NORBA series, Swiss rider Thomas Frischknecht won the race at Mount Snow, Vermont, and was a challenger here at Winter Park, Colorado

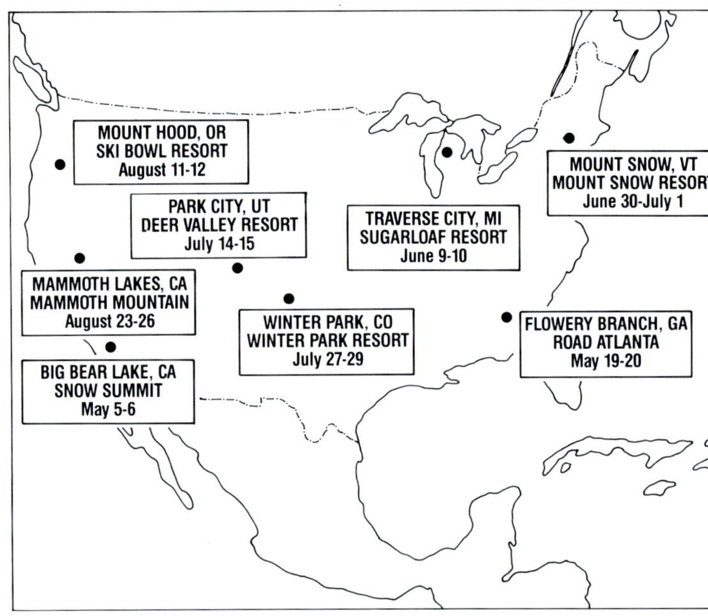

NORBA Series, USA

Traverse City, Michigan were the exclusive preserve of Michigan-born John Tomac. In Vermont, the course stretched the ideal of diversity to the limit, with a technical, grotesquely muddy course over slippery, tangled roots, and for the first time European riders dominated a NORBA event, Switzerland's Thomas Frischknecht beating Polish-born Jan Wiejak.

Continuing its westward path across the country, the series finally hit high altitude in Park City for the fifth round. The more experienced riders coped better with the hazards of the Wasatch mountains – thin air, dusty soil, long climbs and breathless descents – and it was Wiens who overcame challenges from Tomac, Overend and KHS's John Weissenrieder to take the race. Steeper climbing was encountered in the Rocky Mountains: the Winter Park event, held at an altitude of 2800m at the base of the Continental Divide, saw the European-based American, Mike Kloser, perform well to come in fourth behind hot-shots Wiens, Overend and Tomac.

Most of the events in the series were held on highly technical courses with lots of tight, single-track racing through trees, with courses between 5 and 8km long and total race distances of 40-50km. The final two events of the series, at Mount Hood, Oregon and Mammoth, California, were both much longer and at higher altitude, and would thus provide crucial preparation for the World Championships, which were to be held at 2700m over a 13km course at the Purgatory ski area.

The man on form at the Mount Hood race was Rishi Grewal of Coors Light, who notched the biggest victory of his off-road career, racing flawlessly on a course that proved to be the most extreme encountered on the 1990 circuit. Even so, the 3-lap, 48km men's cross-country yielded the closest finish of the year, with only 15 seconds separating the top three riders. Flashing in on Grewal's heels were Weissenrieder, and Ritchey's Tim Rutherford, while early leader Overend faded to fourth, a minute back. 'I led from early in lap 2, and in this

Americans John Tomac, Tim Rutherford and John Weissenrieder – seen here on the Mount Hood, Washington, course – were top-five contenders throughout the series

sport you've got to work that advantage, even if it means sacrificing your pacing,' explained Overend, 'but I just blew up, and when Weissenrieder and Rutherford came by, I didn't even fight for it because I had to save something for that last descent. It's too risky if you're totally blown.'

The result was that Overend went into the finals at Mammoth with only a 12-point lead over Wiens, and Rutherford, with Tomac and Jones also within shooting distance. Most observers were anticipating a dogfight, especially as Mammoth race director Bill Cockroft added a $10,000 bonus for the race winner. That bonus, and the title, eventually went to a patient Overend, who waited out early charges by the aspiring Rutherford, Tomac and Grewal, to seal his only win of the series.

At 19km, the circuit was the longest of the eight-race series, with the men completing 3 laps (57km). But several sections of wide ski runs made it the least technically demanding course of the series, so the racing was more open than usual. The main difficulty was a 3km climb that gained 300 metres on a combination of access roads and single track roads through the loose, pulverized pumice for which Mammoth is notorious. Rutherford, Tomac and Grewal went hard from the start, while Overend held a steadier pace in fourth place. After half a lap, Rutherford led Tomac by 12 seconds, with Grewal at 45 seconds, and Overend more than a minute back with Weissenrieder clinging to the reigning champion's wheel.

By the end of the first lap, Tomac and Rutherford were together in the lead, still the same time ahead of the pursuers. But as they mounted the main climb a second time, the early pace began to take its toll on the three leaders. Rutherford was the first to fold, dropping back to third, and Grewal assumed the lead, passing Tomac two thirds of the way up the mountain. Then Tomac was swallowed up by Overend and Weissenrieder on the course's second uphill stretch. Grewal completed the second lap 30 seconds ahead of Overend and Weissenrieder, but visibly fatigued, and he was caught by the two chasers at the foot of the main climb. Then, when Weissenrieder's chain came off, it was Overend, followed by Grewal, Weissenrieder and a resurgent Wiens, who rode away to claim the loot.

Defending champion Ned Overend conquered the impressive high-altitude course at Mammoth, California to win his only race of the series and clinch the overall title

Grundig World Cup series: 29 April–8 September

The name on everyone's lips in road racing is Perrier, which sponsors the World Cup and the FICP world rankings. In mountain biking – in Europe, anyway – the name is Grundig. For the third year, this German electronics manufacturer was the driving force behind the Grundig Challenge Mountain Bike World Cup. In 1990, this series covered nine events in nine countries, starting in April and culminating with a final meeting in Lenzerheide, Switzerland, in September. One criticism of the series was the scheduling, which put the final just one week before the World Mountain Bike Championships in the United States, and the Grundig organisers stipulated that participation in the final was mandatory. So many riders had to make the difficult choice between the Grundig final and the Worlds in Durango, and Britain's Tim Gould was one who opted for the Worlds.

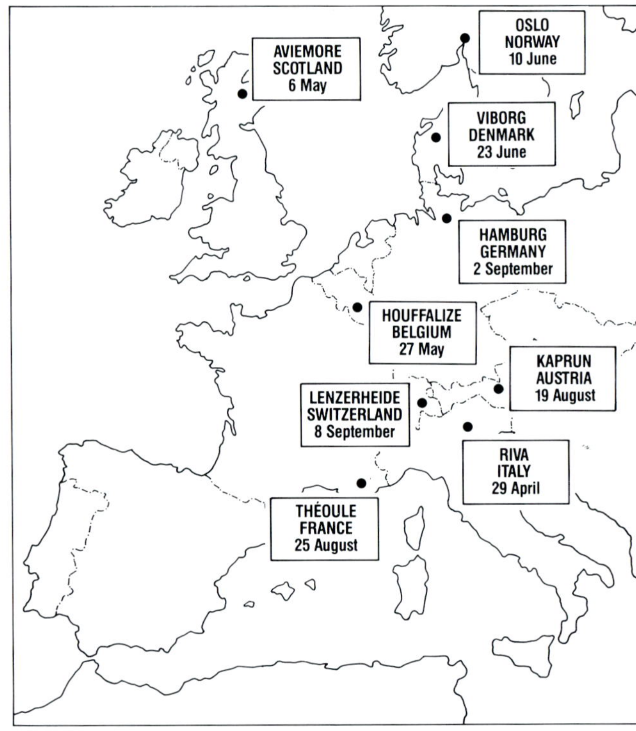

Grundig World Cup series

29 April: Riva, Italy
West German rider Mike Kluge, a former world cyclo-cross champion, was the dominant rider when the series kicked off at Riva, on Lake Garda in Italy. A relative newcomer to mountain biking, Kluge won this first leg on a spectacularly beautiful course. Gould played second fiddle in Riva, with Mike Kloser, from Vail, Colorado, in third place.

Mike Kluge on his way to a comfortable victory in the first event of the Grundig series, held in a spectacular setting on the shores of Lake Garda, Italy

6 May: Aviemore, Scotland
Kluge won again a week later in Aviemore, where he and Kloser had been shadowing each other until the American was forced to stop and make a repair to his bike. Gould also had mechanical problems, and slipped down to 50th place before surging back through the field to take ninth place.

27 May: Houffalize, Belgium
Round three had originally been scheduled for Spa, host in 1989 to the European Worlds, but an eleventh-hour change took the race to nearby Houffalize. Kluge was in contention yet again, with Gould and Czechoslovakian Andrej Glajza also in the running. A puncture forced Kluge to the sidelines, but he managed to repair it and reduce his one-minute deficit to 25 seconds. But the two leaders then turned the screws a little more tightly, and Kluge dropped back – as did Gould when Glajza changed into another gear on the final climb, riding away from the Englishman for his first Grundig victory.

10 June: Oslo, Norway
Kluge, Kloser, Gould and Glajza, the big guns in the men's series, all suffered setbacks of one sort or another: Glajza crashed in Riva, Gould had a loose saddle bolt in Aviemore, and Kloser dropped out in Houffalize after a crash. Oslo was Kluge's turn. With one-and-a-half laps left, he jumped, dropping Gould. But then one of Kluge's derailleurs broke. After two pit stops, his entire shifter was changed, costing him five minutes and first place – which went to Gould. Kloser and Glajza finished second and third, after both had punctured on a course that proved the biggest wrecking ground of the series.

After the previous day's qualifier in blizzard conditions, more seasonal weather prevailed for the Grundig final at Lenzerheide in Switzerland. Here Mike Kloser nears the top of the course on the third lap of the men's cross-country circuit

23 June: Viborg, Denmark
With its cyclo-cross characteristics, the Viborg course seemed ideally suited to Kluge, Glajza and Gould. In fact Kluge and Glajza did prove the strongest and, with Henrik Djernis of Denmark and Germany's Volker Krukenbaum, they soon led the field by a comfortable margin. Kluge and Glajza shook off their two shadows in the closing laps, then Glajza left Kluge floundering, to earn his second win of the series, in which only a rider's best five results counted.

19 August: Kaprun, Austria
After a six-week break, the series continued in Kaprun, one of Austria's most beautiful ski resorts, which staged the Grundig's only downhill event. The races were run on a time trial basis, on an 8.5km course that started at the top of the Maiskogel mountain, and finished in the heart of Kaprun.

The first rider to pull out all the stops was Belgium's Filip Meirhaeghe, whose daredevil tactics brought him home in 12:52. West Germany's Volker Krukenbaum (Rudy Project), the 1989 Grundig winner, had qualified four seconds faster than Meirhaeghe, but couldn't match the ex-BMX rider's performance, with his 13:00. Krukenbaum's compatriot, Jürgen Sprich, who had yet to win a Grundig race, then scorched down the course in 12:36. It proved good enough for victory: only Kloser came near, his 12:49 bringing him second place.

25 August: Théoule-sur-Mer, France
Round seven was held on a hilly, spectacular course on France's Mediterranean coast. Kluge led from the start of the men's race, followed by Kloser and Sprich. But mechanical difficulties forced Kluge back into second place . . . and worse luck was to come.

As he hammered past Théoule's harbour, Kluge crashed and watched helplessly as his bike slid towards, then over the seawall . . . and into the Mediterranean! Kluge leapt in after the bike and rescued it from sinking, but effectively put himself out of the reckoning. The West German did recover sufficiently to finish third, while the battle for first was between Kloser and Sprich. And with 4km to ride, it was Sprich who opened a 30-second lead to win.

2 September: Hamburg, West Germany
Nearly 600 contestants assembled for round eight of the Grundig series. The short, steep climbs of the course called for strong sprinting muscles; ideal for Kluge rather than Kloser, who is better known as an endurance rider, and most eyes were fixed on these two men. Victory for the American here would mean that he and Kluge would go into the final on equal points. However, both Kluge and Kloser were beaten soundly by a marauding Krukenbaum.

8 September: Lenzerheide, Switzerland
Much to the relief of racers, organisers, and spectators alike, after snow the day before, the weather was autumnal for the Grundig final. For Kloser, Lenzerheide offered one last chance to score top marks in the Grundig series. And the course profile seemed suited to the American. He crested the gruelling opening climb in a lead group of four, with Kluge already over a minute down in a chasing group of six. And after only the first of four laps of the cross-country circuit, Kloser had split the lead group asunder, putting a minute between himself and his closest chaser, Uli Rottler of West Germany. As Kloser came into view at the top of the final descent into the finish area, Rottler's attempts to rein in the determined American had obviously come to naught, and Kluge's deficit had grown to over five minutes. There were tears of joy in the popular Kloser's eyes as he rode across the finish line punching the air, a clear winner on one of the Grundig's toughest courses.

Kloser finished the nine-race series equal on points with Kluge – but the West German took the title, thanks to winning two races, to Kloser's one. The Grundig series visited virtually every corner of Europe: 1991 should see a couple of new countries added to the list. 'Mondialization' – the internationalization of cycling – is the catchword on the road scene. Thanks to the Grundig series, road racing's younger brother is beginning to speak the same language.

World Mountain Bike Championships: 11-16 September

Ned Overend was never happier than when he cruised into the crowd-lined finishing straight at the ski resort of Purgatory, near his home town of Durango, Colorado, more than two minutes ahead of his nearest challenger, Thomas Frischknecht. He had just won the senior men's cross-country, the most prestigious title of the inaugural World Mountain Bike Championships, and like the hundreds of other off-road racers who had travelled from 25 countries to compete at the spectacular Rocky Mountains location, Overend knew that this first official championship meant much more than the unofficial world titles he had won in previous years.

The cross country races completed a week of mountain bike racing that matched the ruggedness of the surrounding terrain, where splashes of autumn gold were starting to colour the mountainsides. Home competitors did particularly well: of the ten world championships contested, American riders won eight gold, five silver and six bronze – a total of nineteen medals. The other eleven medals went to Great Britain (one silver, two bronze), Switzerland (two silver, one bronze), Canada (one gold, one silver), France (one gold), Belgium (one silver) and New Zealand (one bronze).

The highlight of the championships was the senior men's, four-lap, 52km race – and it didn't all go Overend's way. By the time the 140 starters emerged at the top of the first, curving uphill – riding one behind the other like a Tour de France peloton – Overend was back in 18th position. The line was led by Italian roadman Claudio Vandelli, ahead of Belgium's Filip Meirhaeghe, American Rishi Grewal, Italian off-road champion Mario Noris, and Britain's Tim Gould. Others who had already worked their way into the top 20 included American star John Tomac (10th), Swiss cyclo-cross specialist Frischknecht (13th) and Italian road sprinter Paolo Rosola (15th). By the initial, 2956-metre summit, before the course cut through the trees and headed for the top turn, Vandelli had been joined by Frischknecht, Gould, Overend and Tomac. Fiercely determined, Tomac launched himself into the terrifyingly bumpy Swire's Gulch descent – to take the lead dramatically from Frischknecht and Overend.

In defiance of conventional wisdom, Tomac clearly wanted to try and win the race on the downhills, rather than the uphills. Whether he was right we will never know, because he punctured just as he reached the 2728-metre base level. And as the Durango-based rider spent a frustrating two minutes changing his tube, a dozen riders – headed by Frischknecht, Overend and Gould – flashed by him. These three – the ultimate medallists – completed the first lap in a bunch, followed by a fading Vandelli, Americans Mike Kloser, Grewal and Paul Thomasberg, Noris . . . and Tomac. Shouting at the riders ahead of him to move out of his way, the demonstrative Tomac was determined to make good his deficit as quickly as possible.

But now the race became an uphill battle, an exercise that suited the leading trio much better than Tomac. On the steepest, 30 per cent section, Overend stayed in the saddle, persevering with his smallest gear, while former

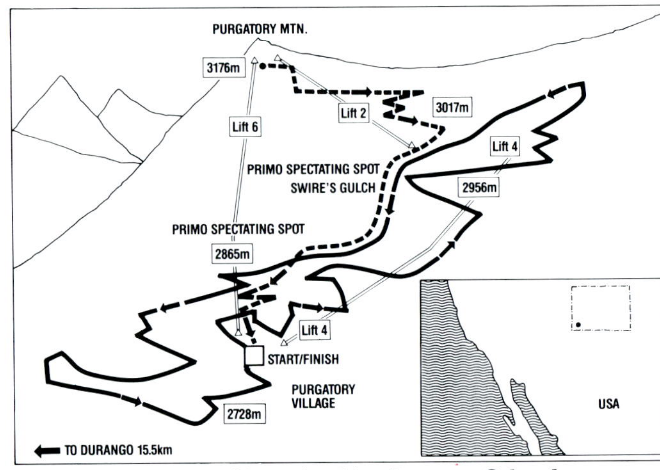

World Mountain Bike Championships, Durango, Colorado

Thirty-five-year-old American Ned Overend set the pace on the toughest parts of the principal 300-metre climb at the Purgatory ski resort course to win the inaugural world cross-country championship

world junior cyclo-cross champion Frischknecht shouldered his bike and ran alongside the American. Gould used a combination of riding and pushing to overcome the fierce, gravel-strewn gradient. By the top of the climb on this second lap, the three leaders were 1:30 ahead of a still surging Grewal, who was closely followed by Tomac. At the front, Overend was more afraid of Gould than Frischknecht, having finished almost a minute behind the 26-year-old Englishman in the non-championship uphill race earlier in the week. However, Gould now experienced some mechanical problems, and was soon 45 seconds behind the two leaders.

Another two minutes down, Tomac had fought his way back to sixth place; but the battle for victory was taking place without him. On the third lap, and ascending the ultra-steep part of the principal climb, 35-year-old Overend and 20-year-old Frischknecht were again neck and neck. When the Swiss remounted, he was still with the American. Then, Overend started to open up a slight lead . . . first one metre, then two . . . and Frischknecht could not respond. Riding in the saddle, with his chain on the middle of his three chainrings, Overend was working hard, clearly more comfortable in thin air than his challenger. At the fourth of the climb's turns, before disappearing into the trees, the US champion was 15 seconds clear of Frischknecht, and 1:10 ahead of Gould. Overend continued to open up his lead, and was 2:36 ahead at the finish.

In the senior women's race, a lone rider took the lead on the first climb, extended it throughout the three-lap, 39km event, and finished an easy winner. However, she wasn't the odds-on favourite, Sara Ballantyne of the US national team, but her neighbour in Boulder, Colorado, Julie Furtado. It was the upset of the championships, and the result left Ballantyne tight-lipped. 'I was waiting for her to collapse. I usually wait until she falls on a pile of rocks – but not this time,' said Ballantyne, after finishing 2:27 behind an exuberant Furtado.

Canada's Elladee Brown made a brief appearance in the lead at the start, but the race quickly became a battle between Furtado, Ballantyne and a third Boulder resident – the recent world road race championship silver medallist, Ruthie Matthes. These three were well clear by the top of the main climb, and by the end of the first lap Furtado had already pulled 45 seconds ahead of the other two, with US national champion Susan DeMattei a further minute behind, in fourth position. Matthes surprisingly outclimbed Ballantyne on the second lap, and briefly held second spot, with DeMattei holding strongly in fourth and yet another US national team member, Julia Ingersoll, passing both Brown and West Germany's Susi Buchwieser on the main climb to take a tenuous hold on fifth position.

On the final lap Furtado continued to extend her lead, while Buchwieser, only 19 years old, showed surprising stamina. She caught Ingersoll again, raced by a suffering DeMattei, and was only 30 seconds behind bronze medallist Matthes at the finish. The remarkable recovery of this young West German rider indicated that the American women may not have everything their own way in future years.

After finishing third at the World Amateur Cyclo-cross Championship in February, the twenty-year-old Swiss Thomas Frischknecht was a worthy winner of the silver medal in Colorado

A bronze medal was the reward for British off-road star Tim Gould, who decided to miss the last part of the Grundig series in Europe to acclimatize to the high altitude of the Worlds course

World Championships: 20 August-2 September

Cycling history was made when the 1990 World Championships were held in Japan, the first Asian, and only the fourth non-European, country ever to host the event.

Locating the two-week-long event in Japan was a contentious decision. There were doubts about training facilities (dispelled once everyone arrived), the language barrier, exhausting heat and humidity, the cost of travel and the inevitable jet lag. In the event, however, the fears turned out to be greatly exaggerated and Japan proved a perfect host. The organizers went to great lengths to ensure that the operation ran like clockwork, and whilst the number of spectators at the track events was disappointing, Japanese cycling *aficionados* flocked in their thousands to the road races.

In all, there were twenty world titles to be decided between August 20 and September 2. The fifteen track events were held at the new, 18 billion yen, 333-metre velodrome at Maebashi, 150km north-west of Tokyo, and the five road events at Utsunomiya, 120km north of Tokyo.

As always, the Worlds provided exciting racing, some surprise winners and losers, and a touch of controversy and intrigue. Win or lose, there's no doubt that few of the participants will ever forget the enthusiasm and courtesy of the Japanese people and event organisers, and at next year's championships, at Stuttgart in Germany, the Japanese Worlds will still be fresh in the memories of everyone who was there.

Road events

Men's professional road race: 2 September
There were two schools of thought about the result of the men's professional road championship.

Was Rudy Dhaenens that much of a surprise winner in the 261km, 18-lap race at Utsunomiya? Those who looked at his slender tally of victories would say yes. Those who had studied his season form and the circumstances of his tally of near misses – consistent top-five placings in the one-day classics – would say a great victory was long overdue, and that the Belgian PDM rider was a worthy wearer of the rainbow jersey.

Throughout his eight-year career as a professional, Dhaenens has been plagued by bad luck. One only has to recall his crash in the 1989 Tour de France: attacking alone on the stage to Blagnac, and seemingly assured of a stage win, his tyre rolled on a turn with only a kilometre to go, and the peloton swept past as he picked himself up. Other 'if onlys' include his second place in this year's Tour of Flanders, where he had the misfortune to draw Italy's Moreno Argentin as his partner in the winning two-man break; his second place to Sean Kelly in the 1986 Paris-Roubaix and third in the 1987 edition, when an unbeatable Eric Vanderaerden caught Dhaenens and two others with five kilometres to go. At Utsunomiya, though, fate shone more brightly on him.

While other, more illustrious names hesitated to commit themselves in the crucial final stages of the race

Despite the misgivings of the international cycling community, the Japanese World Championships turned out to be one of the best organised, and certainly the friendliest, of recent years

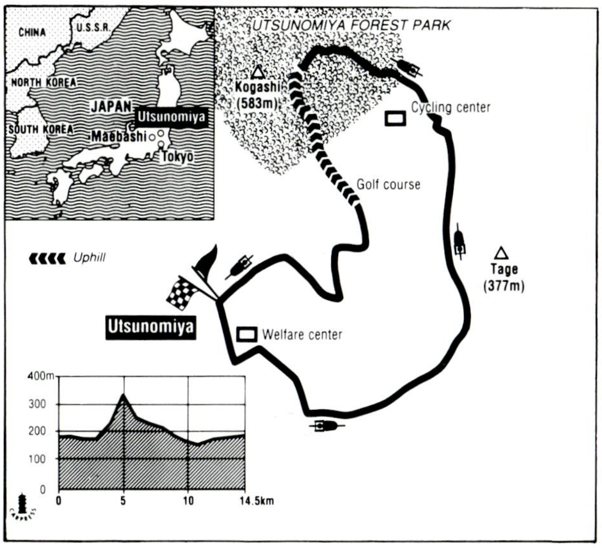

Road circuit, Utsunomiya, Japan: 14.5km

Dag-Otto Lauritzen attacks with two laps to go, little expecting that Dirk De Wolf – behind him here – would ruin his dreams of being world champion

His knee still bloody from the fall with Lauritzen, De Wolf tows Dhaenens into the last lap. Behind Dhaenens is the Spanish rider Alberto Leanizbarrutia

Dhaenens made a bold attack on the second to last ascent of the twisting 1.8km climb which was the focus of the 14.5km circuit. This climb played a vital role in the race pattern, although it was less severe than everyone expected. Out of the 145 starters, 88 failed to finish: at Chambéry the previous year, of the 190 starters 148 did not complete the full distance – a much higher rate of attrition. Discussing the merits of the Japanese course, ex-champion Greg LeMond voiced the prevailing opinion when he commented, 'The hill was hard, but not as hard as everyone said. It didn't make a big selection. And I knew it would come down to a sprint, because the hill is too far from the finish.' But then he added that Dhaenens rode a smart race, and that his attack was well suited to the route.

The crucial moment for Dhaenens came on lap 17, as he and several other chasers, including Frenchman Bruno Cornillet (Z) and Denmark's Johnny Weltz (ONCE), were about to catch the two-man break of Belgian Dirk De Wolf (PDM) and Norway's Dag-Otto Lauritzen (7-Eleven).

These two riders had a potentially winning attack going, but it came to an untimely end when De Wolf, who was setting the pace at the time, brought them both down in a heap half-way up the climb when he fell whilst turning round to call for his team car. The fall incensed Lauritzen, who had instigated the break, and when he had picked himself up he tried to clobber De Wolf. 'It was so frustrating,' he said later. 'That was the moment of my life to win. And then De Wolf turns and falls in front of me . . .' This mishap allowed Dhaenens to break free as his group passed the awkward tangle of Lauritzen and De Wolf, and to add insult to injury, De Wolf managed to remount and join Dhaenens and his two companions, Spaniard Alberto Leanizbarrutia (Teka) and Frenchman Martial Gayant (Toshiba). Passing the summit, with just over 1 lap and 8km to go, the four men had a dangerous 36-second lead.

Behind them was the peloton, numbering about 55 riders and including all the pre-race favourites. There

A dream come true: Rudy Dhaenens celebrates his unexpected victory in the professional road race

was the 1989 champion, in-form American Greg LeMond (Z), who had created a flurry of interest with his plan to travel from Tokyo to Utsunomiya in a private helicopter. Also there was Italian Gianni Bugno, whose Chateau d'Ax team-mates 'saved the race', as Ireland's Sean Kelly (PDM) later said, by leading the peloton's chase of the original 22-man break which at one point had a 6:15 lead. Other notables in the peloton included the stoic Irishman himself, Italy's 1988 champion, Maurizio Fondriest (Del Tongo), Belgian champion Claude Criquielion (Lotto), West Germany's Andreas Kappes (Toshiba), Canada's Steve Bauer (7-Eleven), the Soviet Dmitri Konyshev (Alfa Lum), Frenchman Laurent Jalabert (Toshiba), the Spaniards Pedro Delgado (Banesto) and Marino Lejarreta (ONCE), and Weltz.

Passing the finish line for the penultimate time, the four leaders had 37 seconds on the peloton, although Australia's Stephen Hodge (ONCE) came close to pulling off an impressive solo chase. Hodge, passing the bell-lap only four seconds behind the leaders, joined them one kilometre into the last lap, at the foot of the final climb.

It was on this newly-paved ascent, emblazoned with the names of French, English and even Japanese riders, that the two Belgians shed their three companions. It was clear that nationalistic priorities were in Dhaenens' and De Wolf's minds, and not even Gayant was able to stay with the two Belgians as they accelerated to the summit for the last time.

Hitting the flat 8km stretch through the rice fields to the finish, the hopes of the two escapers hinged on their rivals not chasing. The peloton was strung out behind them, and for any aspiring favourite, this was the time to attack: all eyes, of course, were on LeMond, Bugno, Bauer or even Delgado to try. But alas, no one did.

The peloton eventually did begin a belated charge, and it would still have been possible for the race to be decided in the final sprint. As Sean Kelly said later, 'In the final few kilometres I knew they had a good gap. But with two kilometres to go, we came very close to them. At one moment I said we might catch them in the sprint.' At the same time, De Wolf suddenly cracked. 'When Dirk told me with one kilometre to go that he had cramps all I thought of was who could catch us. I urged him on to work with all he had. Finally, it was my turn to win but . . . (smiling) . . . I've learned to become patient,' said Dhaenens later.

De Wolf was nevertheless as joyous as Dhaenens was when the two took home both the gold and silver medals. The bronze was decided eight seconds later when Bugno took third place for Italy. The expected sprint never materialised: no doubt fourth-placed LeMond and fifth-placed Kelly came for gold, and nothing else was likely to stir their imaginations.

And so ended another world championship road race. Dhaenens, with new privileges and responsibilities as world champion – and no doubt as a team leader for next year's classics – will certainly remember the experience of Japan. And, for those who remain bewildered by his win, the sense of surprise caused at Utsunomiya will provide food for thought for a long time to come.

The rivalry between East and West Germany that began at the track championships continued in the team time trial. This time, however, the West Germans (above) had to concede to their future compatriots and last year's champions in the battle for the silver medal

A jubilant Catherine Marsal followed in the footsteps of Jeannie Longo by winning the women's road race

Men's and women's team time trials: 29 August
The Soviet Union and the Netherlands asserted their mastery of team time trialling by winning the men's and women's titles respectively. And the Soviet's gold medal victory over East and West Germany was complemented by a bronze in the women's race.

Run on a motorway connecting the cities of Utsunomiya and Nikko, the team time trials were the opening event of the road programme. And the course, 50km for women and 100km for men, contained its hazards, particularly the constantly changing winds and a testing 1.36% gradient on the 25km outward stretch of the course.

In the men's title, the Soviets raced through to the lead in the third quarter, the final 25km to the finish. It was here that the United States ran out of steam after setting the fastest times through every previous split; they also dropped one man, Nate Reiss. The Americans, fourth in 1989, finally collapsed to finish a disappointing seventh in 1:59.18, 2:28 behind the Soviets who were third last year. The Soviets' winning time of 1:56.50 was 0:15 faster than East Germany, who clocked 1:57.05 to win the silver medal. West Germany, using for the first time the East German-styled carbon fibre bicycle frames, finished in 1:57.09.

This Dutch quartet survived a crash during their warm-up to win the women's team time trial

The womens' championship was touched with drama even before it began. The eventual winners, the Netherlands, crashed while warming up near the start. The obstacle was an aged farmer pedalling his way between the paddy fields, and the ensuing fall, 30 minutes before their start, involved three Dutch cyclists, world pursuit champion Leontien Van Moorsel being the lucky escapee. For the others, cuts and grazes were the main problem, although Astrid Schop's cut to the head produced urgent demands from the attending medical staff that she should not race but should go to hospital.

Her decision to race on soon looked like the right one; Schop and her team-mates held the fastest time for three-quarters of the race. As in the men's race, it was the United States who set the dominating pace at 12.5km, but by 25km they were in second, and thereafter the Dutch team never faltered, despite an American attempt to come back in the third split to 37.5km. Riding with only two members of their 1989 team, which finished fourth, the Netherlands finished together in 1:03.51.

The United States women's team finished better than their male colleagues. Their time of 1:04.07 was enough to edge the Soviet Union out of the silver medal. The Soviets, although they failed to repeat their 1989 gold-medal-winning performance, nevertheless took an easy bronze medal with a time of 1:04.21.

Women's road race: 1 September
Catherine Marsal of France was always favoured to win the 72.5km road title. She won the silver medal to the now-retired Jeannie Longo's gold in 1989, and since then she has won nearly every race she has entered.

At Japan, she dominated the racing more conclusively than Longo ever did, although the event, which took place in hot, humid conditions, was arguably marred by the absence of Dutch sensation, Leontien Van Moorsel, who won the women's pursuit title and was a member of the Dutch team time trial squad which won the gold medal. Van Moorsel was regarded as the only real threat to Marsal, but the Dutch road champion was forced to scratch from the race when she came down with a fever the day before.

Yet Marsal's sparkling form makes it doubtful that anyone could have beaten her. Marsal, the winner of the Tour of Texas, Norway's Post Giro, the Tour of Italy and Tour de l'Aude this year, seemingly played with her rivals, establishing her authority on the very first lap of the 5-lap race. Her break on the first ascent of the 1.8km climb, although it was caught after 9km, exhausted the 75-strong field, and it came as no surprise when she attacked again on the same climb on lap 2. By the end of the second lap, Marsal was 0:57 ahead of the field, and it was clear that the women's road title would once again see a field outraced by one very classy rider. Her lead grew to 2:03 on lap 3 and 3:19 on lap 4, and by the finish she was 3:24 ahead of Ruthie Matthes of the United States, who took the silver medal, and Luisa Seghezzi of Italy, who took bronze.

Men's amateur road race: 1 September
Mirko Gualdi became the 17th Italian world amateur road champion at Utsunomiya, thanks to a victorious solo attack on the eighth of twelve 14.5km circuits. Gualdi, 22, attacked on the climb and by the finish of the 174km race had 54 seconds on two chasers – his second-placed compatriot Roberto Caruso and Frenchman Jean-Philippe Dowja, trailing a strung-out field of 65 finishers.

Gualdi is not a newcomer to success. His win at Japan was his fourth this year and he is remembered for a similar world title attack in the 1989 world titles at Chambery, France, which lasted three laps before he was caught. On this occasion, however, nothing impeded Gualdi's progress to victory in a championship characterised by the international nature of its racing. The contribution of two Americans, Lance Armstrong (11th) and Nathan Sheafor (23rd), particularly, indicated that amateur racing is finally making world-wide progress.

Armstrong, in his first year of senior racing after leaving triathlon, was in the first attack of the day on the third lap after 40km. He, Dowja, Caruso, Denmark's Peter Meinert, Brazil's Wanderley Azevedo, France's Christophe Capelle and the Soviet Union's Pavel Tonkov had a 1:08 lead on the main field after the third circuit. Then, after the fourth lap, 10 chasers, including Gualdi and the American Sheafor, joined, bringing the number of riders in the lead group to 17.

These riders were soon defined as the shortlist of candidates, and most of them tried their hand at dominating the race. After six laps, Switzerland's Fabian Jeker was away alone, with 0:11 on a pursuing Armstrong and 0:57 on the rest of the group. And one lap later, it was Meinert who was on the attack.

But Gualdi proved the strongest. His eighth-lap attack started a chase – led by Sweden's Michael Andersson

With gold and silver medals in the amateur road race, Mirko Gualdi (above) and Roberto Caruso gave rise to ecstatic celebration in the Italian camp

and Shaefor – which was joined by three others by the end of lap 9: Meinert, Dowja, and Norway's Bjorn Stenersen. They were then 1:31 down on Gualdi, with Armstrong and four others at 1:55. The remaining members of the 17-strong break were further adrift and hoping only for a finish.

Gualdi was never assured of victory, the aggressive series of chases behind him indicating that the bunch had not lost its appetite for victory. But when he still had a 1:30 lead with two laps remaining, the others began to adjust their ambitions towards a bronze or silver medal. Meinert, Dowja, Caruso, Jeker and Heppner were clearly the strongest contenders for second and third places as the pace took its cruel toll on the field. Meinert tried to go it alone, but was caught on the climb of lap 11 by the other four. Then, as they passed the summit together, Dowja and Caruso took off in a move that could not be reeled in during the one remaining lap.

Finishing 0:54 seconds behind Gualdi, Caruso's silver medal was met with a chorus of cheers from the 500-strong contingent of Italian supporters, who had flown to Japan together on a chartered flight. Dowja's third place – at 0:56 – ensured that his name would go into the hat of aspiring new French professionals to watch for in 1991.

Track events

Men's amateur 1000-metre time trial: 21 August
The Soviet Union announced its gold medal ambitions at Maebashi by winning the first title final, the men's amateur 1000 metre time trial. Known as the 'kilo', the title's gold medal went to Aleksandr Kirichenko.

It was Kirichenko, the Olympic champion, who suffered *the* misfortune of the 1989 Worlds, when his handlebars broke with half a lap to go in the final of the time trial, and the winner of an almost certain gold medal had to be content with the bronze. This year there was no doubt about it; nearest to his winning time of 1:03.565 was Australia's 1989 silver medallist Martin Vinnicombe, who thus became only the second rider to win medals in the discipline in six consecutive years of

The superbly spacious 18-billion yen stadium at Maebashi

Aleksandr Kirichenko made sure of his gold medal in the amateur time trial this year

World and Olympic competition.

Last year's winner, Jens Glüklich of East Germany, recorded a time of 1:04.210, and had to be content with a bronze medal this year.

Men's amateur 4000-metre pursuit: 22 August
The decision of defending champion, Soviet Viatcheslav Ekimov, to turn professional, threw this championship wide open. But an all-Soviet final made sure the title stayed in Russian hands; Evgenii Berzin took the gold medal from his compatriot, Valerii Baturo, clocking 4:33.01 against Baturo's 4:42.91. The bronze was between two Americans – the two Soviets had both beaten Americans in their semi-finals – but because Mike McCarthy clocked a faster losing time in his semi-final against Baturo, he won the bronze medal over Steve Hegg, who had lost to Berzin in his semi-final.

Men's professional sprint: 22 August
Former world amateur champion Michael Hübner became the first and last East German professional world sprint champion at Maebashi. The 100kg Hübner, who lost not a single race on his way to the final, won the flying 200 metre sprint's gold medal from defending champion, Claudio Golinelli of Italy.

Golinelli, Hübner and Australia's Stephen Pate were the favourites to battle out the medals. But when Hübner recorded 10.345 – the fastest qualifying time from the 12 starters – it was clear that he was the man to beat, and he won the final in two straight race-offs against Golinelli, while Pate secured the bronze medal with his 2-0 victory over Japan's Hideyuki Matsui.

A euphoric Michael Hübner beating Golinelli to win his first ever professional sprint title

As predicted, Viatcheslav Ekimov won the professional pursuit

Men's amateur motorpaced: 23 August
The 150-lap amateur motorpaced championship, covering 50km, once again went to Austria's Roland Konigshofer, over Italy's Australian-born David Solari and Switzerland's Andrea Bellati.

Konigshofer, who lapped his nearest rivals, has always dominated in this event. As well as winning last year, he was a bronze medallist in 1986 and 1987, and a silver medallist in 1988. His gold medal win in 1989, when he also lapped the field, was Austria's first ever gold medal in a Worlds track event.

Men's amateur sprint: 23 August
An old hand met a new boy in the amateur sprint final, but despite an initial exciting tussle in the first of two heats, in the event East Germany's defending champion, Bill Huck, took the gold easily with an unchallengeable ride in the second. His victim was up-and-coming Canadian Curt Harnett who, after winning gold at the Goodwill Games in Seattle at the end of July, came to Japan looking only for a top four place.

Huck's winning rides of 10.811 and 10.853 provided East Germany with its eighth sprint title in 11 years; with German unification imminent, however, it was also the last.

The race for the bronze medal also produced fine performances from East Germany's Jens Fiedler and the Soviet Union's 1989 bronze medallist, Nikolai Kovsh. In their three race-offs, the two had to meet each other as many as eight times as lengthy stand-ups and falls forced re-runs, but finally, Fiedler got the better of Kovsh and secured his place on the podium.

Men's professional individual 5000-metre pursuit: 23 August
Viatcheslav Ekimov of the Soviet Union came up to expectations with his easy win in this event – his first as a professional. His rival in the final was Frenchman Francis Moreau, a newcomer to pursuiting but well-suited to the event by virtue of his expertise as a prologue racer in stage events. (His successful world record attempt later, at the world indoor 5000 metre distance, clocking 5:41.104 to beat the 5:54.344 set by Denmark's Hans Henrik Oersted in 1987, provided further confirmation of his aptitude for the discipline. Ekimov had himself beaten Oersted's time in April, but failed to have his time ratified by the UCI, his main objective being to win the world pursuit title.)

In the final, Ekimov clocked 5:39.04, and Moreau took the silver medal with 5:40.66. Frenchman Armand De Las Cuevas won the bronze medal from Australia's Dean Woods, having recorded a faster losing semi-final time – 5:44.06 – than Woods, whose time was 5:47.78.

Men's keirin: 24 August
Australia's Stephen Pate caused a sensation in this motor-paced sprint event by winning the race and then being disqualified for illegal riding.

The final of nine riders was as action-packed as anyone could have wished, despite the absence of Japan's Koichi Nakano, ten times world sprint champion, who had come out of a four-year retirement to contest the keirin crown on his home turf. But Nakano was clearly outclassed, and never even qualified for the final.

The reason for Pate's disqualification was twofold. Firstly, on the final bend he rode into the sprinter's lane, occupied by Hübner. And then, as they came into the finishing straight, Frenchman Patrick Da Rocha crashed, and Pate was held to be the cause of the accident.

Pate's misfortune was Michael Hübner's good luck – the gold medal was awarded to the East German, who finished behind Pate in the final. The silver medal went to Belgium's Michel Vaarten, while Italy's defending champion, Claudio Golinelli, took the bronze.

Curt Harnett fought his way into the final of the amateur sprint against Bill Huck with an impeccable series of rides. Here the Canadian holds off Jens Fiedler on his way to the final

Stephen Pate beats Hübner across the line in the keirin, but was disqualified for illegal riding. The fallen cyclist in the background is the Argentinian rider Marcello Alexandre

Women's sprint: 24 August
American Connie Young claimed her fourth world sprint title in Japan with a 2-1 win over compatriot Renée Duprel. Young, the world champion in 1982, 1983 and 1984, lost the first of three race-offs, but came back in formidable fashion to win the second and third with times of 12.298 and 11.960. The bronze medal went to the Soviet Union's Rita Razmaite, who defeated Felicia Ballanger of France in two straight race-offs.

The contest might have been closer, but with the Olympic and defending world champion, Erika Salumiae of the Soviet Union, absent due to injury, Young was always tipped to end her six-year spell in the wilderness with a gold medal this year.

The women's sprint final was an all-American affair. Here Connie Young defeats Renée Duprel in their first match

Men's amateur team pursuit: 24 August
The Soviet Union avenged their defeat by the East German pursuit team in the 1989 World Championships at Lyon, France, with a gold-medal-winning ride at Maebashi to beat the title surprises, West Germany, in the final. With only the third fastest qualifying time, the Soviet team nevertheless rode a faultless series, defeating Czechoslovakia in the quarter-final and Australia in the semi-final.

West Germany had astonished everyone with their semi-final win over East Germany, but in the final the Soviets were just as dominant over them, with a winning time of 4:09.28 as against the West Germans' time of 4:15.91.

Australia, having recorded the fastest semi-final losers' time, were awarded the bronze medal over fourth-placed East Germany.

Michael Hübner was the most impressive cyclist of the 1990 World Track Championships

Leontien Van Moorsel entranced everyone with her looks and talent

The final of the men's tandem had the huge crowd on the edges of their seats, but ultimately the Italians' speed was too much for the Japanese teenagers

Stephen McGlede was a delighted winner of the amateur points race

Women's pursuit 3000 metres: 25 August
Leontien Van Moorsel of the Netherlands left Japan as the undoubted queen of pursuiting. Her slimmed-down, glamorous appearance, together with her undeniable talent, left a strong impression on those who witnessed the track events at Maebashi.

In the final against New Zealand's Madonna Harris, 20-year-old Van Moorsel, in her second ever pursuit series, clocked 3:44.348 against the New Zealander's 3:46.982.

Switzerland's Barbara Ganz, with a faster losing semi-final time than Canada's Kelly-Ann Carter, won the bronze medal.

Men's amateur tandem: 26 August
Not an event that often receives top billing, this year's tandem title became a major crowd-puller at Maebashi after two local teenagers, having teamed up only two weeks previously, suddenly found themselves in the final.

When Toshinobu Saito and Narihiro Inamura clocked the fastest qualifying time of 10.556 one sensed their potential was there. And come the semi-finals, their ability to upset the apple-cart became even more obvious when the Japanese duo once again defeated the French pair of Frédéric Magné and Fabrice Colas, three times world champions.

In the final against Italy, the Japanese pair were given every encouragement from a crowd totalling nearly 9000 – the biggest of the week-long meeting. But the Italians, Gianluca Capitano and Federico Paris, were too strong for them and won the first two race-offs easily to take the gold medal – although their win was quite eclipsed in the eyes of the crowd by Saito and Inamura's silver! France, hoping to salvage a bronze medal, lost out there as well, to West Germany.

Men's amateur points race: 26 August
Australia's Stephen McGlede overcame the favoured Danish and Swiss contingents to win his country's first gold medal here in the 50km amateur points championships.

21-year-old McGlede, a member of Australia's bronze-medal-winning pursuit team, was part of a seven-man break which lapped the field of 23 riders with 55 of the 150 laps to go. He had a close fight with Switzerland's Bruno Risi and Denmark's Jan Petersen. But McGlede finally took the gold with 42 points, against Risi's 32 and Petersen's 24.

Men's professional motorpaced: 25 August
Italy's Walter Brugna came from behind to win the world motorpaced crown from Switzerland's Peter Steiger and Australia's Danny Clark. Of the nine finalists, Brugna, the silver medallist in 1989, started in second position, just behind Steiger, whose winning time in the qualifying heat was faster than the Italian's.

One of the biggest surprises was the effort of Danny Clark, the 1988 world champion. He drew the last position – 9th – but after forcing two re-starts, made up five places in the very first lap and eventually managed to fight his way up to a bronze medal.

Women's points race: 25 August
One of the most startling results of the World Championships was New Zealander Karen Holliday's gold medal in the women's points race. Leading the race with eight laps to go, she was one of two riders to crash on the velodrome's steep, 42° banking as the field wound up its pace for the finish.

The spill was caused by American Karen Bliss, who touched wheels with Australia's Julie Speight and came tumbling down into Holliday's line. Bliss abandoned, but Holliday miraculously was able to recover, remount and rejoin the race with six laps to go, just before the penultimate sprint.

She took the race with a tally of 33 points; in second place was the Soviet Union's Svetlana Samokhvalova with 26 points, and Belgium's Kristel Werckx took the bronze medal with 25 points.

New Zealand officials hurried to get Karen Holliday back into the race after a crash threatened her gold medal

Men's professional points championship: 26 August
France's only track victory at Maebashi came in the very last event to be contested, the professional points race over 50km.

Little Laurent Biondi was the winner, after he and Denmark's Michel Marcussen lapped the field with 35 of the 150 laps to go. Until then, Australia's Danny Clark looked certain to win his tussle against Switzerland's fancied Urs Freuler with ease. But Biondi, only 53kg in bodyweight and 1.64m tall, surprised everyone with his attacking style (which he used last year as well, but less successfully). Finally scoring 38 points to Marcussen's 15, Biondi secured the gold medal. Marcussen took home the silver; Clark, despite having 65 points, was one lap down and had to be satisfied with bronze.

The Japanese people responded enthusiastically to the friendly invasion by the western cycling world

UTSUNOMIYA
(個人)9 1·2
宇都宮市森林公園周辺道路
'90 自転車世界選

Grand Prix de la Libération: 16 September

After taking a narrow lead in the Perrier World Cup teams competition at the San Sebastian Classic on 11 August, the pressure was on the Dutch PDM team to assert their dominance at the Grand Prix de la Libération a month later. For after overhauling Panasonic-Sportlife and Helvetia-La Suisse on the points table at San Sebastian, PDM's lead was slim: only two points on Helvetia and three on Panasonic. And after the Championship of Zurich on 14 August – round eight of the World Cup – PDM was still only three points up on its Swiss rival, although a more comfortable 11 on Panasonic. So, racing on their team's home territory, at Eindhoven in the Netherlands, PDM intended nothing less than a victory in this 88.1km team time trial.

Being the only team time trial on the World Cup calendar, and coming as it does at the latter end of the year, the two-lap Grand Prix de la Libération – round nine – provides a vital key to every team's final positioning in the World Cup. However, despite its significance to the top ranked teams, the Grand Prix de la Libération this year – its third – once again proved that it is far from a seasonal highlight. In a year already rich in glorious images of riders struggling up the highest peaks, barrelling over the ancient cobblestones, fighting and muscling their way through terrifying bunch sprints, the sight of teams heading backwards and forwards across the network of autoroutes outside Eindhoven was more confusing than impressive. Still more unfortunate was the absence of many noted stars and several major league teams because of World Cup rulings which declare that the event does not carry individual World Cup points. Greg LeMond's Z team (but without LeMond) was the only French participant there; Castorama with Laurent Fignon, Toshiba with Laurent Jalabert and RMO with Charly Mottet all abstained. So did the World Cup leader Gianni Bugno of Italy (Chateau d'Ax), who opted for training, as did Spain's Pedro Delgado and Miguel Indurain of Banesto and Australian Phil Anderson (TVM). Some of these riders, and many others, had contested the previous day's Barrachi Trophy (a 94km two-man time trial classic in Italy) and did not want another similarly lengthy onslaught; although riders like Great Britain's Sean Yates and Norway's Dag-Otto Lauritzen appeared for 7-Eleven after taking third in Italy.

Even newly crowned world champion, Belgian Rudy Dhaenens (PDM), was scratched – although only when a tendon strain decided his coach Jan Gisbers to withdraw him from the Grand Prix de la Libération, Paris-Brussels and several other post-World Championship events. Fortunately for his team, Dhaenens' presence was not necessary this time – for a change, after his regular up-front presence in every one-day classic. PDM finished as they intended . . . first. And in doing so, the team widened its World Cup tally from 53 points to 71 points, now 13 more than Helvetia-La Suisse, who finished ninth at Eindhoven.

This year's Grand Prix de la Libération proved as popular as the 1989 inaugural edition, with crowds of 50,000 in the centre of Eindhoven

So near, and yet so far . . . the Lejarreta-inspired ONCE team nearly pulled off a dream victory in Eindhoven, but PDM pipped them to the post by just 24 seconds

However, PDM's victory was not as clearcut as its eventual 1:41.03 time and its margins of 0:24 over the powerful Spanish ONCE team and 0:53 on another Dutch team, Buckler, indicated. It was never really expected to be. Despite the absentee list, there was still plenty of team time trialling clout from the 15-team start-list, which included Panasonic-Sportlife, the Tour de France team time trial winner; ONCE, proving one of the strongest teams this year; Buckler, with its line-up including Belgian riders Eric Vanderaerden and Edwig Van Hooydonck, and Jelle Nijdam, Frans Maassen, Gerrit Solleveld and Gerrit De Vries of Holland; TVM, last year's winner; and Chateau d'Ax of Italy.

In fact, it was Buckler who looked like the 'Untouchables' on this overcast Sunday afternoon. Their early domination was in clear contrast to the Panasonic team, who would do no better than 10th and 3:09, after losing John Talen and Viatcheslav Ekimov through punctures. For Panasonic, it was a worse performance than their failure of 1989 when, on a longer 114km route, a crash and puncture by Australia's Allan Peiper – on two separate occasions – broke their rhythm and saw them finish a disappointing fourth.

Buckler, despite losing Tour de France stage winner Solleveld after only 10km, clocked the fastest time on the first 55km lap. And on the second, shorter, circuit they maintained the lead up until the last 20km – when Van Hooydonck, unable to match the Buckler pace, was dropped. The result was a near-immediate collapse to third place as PDM and ONCE respectively pulled their way through to the front.

One of the key figures in PDM's fight from behind was Dutchman Eric Breukink, who was working up his condition for the coming Grand Prix des Nations time trial the next week. His double turns at the front of the PDM 'train' nearing the finish certainly improved his standing as a favourite for the French time trial classic. After passing the finish line, where a huge crowd vindicated the organisers' belief in the event being a World Cup round, criticism or not, Ireland's Sean Kelly was the first to compliment this blossoming Dutch star: 'Eric was very strong, we all were. But, if he hadn't taken twice as many turns as the rest of us did near the finish, we would have been beaten,' he said.

PDM finished with five of its six riders still intact: Kelly, Breukink, Dutchman Gert Jacobs and East Germany's Uwe Raab and Uwe Ampler. Mexico's Raúl Alcalá finished alone after being dropped in the last kilometres where Breukink's 'double turns' took place. Breukink was certainly full of confidence for the Grand Prix des Nations after showing his muscle here. 'I prepared so well for the World Championships and I was disappointed not to have been able to show my potential there,' he said. 'But I have still kept the form. And the way I felt today has given me great confidence for the Nations. There, there is 90 kilometres . . . a bit like here.'

The PDM team on the last lap; still trailing ONCE, but confident of the ability of riders like Uwe Raab (leading here) to pull them through to victory in their home town

Paris-Brussels: 19 September

Yet another chapter in the Italian success story of 1990 opened on 19 September, in the 'Race of the Two Capitals', Paris-Brussels. This time, though, the key character was not Gianni Bugno, Maurizio Fondriest or Moreno Argentin. It was a rider who had quietly been one of the most consistent riders of the year, but who, until 19 September had yet to win a major event.

Franco Ballerini is a 25-year-old Italian who has been a professional since 1986 and is a Del Tongo team-mate of Fondriest. He is also, now, the reigning Paris-Brussels champion. Amid the hype paid to the season's winners, it is easy to overlook Ballerini's search for a big win. Reflection upon his eventual success, however, sheds light on why many people say it was only a matter of time before it came his way. Certainly, the 1990 record books support the notion that he has been one of the most consistent classic riders; and his seventh place on the World Cup ladder at the time of winning Paris-Brussels from Belgium's Michel Dernies is added testimony.

In a manner previously thought as unbefitting of an Italian, Ballerini apparently adores the wet, windy, fast and cobbled classics of northern Europe. At the Tour of Flanders he was 10th at 0:37. In Ghent-Wevelgem he was 3rd in a sprint finish. He went on to Paris-Roubaix four days later to take 19th at 1:48, the first Italian placing. In both the Amstel Gold Race and the Championship of Zürich he was placed fifth. Ballerini's victory at Paris-Brussels was his second in the year; he had already won the Tour of Campania in Italy on 23 April. But as he crossed the finish line in downtown Brussels' Avenue Emile Jacqmain, it was easy to tell it was his finest and most popular. Ballerini was one of the most determined riders in this 246km classic, which was first raced in 1907 and had only been won by an Italian on four previous occasions – the last was Guido Bontempi in 1986.

Paris-Brussels: 250km

Franco Ballerini demonstrated his fondness for Belgian classics (he was third in Ghent-Wevelgem – by winning Paris-Brussels ahead of Michel Dernies and a chasing group of 17 men

One of the factors in Ballerini's run of 'failures' to win a race of similar importance earlier this year was undoubtedly the lack of support from others who would not trust his abilities. His frustration hit its peak in Japan, in the professional world road race championship, when he and two other Italians were in the early 22-man lead group which faltered under the impact of his chasing Italian team-mates. To this day, Ballerini feels he was robbed of a chance to win, a chance he felt he deserved: 'In the world titles, I found myself in the lead group. That day, I hardly felt the pedals, I was so strong. I really believed that I had it to do something that day. But unfortunately, the Italian team rode us down. It was proof to me that nobody believed in me,' he said. 'At the time I didn't want to get involved in a big fight with Alfredo Martini [the Italian national technical director]. But I was really angry with him and I waited for this moment to show him he was wrong not to have had confidence in me . . . to say what I felt. Voilà . . . it's done.'

This year's Paris-Brussels literally started with a difference, with the start-town not even being Paris, but Noyon, half-way between Paris and the Belgian border.

Danny Neskens took the sprint for third place in Brussels' Avenue Emile Jacqmain

But as is the case with so many ancient classics which are forced to re-locate their traditional starts because of urban sprawl, the event name stayed the same.

Beginning and continuing under a blanket of grey sky, showers and wind, it was not surprising that the first break did not occur until after 168km. It was well into Belgian territory, on a short cobbled climb just out of the southern Belgian town of Binche, that Ballerini, together with Belgium's Yves Godimus (LA William) and Dutchmen Wiebren Veenstra (Buckler) and Eddy Schurer (TVM), pedalled off. It was a futile attack, though, and never got more than a 0:20 lead before being caught.

The vital break came at 206km, with 40km to go, on the uphill exit from Tienne St Roche at Nivelles. Significantly, it was an area Dernies knew well, and he had premeditated his 'kill'. With cool precision, he launched an attack and took with him four others – including his Weinmann team-mate, fellow Belgian Jean-François Brasseur, with whom he had rehearsed the manoeuvre the day before. With Dernies and Brasseur went Ballerini, Denmark's Soren Lilholt (Histor) and Belgium's Peter De Clercq (Lotto). Soon they were joined by three more: Dutchman Jelle Nijdam (Buckler) and the Italians Marco Lietti (Ariostea) and Stefano Zanatta (Chateau d'Ax).

The leading eight quickly notched up 0:30 on the peloton as the shadowed dusk images of inner-city Brussels grew bigger and bigger. But then, with 16km to go and 5km after Dernies, Brasseur, Nijdam and Ballerini had shed the others, drama broke unexpectedly. After passing the Côte d'Alsemberg at 231km, on the exit from Linkebeek at 234km, the leaders – now minus Brasseur who was dropping off the pace – misjudged a turn and were forced to backtrack onto the route proper. The error proved most costly for Nijdam, who was leading the four at the time. Dernies was the quickest to react and attacked. Ballerini followed, but Nijdam was too far down the wrong route and could not. By the time he rejoined the route, and a struggling Brasseur who was not about to start chasing against Dernies now, Nijdam knew his hopes of victory were gone.

Passing through the plush green Bois de la Cambre at 240km, Dernies and Ballerini were clearly on target to fight out the winning sprint, despite the fact that their 0:43 second lead of 1km earlier was now down to 0:38 under the impact of a chasing group of seventeen riders. But by the finish line, where Ballerini was clearly victorious over Dernies, those seventeen led by Belgium's Danny Neskens (LA William) – were 0:05 short of succeeding. Ballerini had achieved his big win.

Will it never end? Ballerini celebrates yet another Italian victory

Grand Prix des Nations: 23 September

Thomas Wegmüller's peers call him 'Thomas the Tank', so strong is this lanky, big Swiss when he rides at the front of the peloton during those tense last-kilometre finales to continental road races. Ireland's Sean Kelly once said of his former Kas team-mate that whenever Wegmüller (now of Weinmann) moved up to the head of the group, it became a challenge merely to keep up with his pace, let alone attack or catch the forward attackers. To this day Wegmüller is one of the peloton's most frequent aggressors. He may not be the most graceful, agile or naturally gifted cyclist on the circuit, but he is certainly one of the most courageous. And what better place to test his aptitude, or any riders' for that matter, than at the most prestigious and difficult time trial on the calendar, the 89km Grand Prix des Nations in southern France.

The Grand Prix des Nations, starting and finishing at the rich Mediterranean seaside centre of 'high society', Cannes, provides a thorough measure of an individual rider's soloing strengths. The anti-clockwise circuit, covered twice by the field of 22 selected time triallists, is punctuated by several testing climbs and twisting descents with an even seasoning of flat, oceanside and windswept stretches. It is a course only the fittest, most confident and aspiring riders can tackle successfully.

History now shows that Wegmüller, five days short of his 30th birthday, was the most qualified to fit those criteria in 1990; his come-from-behind victory over Dutchman Eric Breukink (PDM) and Switzerland's Toni Rominger (Chateau d'Ax) bettered his impressive second to Laurent Fignon in 1989. He was also the first Swiss winner since two-times winner Daniel Gisiger won in 1983.

It was only unfortunate for Wegmüller that this year's Grand Prix des Nations lacked the sparkle of previous editions since its inception in 1932. It was certainly no fault of Wegmüller's, but curiously the usual atmosphere and sense of prestige was missing. Perhaps it was due to the prospect of the event's historic move to Italy in 1991, where it will be the final round of the World Cup. Or perhaps it was the fact that for a French race, so steeped in French glory (non-French riders have won on only nineteen occasions), the domination of Wegmüller and the lack of panache of the French contingent diminished local interest. Certainly, Fignon's absence was missed. And the poor form of 1988 winner Charly Mottet (RMO), normally a key figure here, who finished a sorry 12th at 5:15, no doubt influenced the mood of the spectators; though that was no direct fault of Mottet's, since he had only just taken off a plaster cast on his left hand after fracturing his wrist before the world titles. Even professional bicycle racers need a little time to recover.

Another factor may have been that Thierry Marie (Castorama), who is billed as a prologue rider, not a long distance time triallist, finished ninth at 5:01 to become the top-placed Frenchman. If not any of these things, maybe the hazy, dull climate was to blame; winds and milky blue waters decorated the finishing area, rather than the crystal blue seas and rich blue skies normally attributed to a Grand Prix des Nations finish.

Whatever the problems, Wegmüller was always up amongst the best-placed riders through each of the timed splits. He went through the 11.5km mark in third place, 0:32 behind Breukink, who was the pre-race favourite and leader until the dying kilometres. By 30km Wegmüller had overtaken Australia's Stephen Hodge (ONCE) to take second place, although Breukink had widened his lead to 0:43. By the end of the first lap, at 44.5km, it was clear that Wegmüller was starting to make

Wegmüller improved on his 1989 second place by winning the last Grand Prix des Nations to be held in Cannes

Just when he seemed certain to add his name to the illustrious roll of Nations winners, Breukink faded in the last 30 kilometres

some impression. He hurtled through Cannes and out on to the second lap only 0:28 behind Breukink. Meanwhile, Rominger's strength also started to show as he finished the first lap in third place, having passed fourth-placed Hodge.

It was common belief that the second lap would produce the winning move. Breukink, riding as gracefully as he did in the Grand Prix de la Libération and in his winning time trial to Villard-de-Lans during the Tour de France, had been the foremost proponent of this thinking. And when he widened his lead on Wegmüller to 0:36 by the 56km mark, it was felt he would fulfil such expectations without difficulty.

Breukink's advantage was always gained on the ascents, the first of which came 6km into the circuit and lasted 4km. The other two followed soon after; they began at the 200m altitude of the first ascent and were less severe. But it was on these 'rolling' portions on the second lap that Breukink began to fade, just as a dogged Wegmüller started to harden his attack. By the 75km mark, the Swiss giant was finally in the lead, 0:42 seconds clear of second-placed Breukink and 1:42 ahead of third-placed Rominger.

With 14km to go, and all of it downhill and flat, Wegmüller knew Breukink's climbing weaponry was useless from here. He also knew that his greater bodyweight would better suit the descent, and that his increasingly high morale would help him bully his way through a closing 5km run along the coast, battered with rising winds. And when he crossed the finish line in 1:57.57 – one minute slower than Fignon's course record of 1989, but the fastest on the day – he had time to spare to witness Breukink's painful fight to the line, 1:47 in arrears. And so, for the third time this year, glory became Wegmüller's to savour.

Hodge, still enjoying the good form he first found in the Giro d'Italia, snatched 4th place from his team leader Lejarreta in Cannes

Grand Prix des Amériques: 30 September

Under a day-long downpour on the rugged Mount Royal circuit, Italian rider Franco Ballerini of Del Tongo took home his first World Cup victory – and his second classic in 12 days – when he won Canada's Grand Prix des Amériques. Out of ten races in the 1990 season's Perrier World Cup Ballerini's was the fourth win by an Italian. His compatriot Gianni Bugno, who finished 11th in the Montreal race, maintained his leadership of the series with an 18-point advantage over runner-up Rudy Dhaenens.

The abominable weather that persisted throughout upset most of the prerace predictions and tactics. After only 30km, near the end of the hilly 16km circuit's second lap, the first attack was launched by another of this season's Italian revelations, Claudio Chiappucci of Carrera. He was quickly joined by Soviet star Viatcheslav Ekimov (Panasonic-Sportlife); and on the fourth lap, a successful bridge was made by Swiss rider Heinz Imboden of Helvetia-La Suisse.

This trio battled the hills and the elements until, at half-distance, its lead was more than two minutes over a bedraggled looking pack. However, within another lap, both Ekimov and Imboden lost contact with Chiappucci – who then awaited the reinforcement of five chasers. This chase group comprised American Frankie Andreu (7-Eleven), who had won the warm-up race at Hamilton, Ontario, two days earlier; the talented Belgian Sammie Moreels (Lotto-Superclub), on the comeback trail after breaking a leg in the Tour of the Americas in February; Danes Rolf Sörensen (Ariostea) and Jesper Skibby (TVM); and Ballerini, who had won the Paris-Brussels classic the previous week.

Within another 20km, both Andreu and Skibby lost contact with the break, leaving Ballerini, Chiappucci, Moreels and Sörensen at the front, with a lead of 1:20 over the peloton. Several bridging attempts were made – including accelerations by home favourite Steve Bauer (7-Eleven), 1989 World Cup winner Sean Kelly (PDM) and Bugno (Chateau d'Ax) – but the next two to join the

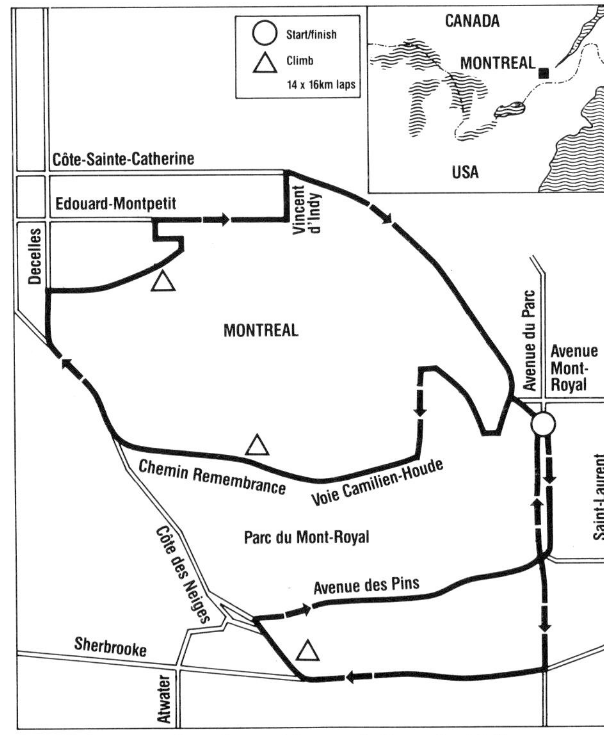

Grand Prix des Amériques, Montreal, Canada: 224km

Ballerini and Moreels dropped the rest of the breakaway group on Mount Royal, 30km from the finish

On the final lap Bauer, Kelly and De Koning fighting the gradient and the rain in pursuit of the leaders

Ballerini finished more than a minute ahead to take his second classic race in two weeks

leaders were world champion Rudy Dhaenens (PDM) and Brazilian Mauro Ribeiro (RMO). At the same time, Sörensen dropped back, leaving a now five-strong break 1:40 ahead.

Clearly, with the principal Mount Royal climb splitting the pack on every lap, the situation was far from definitive. And another flurry of counterattacks saw a 16-strong chase group take shape. It was powered by Bugno, Bauer, Robert Millar (Z), Thomas Wegmüller (Weinmann) and Andy Bishop (7-Eleven), and marked by the PDM pair, Kelly and Eric Breukink, who were riding defensively on Dhaenens's behalf.

Then, with about 30km still remaining, Ballerini and Moreels dropped Chiappucci, Dhaenens and Ribeiro. And these three were caught by Bauer, Wegmüller, Kelly, Dutchman Louis De Koning (Panasonic-Sportlife) and Frank Van Den Abbeele (Lotto-Superclub).

On the final climb of Mount Royal, Ballerini dropped the tiring Moreels, and went on to take a brilliant solo victory. The elated Ballerini, 25, from Florence, observed, 'I don't usually race very well in the rain, but with the victory in sight . . .'

Behind him, Moreels was caught by a flying Wegmüller, fresh from his Grand Prix des Nations success. The Swiss went on to take second place, at 1:22, by outspeeding Moreels on the finishing straight, while the lone Chiappucci was just behind in fourth place. A further minute back, Bauer outsprinted Kelly, De Koning and Dhaenens to take fifth place.

Wegmüller, whose second place recalled his disappointment at being runner-up in the 1988 Paris-Roubaix, agreed that he had mistimed his effort. 'I left it a little too late,' he said. 'When I was in the group with the three PDM riders [Dhaenens, Kelly and Breukink], I thought I would let them do the work. But when I realised they were all cooked, I went away on my own. I realised that I couldn't possibly catch Ballerini as he'd ridden a superb race, but I knew that I *could* catch Chiappucci and Moreels.' Commenting on his race, fifth-placed Bauer said, 'When Wegmüller took off, I wasn't capable of countering him. I looked at Kelly, and he looked about as good as me. I didn't have the legs. At the start of the race, I was even having a hard time staying with the pack. I even considered abandoning.' Bauer's reward for fighting through his pain was a precious 16 points, which lifted him from 12th to seventh place in the Perrier World Cup. At the same time, Dhaenens's eighth place here allowed him to regain three points on overall World Cup leader Bugno, with three races remaining in the competition.

The Montreal race again proved one of the most difficult of the season. As winner Ballerini pointed out: 'This is a very difficult course that leaves little time for riders to catch their breath. You had to concentrate the whole time, as you were always having to fight against a crosswind. Regardless, I always thought my chances of catching Chiappucci were good.'

Only 42 riders managed to complete the full distance: two more than last year, despite the awful weather. Among those who quit were last year's winner, Jörg Müller (TVM-Yoko), and three men still recovering from injuries: Moreno Agentin, Laurent Fignon and Charly Mottet. Greg LeMond also failed to finish, lamenting 'This was my first [international] race since the Worlds in Japan, and it rained, rained, rained . . .'

Nissan Classic: 3-7 October

When the 1990 Nissan International Classic rolled away from Dublin in early October, victory in a major stage race was still eluding Dutch PDM rider Eric Breukink. After a season in which he had taken second place in the Tour of Holland and thirds in the Tour de Trump and Tour de France, Breukink wanted such a victory to finally lay the ghost of his unfortunate 1989 season with Panasonic. But with the end of the season looming, his last hope was the Irish Tour.

In the light of the intense pressure on him to win, therefore, his eventual victory by 0:15 from Belgium's Johan Museeuw (Lotto-Superclub) was all the more impressive. Breukink was in his element in the stage 2a time trial, and nobody was surprised when he took the yellow jersey there, but thereafter he and his PDM team-mates defended it in as solid and well-executed an operation as Sean Kelly's win in the Tour of Switzerland.

Since its inception in 1985, the Nissan Classic has matured into a highly regarded race. It is usually a testing route, winding up and down the rugged, narrow and, more often than not, windswept and rain-sodden roads of southern Ireland, and it takes nothing less than a champion to win it. The previous winners attest to that: Ireland's hero Sean Kelly won the first three editions of the race, in 1985, 1986 and 1987; then Germany's Rolf Gölz in 1988; and Belgium's Eric Vanderaerden in 1989.

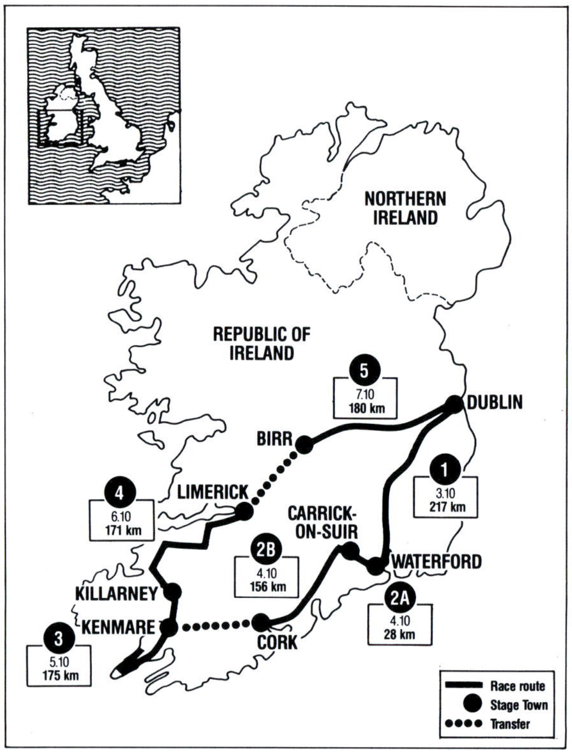

Nissan Classic, Ireland: 927km

Johan Lammerts catches his breakaway companion of the previous day, Graeme Miller, on the finish line of the time trial at Carrick-on-Suir

As in past years the Nissan Classic lured a very high-class line-up, whose ambitions ranged from overall victory or stage wins, to simply getting into condition for the end of season World Cup races and classics.

The principal riders to watch were Breukink, Kelly and Mexico's Raúl Alcalá from PDM; Vanderaerden, Dutchmen Jelle Nijdam and Frans Maassen and Belgium's Edwig van Hooydonck from Buckler; Soviet Viatcheslav Ekimov, Belgium's Eric Van Lancker and Germany's Olaf Ludwig from Panasonic-Sportlife; Frenchman Laurent Fignon of Castorama; Canadian Steve Bauer, Great Britain's Sean Yates and Norway's Dag-Otto Lauritzen from 7-Eleven; Australia's Phil Anderson from TVM; Switzerland's Thomas Wegmüller and the Netherlands' Adrie Van der Poel from Weinmann; and the man Irish cycling fans have not seen since the 1987 Nissan Classic – Greg LeMond.

There was no question but that LeMond, the American Tour de France champion, brought a smile to the organizers' faces by arriving on the start line of stage 1 from Dublin to Waterford. Since 1987, Sport for Television had failed to secure the American's participation. At last, or so they thought, they had succeeded. But before the first day's racing was over their satisfaction had evaporated. LeMond, who had complained of fatigue before the start and a stomach infection during the stage, abandoned just before the end of the stage.

LeMond's poor form had been evident ever since his fourth place at the world road race title in Japan, and apart from a local mountain bike race in the United States, he had failed to finish an event since. And on 14 October, the eve of Paris-Tours, it was confirmed that he

Breukink's time trialling won him the Carrick-on-Suir stage, and with it eventual victory

was suffering from intestinal and blood infections, and would cut short his season in order to recuperate at home. But all this was in the future on stage 1 of the Nissan: his abandonment was a blow not only for the organizers, but also for his sponsor, Z, and far from appreciated by the locals, despite the American's pledge to stay in Ireland and train until the Sunday finish.

Stage 1, 217km from Dublin to Waterford, was also marred for Z when Robert Millar, their Scottish climbing specialist, crashed after 160km. His French team-mates, Bruno Cornillet and Ronan Pensec, joined LeMond in an unsuccessful attempt to help Millar rejoin the peloton. But stage 1 was not a total disaster for the Z team: Dutchman Johan Lammerts saw to that.

Lammerts, the former Tour of Flanders winner who did not get a Tour de France ride because of poor form this year, and New Zealander Graeme Miller (Bolla), broke away from a complacent peloton on this long first stage, building up a 17-minute lead at one point. They held on to their advantage until the final sprint, which Lammerts took from Miller, a mere 0:25 clear of a chasing group of 37 riders.

LeMond abandoning, Lammerts' victory, and the belated finish of Millar and his Z companions 13:08 after Lammerts came in, must have given the Z *directeur* sportif, Roger Legeay, some conflicting sensations to ponder that night!

Sean Yates' form in the time trial earned him third place overall and made up for a season which he would otherwise sooner forget

The yellow leader's jersey would not be Lammerts' for long, despite starting the following day's split stage with 0:02 on Miller overall, 0:23 on Belgium's Hendrik Redant (Lotto-Superclub) and 0:28 on the main field, which included Breukink.

In the morning's 28km time trial, stage 2a from Waterford to Carrick-on-Suir, Lammerts finished 1:39 behind a dominant Breukink, whose win there put him in the overall lead. Evidence of Breukink's prowess was not merely his 0:22 advantage on Museeuw, but his margin on many of the other time trialling specialists. Yates was third, also at 0:22. Ekimov, blocked in the last kilometre by a truck parked where it shouldn't have been, was fourth at 0:41, with Alcalá and Maassen fifth at 0:55 and sixth at 0:59 respectively. Wegmüller, the man who beat Breukink in the dying kilometres of the Grand Prix des Nations time trial, was seventh at 1:00.

For those who witnessed the reshuffle of the top order, it was a magnificent display. Inevitably, of course, most hearts at Carrick-on-Suir were beating for their home champion Kelly, but sadly, a loose rear wheel hampered the Irishman's racing and he could do no better than 13th at 1:20. So Breukink's success relegated Kelly to domestique duties for the remaining stages to Dublin. And although Breukink's defence never faltered, or even looked like doing so, there was still some good hard racing to come.

Not yet, however: stage 2b, a 156km race from Carrick-on-Suir to Cork, saw all but one in the field happy to rest up. The only renegade was Cornillet, whose sorry time trial performance – he finished in 92nd place, at 8:47 – had put him in last place overall and at more than 21:00. So when Cornillet attacked after 27km, he did so with the intention of demonstrating the meaning of 'bravado': the finish line and any hope of a stage win was 122km away, and in between lay the challenge of three passings of the notorious Patrick's Hill in the centre of Cork.

Patrick's Hill, a brutally steep 600-metre-long wall or *mur*, as the French call such ascents, had been one of the Nissan Classic's early highlights, and the narrow ancient roadway was regularly jammed by the thousands of spectators who flocked to see the Nissan Classic struggle up Patrick's Hill. The climb was back this year, after a three-year absence, and as before it took many of the field to the limit of their endurance, several riders being forced to walk up.

By the time Cornillet was on the third and final circuit, his lead was more than 10:00; a margin reduced from 17:00 with 50km to go. By then, there was no doubt that he was going to further compensate the Z team for their stage 1 troubles. 'After having raced the Nissan Classic in 1987, I knew the circuit and knew that to win you needed to be courageous and willing to go to the limit. And today, I felt that way,' said a happy Cornillet, after fending off second-placed Yates and the rest of the main field by 10:03.

Still, the overall order was unchanged; and it remained unchanged after stage 3 from Kenmare to Killarney over

The Nissan peloton encountered Patrick's Hill for the first time in three years

175km. Breukink was not troubled by Museeuw winning the field sprint and stage from second-placed Belgian Etienne De Wilde (Histor-Sigma) and third-placed Kelly, for time bonuses were not on offer here. So the Dutchman's 17th place was not a matter for concern.

This picturesque stage was not billed as the sprinters' race it eventually became. The highlights of the stage, the climbs of Healy Pass and Moll's Gap near the mist-shrouded Atlantic coastline, were expected to split the field of 91 survivors. However, strong headwinds soon put paid to that: even after an hour and a half, they had only covered 40km!

Now, the Nissan Classic hinged on time bonifications. And over the last two stages to Dublin, a handsome booty of 0:96 in time bonuses was up for grabs. For a sprinter like Museeuw, second overall at 0:22, that was a tempting challenge to contemplate. But this final weekend, blanketed in wet, miserable weather, held disappointment in store for the Belgian runner-up. On Saturday, the 171km stage 4 from Killarney to Limerick, Museeuw only cut back his deficit to 0:15, for Germany's Markus Schleicher (Stuttgart) attacked with 50km to go and secured his first professional victory. Museeuw – wearer of the green points jersey – finished second on the stage, leading the main field 0:48 behind Schleicher, but significantly, Schleicher's win denied Museeuw a 0:10 bonus.

PDM knew that by helping Schleicher, they were depriving Museeuw of extra time bonuses, so Breukink's team-mates worked tirelessly to help contain any chase by Museeuw's Lotto-Superclub team on this critical stage. But Lotto-Superclub's chasing efforts were already undermined by two setbacks, a silly crash by Museeuw himself and then, during their attempt to chase down Schleicher, their powerful Belgian, Hendrik Redant, punctured.

The final day, stage 5, would have had to produce a miracle for Museeuw to take the yellow jersey off Breukink's back. His impossible task was to win two intermediate sprints, together with the stage, but PDM were just too powerful. Museeuw failed to secure any of the intermediate sprints, and as the race went into the twelve finishing circuits of Dublin's O'Connell Street, all that was left for him was to try for a consolatory stage win. After his victory in the final stage of the Tour de France on the Champs Elysées, many people felt he might pull off an 'encore' on Dublin's O'Connell Street – aptly nicknamed 'little Champs Elysées'.

The entire field descending through the mist. Healy Pass, near Kenmare

The ravaged expressions on these faces is testament to the gruelling pace that took stage 4 into Limerick

However, not even that compensation came Museeuw's way. Ludwig, Museeuw's rival in the Tour de France and the green points jersey winner there, reversed the roles they had in France and won in Dublin.

Ludwig surprised everyone by jumping away from the field 200 metres from the finish, taking his solitary stage win in Ireland with a 0:01 margin on Kelly, who produced a chorus of cheers from the throng of local fans by leading in the peloton and taking second place. Museeuw, disappointed but already looking forward to Paris-Tours and an opportunity for vengeance, was an inconsequential 10th.

However, Breukink, 20th on the stage, was a very consequential first overall. As with so many previous races this year, the time trial had proved crucial. 'Certainly, my results in time trials put me in a strong situation in every stage race. In fact, in my list of career wins, there should be a lot more victories of this kind,' said the boyish-looking blond Dutchman of 26 years, whose Irish win also stood him in good stead for the Tour of Lombardy in Italy. 'The Tour de France will be my great goal next year. But for now, considering my good form here, my immediate goals will be to take my chance in the Tour of Lombardy. There, it seems the door is open for me. Also, of course, there's the World Cup final [time trial] at Lunel.'

The champagne of victory brought a smile to Breukink's face in Dublin

Paris-Tours: 14 October

A refreshing variation was introduced into a racing season dominated by Italian victories when Denmark's Rolf Sörensen (Ariostea) won the Paris-Tours World Cup race in mid-October. The 25-year-old Dane was accompanied in his winning break by Australia's Phil Anderson (TVM), Germany's Andreas Kappes (Toshiba) and Denmark's Kim Andersen (Z), and had it not been for a late chase by Maurizio Fondriest (Del Tongo) it would have been that rarity in the 1990 season, a finale not featuring an Italian rider.

The weight of tradition supported the belief that Paris-Tours would be won by a sprinter. After trying out several different itineraries between 1974 and 1987, when the route from southern Paris to Tours evolved, more often than not the finale was marked by a bunch sprint. The consensus in the bunch this year was that since the Tour of Lombardy was better suited to climbers, Paris-Tours would be the sprinters' farewell to 1990, and amongst the 186-strong line-up there were certainly some highly qualified candidates. Clear favourites were Dutchmen Jelle Nijdam and Wiebren Veenstra (Buckler), France's Frédéric Moncassin (Castorama), Germany's Olaf Ludwig (Panasonic-Sportlife), Italy's Adriano Baffi (Ariostea) and the Belgian trio of Johan Museeuw and Sammie Moreels of Lotto-Superclub and Carlo Bomans (Weinmann). One had also, in view of the keen competition for World Cup points, to anticipate strong showings from Italian Gianni Bugno (Chateau d'Ax), the World Champion Rudy Dhaenens (PDM) of Belgium, Ireland's Sean Kelly (PDM), Canada's Steve Bauer (7-Eleven) and Italy's Claudio Chiappucci (Carrera), Franco Ballerini (Del Tongo), Fondriest and Moreno Argentin (Ariostea). Two notable absentees were America's Greg LeMond (Z), who had cut short his season to recuperate from

Andersen and Schleicher's 250km breakaway strongly influenced the outcome of the race. Here Schleicher is seen leading as their pursuers close in, but it was the more experienced Andersen who got into the winning move

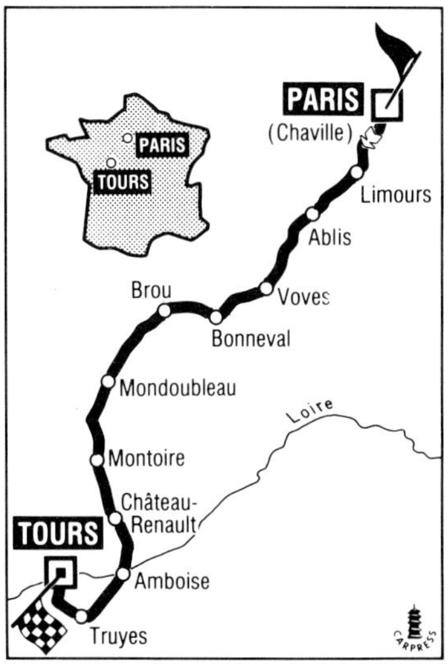

Paris-Tours, France: 284km

infections diagnosed after the Nissan Classic, and Belgium's Eric Vanderaerden (Buckler), who withdrew from the race following the news that his mother had died.

However, despite the weight of tradition and the depth of sprinting talent in the field, this year's edition of Paris-Tours was different. Firstly, the characteristic back-breaking headwinds along the flat and open route were absent. What headwind there was was very slight, and far from strong enough to discourage a strong breakaway. And secondly, there was the underestimated gallantry of the Dane Kim Andersen (Z) and Germany's Markus Schleicher (Stuttgart), who attacked after only 13km. It was a long time before anyone realised that their bold escapade was a threat, and by 63km their lead had grown to 17:20; it was not until the 70km mark that a pursuit, organised by Nijdam's Buckler team-mates, was instigated.

The pursuit reduced their lead to 8:15 after 104km, but the chase was interrupted 68km further on when a crash, involving Argentin and Dutchmen Eric Breukink (PDM) and Frans Maassen (Buckler), blocked about 20 riders and broke the peloton's rhythm. A cut and grazed Argentin abandoned immediately, while Maassen and Breukink dropped out soon afterwards. So it was not until after 230km that Andersen and Schleicher looked like being caught. Spaniard Marino Alonso (Banesto) tried unsuccessfully to chase them down alone, then Fondriest tried a similar move 10km later; his escape was also reeled in, but by then the two leaders were less than a minute in front. Finally, at the 261km mark the three-man chase of Sörensen, Anderson and Kappes made contact, giving the front group a bare 30-second lead on the peloton, now driven by Ludwig's Panasonic-Sportlife lieutenants.

It was an impressive display by the leaders to stay away as they did, although Andersen understandably rested at the rear of the group after his efforts, and Schleicher faded before being dropped with 10km to go on the gradual ascent to the Côte du Crochu. His more than adequate replacement in the lead group was Fondriest, who launched a miraculous solo chase on the next rise

With Schleicher dropped, Kappes, Anderson and Sörensen stormed towards Tours at 60kph – a speed which was still barely sufficient to hold off the Panasonic-led peloton

and caught the four attackers with 4km to go. He looked like being the strongest rider in the group, and, as so often in 1990, the press contingent began composing the storyline of yet another chapter in the Italian renaissance.

However, it was Kappes who was the first to show his hand, breaking free under the red kite with a kilometre to go. Sörensen and Anderson – also looking remarkably strong – were quick to chase, and then, with 500 metres left, the Dane Andersen spent his remaining reserves in leading out the sprint. His lead-out prompted a three-man sprint to the line on the tree-lined Avenue du Grammont in Tours, with Sörensen taking the far left, Fondriest the centre and Anderson the right. But on the line it was Sörensen, confounding expectations that a mass sprint would select the Paris-Tours winner, who had the speed and strength to win, with Anderson in 2nd place, Fondriest 3rd, Andersen 4th and Kappes 5th.

It was Sörensen's fourth win of the year; he took a stage, and overall victory, in the Semaine Siciliane in February, and the Italian Trophy Laigueglia in March. 'This win proves that I am a good rider, something that I haven't really done so far this year,' said Sörensen afterwards. 'But I came here to win; if not, to get a good result. I warned my team-mates of that at Chaville this morning. Last year, I came very close to winning [4th], but this time I had a lot more motivation . . . a sort of interior rage.'

Paris-Tours, round 11 of the 1990 World Cup, left the series leadership unchanged. Gianni Bugno was still in the lead, although his 23rd place earned him no points, and Rudy Dhaenens, who gained one World Cup point with his 20th place, remained in second place. The biggest change to the World Cup standings was the move up from fifth to third by Sean Kelly, whose eighth place (third in the bunch sprint) gave him 13 points.

The finale of Paris-Tours was not the anticipated bunch sprint, but it was still a sprinter who won. Rolf Sörensen bursts across the finish line in Tours

Tour of Lombardy: 20 October

The splendour of the Madonna del Ghisallo owes much to its lakeside setting and Alpine backdrop

Although the scene was set for the Italians to complete the season in triumph at the 84th Tour of Lombardy, this – the only truly mountainous classic – was unceremoniously pulled from their grasp by foreigners for a third successive year. After wins by Frenchman Charly Mottet and Swiss Toni Rominger in 1988 and 1989, the 1990 edition of Italy's toughest one-day race went to another French rider, the multi-talented Gilles Delion (Helvetia-La Suisse). Often runner-up in big races, and second to Rominger in 1989, the 24-year-old Delion was enthusiastic about his breakthrough win. 'Because of all my 2nd and 3rd placings this year, I'd wanted to win a really top race. And the Tour of Lombardy was a bigger race than any of those that I lost,' he said.

The result was a huge disappointment to the *tifosi,* the home country's fanatical cycling supporters, who had been convinced that one of their new heroes – Gianni Bugno, Franco Ballerini or Claudio Chiappucci – would again overcome the opposition in their banner year. In fact, so sure were the organizers that one of the first two, world-ranked professionals would win that the Milan-based race was rearranged to start and finish in Bugno's home town of Monza, and the course was routed through the village where Chiappucci lives – Uboldo, 24km into the 246km event.

However, hopes that a local man would pluck the fruits of victory from this Race of the Falling Leaves were dashed after only four hours: the time it took for the leaders to reach the steepest slopes of the Valico Valcava mountain. There, 5km from the 1336m summit of this spectacular climb – with Chiappucci already dropped from the leading group (and about to abandon the race), and Bugno having a hard time staying in contact with the other protagonists – a break was made by the five riders who would dominate the remaining 98km. They were Delion and his Swiss team-mate Pascal Richard, Spaniard Federico Echave of Clas, Scotsman Robert Millar of Z, and Mottet of RMO. These five men, all lightly built climbers, stayed clear for the remaining 98km to contest a finishing sprint that went to Delion, from Richard and Mottet.

Such a result had looked unlikely before the start on a

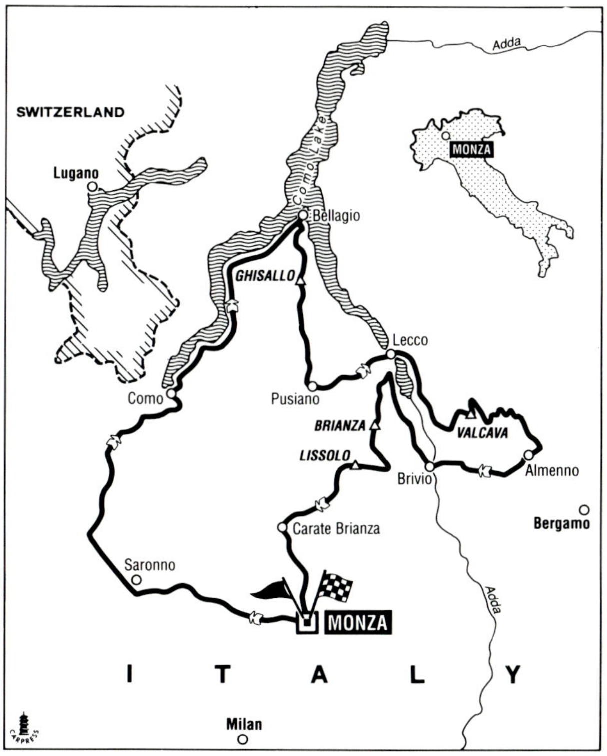

Tour of Lombardy, Italy: 246km

damp, depressing Saturday morning outside industrial Monza's ultra-functional expo centre. This unglamorous venue – a sharp contrast to the recent starting point in Como, where the sun usually illuminates the town's splendid, lakeside main square with its backdrop of impressive peaks – was the price of bringing the finish closer to the mountains than the former, central Milan location. Other course changes included the bypassing of two of the four major climbs, and replacing them by two hills that were much less severe – but closer to the finish. Reflecting on the course changes later, Millar reported, 'It's just as terrible as it usually is, though it's better with the hills at the end – that makes it a little harder – and it's better than going the last 60km on the flat, like last year.'

This time, the 208 starters rode the first 60km on the flat, and despite the miserable weather, it wasn't long before the first attack came. Spaniard Herminio Diaz-Zabala (ONCE) and Italian Fabio Foscioli (Del Tongo) sped clear into the wind after only 4km, gaining 35 seconds before they were reeled in, just before an intermediate sprint at Uboldo – won not by local hero Chiappucci, but by the German Thomas Barth of TVM.

Turning north from Uboldo, Bugno's Chateau d'Ax team took over the front of the peloton, setting an intimidating pace of 40 kph to discourage any more breaks before their team leader had warmed up. Bugno was the hot favourite, having been tipped to win by such experts as Eddy Merckx, Francesco Moser . . . and even Mottet. It was said that in the seven weeks since winning the bronze medal at the Worlds and virtually locking up the World Cup, with 1st place at the Wincanton Classic

Micheal Wilson's mid-race break (above) provoked an acceleration in the group behind and allowed his team-mates Delion and Richard to join the winning break on the Valcava. But the Australian's efforts spelt disaster for World Cup leader Bugno (below), struggling towards the summit of the Valcava with an equally weary Kelly and Caritoux for company

Earlier, everything seemed set for a win for Bugno, as his team set a daunting pace on the approach to Madonna del Ghisallo

and 5th in Zürich, Bugno was focusing all his attention on a victorious conclusion to his season in the Tour of Lombardy.

Apart from a solo break by Spaniard José Oliveira (Clas), who built up a lead of 1:50 after 48km, just before the route passed Como, the Chateau d'Ax control of the race lasted until the foot of the first major climb, the famous Madonna del Ghisallo, at 95km. Oliveira was reeled in after 64km at the top of a long, steady climb to Asso, on a section of the course that had been added at the last minute to bypass a landslide on the original route beside Lake Como. As well as increasing the course distance by 5km, the bypass also added 150m of climbing to the already impressive scheduled 2453m. The extra climb proved too much for half a dozen riders – including Italian Silvano Contini (Gis), a former winner of the Liège-Bastogne-Liège classic, and a runner-up in the 1979 Tour of Lombardy at the start of his career. This was the last big race of his career, but this wasn't the way he'd hoped to end it.

From Asso, by which time the rain had stopped, the field plummeted down a narrow back road, dropping 265m to Lake Lecco, at Onno. The tricky descent split the peloton into several groups, and the rapid pace set by the Chateau d'Ax riders ensured that there was no regrouping in the flat 9km that led alongside the calm waters of the lake to the foot of the mighty Ghisallo.

This awesome climb used to be an unsurfaced track in the heyday of Fausto Coppi, the legendary Italian, who won the Tour of Lombardy four successive times from 1946 to 1949, usually by breaking clear on the Ghisallo, and racing the remaining 50km to Milan on his own. Now smoothly asphalted, this 9km ascent is much less destructive, and a group of 28 riders crested the steep, wooded ridge in the front.

Helvetia-La Suisse was already showing its strength here, with its Swiss rider Guido Winterberg pulling the peloton for most of the climb, before Ballerini took over at the front. The half-million lire *prime* at the 754m summit, next to the cyclists' chapel of the Madonna del Ghisallo, was taken in a brief sprint by another Swiss, Fabian Fuchs of Buckler, ahead of Echave and Italian Angelo Lecchi of Del Tongo.

Lecchi seemed unaware that his team leader, Maurizio Fondriest, had fallen on one of the steep, uphill turns – but he wasn't seriously hurt. Much unhappier were some of the other favourites. Chiappucci and fellow Italian Moreno Argentin of Ariostea were in a second group, 1:15 down on the leaders; Australian Phil Anderson of TVM was at 1:50; and Dane Rolf Sörensen of Ariostea (winner of the previous weekend's Paris-Tours) and Dutchman Eric Breukink of PDM, were both 3:20 back. 25km later, at the feed zone, Breukink pulled out of the race.

In that distance – half of it downhill – a solo break was made from the front group by Helvetia-La Suisse's Australian rider, Micheal Wilson, who was still negotiating for a place on another team in 1991, and needed a good performance here. He benefited from a relaxation among the other front runners, who eased back on the descent to the feed zone, allowing another 30 riders – including the Chiappucci-Argentin-Delion group – to catch them. Here, just beyond the halfway point and before descending into the town of Lecco, Wilson was 2:20 ahead of the main group, and 3:05 up on a second substantial pack, from which German Andreas Kappes of Toshiba, and Briton Sean Yates of 7-Eleven, were trying to bridge. They didn't make it, but two others, Sörensen and Dane Kim Andersen of Z, did manage to cross the gap, just before the front group reached the start of the Valcava.

As they turned left onto the climb – that first twists up an escarpment between fruit trees before continuing across the bare mountainside – the main group was still 2:20 behind Wilson. His team director Paul Köchli now unleashed the second part of his game plan, sending Winterberg away on a mission to join Wilson. It was a brave decision by the wily Swiss coach, who had been heartened earlier in the week when his riders – Mauro Gianetti, Jean-Claude Leclercq and Delion – came in 1-2-3 at the Milan-Turin race. By the mid-point on the Valcava – which climbs through 1130m to a 1336m altitude – Wilson was 2:00 ahead of his team-mate, and 2:40 ahead of the group. Chiappucci was about to be dropped for good, and Bugno was riding well back in the group, instead of in his usual place near the front. The day was turning against the Italians, even though Ballerini was still sharing the pace-making with Mottet and Belgian champion, Claude Criquielion of Lotto-Superclub. Mottet's team-mate Eric Caritoux was also aiding his leader – although it was a pleasant surprise to see Mottet climbing so strongly only three weeks after having a cast removed from a broken wrist.

With 4km of climbing left, the race favourites' forcing had closed the gap on Wilson to only 1:30, while Winterberg was still 40 seconds ahead of the group. Within a kilometre, Winterberg was caught, and after more than 75 minutes away on his own Wilson was finally beginning to show signs of cracking. Now came the vital moment of the race – and it was Mottet who was one of the chief instigators of the key break which developed. The break came just after a turn, 3km from the top of the 15km climb, where the gradient suddenly steepened. Millar described the moment. 'I didn't really remember where the hard bit was,' he confessed. 'I'd just moved up to the front to ride beside Mottet and Delion, because they'd been to see the hill [before the race], so I figured they knew where it was going to get hard. It was just around a corner. You just got up there the best way you could – I didn't go past anyone, but nobody came past me. I looked around [at the top], and there was nobody left.'

Indeed, the only riders left with Millar, Mottet and Delion were Echave and Richard. These five riders soon overtook Wilson, who was dropped just as they entered

Fondriest's ascent of the Valcava was one of the fastest of the day, but his efforts later resulted in a bout of cramp which forced his retirement

the final kilometre of the Valcava. By now, the sun was shining on the crowds that had gathered on this windswept mountainside, but the partisan fans were not pleased with the less than stellar performances of their heroes. When Echave pulled clear to take the prime at the top, 15 seconds ahead of the other four leaders, Spaniard Marino Lejarreta of ONCE, Venezuelan Leonardo Sierra of Selle Italia, and Criquielion led a small chase group, which Fondriest had joined, at 0:50; just behind came Wilson and Winterberg, with a few others; and then, at 1:10, came the group of principals, headed by Bugno, Chateau d'Ax team-mate Alberto Volpi, Belgian Eric Van Lancker of Panasonic-Sportlife, Swiss Thomas Wegmüller of Weinmann, and the PDM colleagues, Mexican Raúl Alcalá and Irishman Sean Kelly – whose world champion team-mate Rudy Dhaenens had not travelled to Italy, wishing to be with his wife at the expected birth of their baby.

Normally, one would expect that on descending roads, a group as strong as this would close on a lead group composed of climbers. But on reaching the valley, 71km from the finish, the five leaders had increased their lead to 1:50 over the Lejarreta-Criquielion group (in which Fondriest was suffering from a bout of cramps, and would soon abandon); and to 2:30 over the Bugno-Kelly group, from which Wegmüller and Ballerini had both broken clear. It was clear that the Valcava climb had

The break: it was already clear that Delion was the strongest of the five escapers

The chase: Criquielion and Lejarreta were the prime instigators of the chase. Here they accelerate away after the descent of the Valcava

taken a more severe toll than was first realised, and when the five leaders reached the first of the final hills, 47km from Monza, they were 3:10 ahead of the chasers, and 3:56 ahead of the leading World Cup contenders.

The last three climbs – the first long and gradual, the other two short and steep – only intensified the damage done by the Valcava. The five leaders did remain together, although Millar lost contact momentarily on the last two 'walls', but the chase group was reduced to just three riders (Sierra, Criquielion and Lejarreta), and the Bugno group dropped to 5:55 down. It seemed that Bugno had definitely clinched the World Cup, as only Kelly was now within shooting distance of the Italian, but the outcome of this absorbing Tour of Lombardy still remained in doubt.

It was logical to surmise that team-mates Delion and Richard would be able to work over the other three riders with alternating attacks, but they were both wary of former winner Mottet – who had won a similar sprint to this in the Championship of Zürich against Greg LeMond and Chiappucci – and the two Helvetia-La Suisse riders were also a little jealous of each other. As their director Köchli said later, 'When you have two men in the front like that, you *have* to win, no?'

To this end, Köchli told Richard that he or Delion had to attack before the final kilometre. Richard – whose most significant career win was the Izoard stage of the 1989 Tour de France – felt that as he was the senior rider, Delion should be the hare. But Delion was unwilling to carry out this risky assignment; he explained afterwards that he knew that he didn't have a chance in a technical sprint, but he was psyching himself up to make an aggressive effort at the end. Even so, Delion did make a dummy effort, 1300m from the line, allowing Richard to sprint clear on the far side of the wide road. Initially, the others hesitated, then Mottet took up the chase. Köchli observed, 'I thought Richard might win when he attacked. And if Mottet had hesitated a moment longer, it would have been all over. . .' But Mottet did react, so Richard eased up, wanting to save himself for the sprint.

Contesting such a finish on flat roads is an unusual experience for climbers such as these, but Mottet was the expected favourite. True to form, the senior French rider led out the sprint on the right of the straight boulevard; but Richard almost as quickly started his own charge in the centre of the street, while the new, 'aggressive' Delion made an even stronger effort in between. Both Millar and Echave were beaten, and it was the delighted Delion who crossed the line with his arms high in triumph. This was the first of what should be many significant victories: Delion had already won the prize for best young rider in his first Tour de France, and now he had captured his first single-day classic success. The young French rider from Chambéry could have been tempted to move to some big-money teams after the 1990 Tour de France, but he turned down the offers and re-signed for Köchli's more austere squad for 1991. Such confidence in his mentor should ensure that Gilles Delion will become much more widely known in the future.

Delion's finishing kick was too much for his more senior team-mate Richard

After the final showdown at Monza, where a slight drizzle had again dampened the day, the Italian crowd had to wait 3:35 before 6th place was taken by Criquielion, from Sierra and Lejarreta; while Wegmüller led in the principal group by 50m, with two-time race winner Kelly outsprinting the best of the Italians – Ballerini, his Del Tongo team-mate Angelo Lecchi, and Bugno – for 10th place. It was indeed a disappointing display by the home riders, and perhaps proved that cycling at this superbly high level can never be scripted to meet the expectations of the fans.

World Cup Final: 27 October

Saturday, 27 October: Lunel, France. That was the last major dateline for the 1990 cycling year, and the occasion was the World Cup Final, a 50km individual time trial involving 19 of the best riders of the year.

Succeeded only by the Montjuich hill climb in Spain the next day, this 13th and last round of the World Cup was almost the very last race of the year, and was certainly the last to have such a star-studded start list. Raced on a flat and open clockwise route, and under a warming sun which contrasted pleasantly with the wet, miserable weather of northern Europe, the World Cup Final was contested by an invited field originally numbering 23. It was a field specially selected from three qualifying categories: the top 10 in the World Cup after the Tour of Lombardy and the world FICP rankings, the winner from each of the previous 11 road race rounds, plus the reigning world road champion. But Italy's Moreno Argentin (Ariostea), Germany's Andreas Kappes (Toshiba), Belgium's Luc Roosen (Histor-Sigma) and the Netherlands' John Talen (Panasonic-Sportlife) all scratched, which resulted in the eventual line-up of 19 riders.

The World Cup Final was created this year, and has attracted controversy from the start. Many wondered why it was not staged in a better known and more accessible location than Lunel, near Montpellier in France's Hérault region. In the later rounds of the World Cup, as Gianni Bugno's lead became increasingly unassailable, it started to look as though this final race would in any case have no chance of influencing the outcome of the series. Finally, many people – particularly the riders – resented the season being stretched in this way to the end of October, nearly two weeks after the traditional mid-October ending. Before the race day was over the riders made their feelings known when, led by Rudy Dhaenens, they presented FICP President Hein Verbruggen with a letter formally protesting against such a long racing season. The letter reflected the weariness of the riders. 'Morale is the big problem. It's very hard to have it so late in the season,' said Ireland's Sean Kelly (PDM), who finished 16th. 'It's too late in the season for this. After the Tour of Lombardy I had no morale to train during the week for a final time trial.' Others reported to have signed the letter were Canada's Steve Bauer (7-Eleven), France's Charly Mottet (RMO), the Netherland's Adrie Van der Poel (Weinmann), Spain's Marino Lejarreta (ONCE), Denmark's Rolf Sörensen (Ariostea), Belgium's Eric Van Lancker (Panasonic-Sportlife), and Switzerland's Thomas Wegmüller (Weinmann).

Bugno breezes through the final corner at Lunel. His World Cup victory was already assured, and after a monumentally hard but successful season he was content to let Breukink, Rominger and Echave share the honours at the time trial

Even Bugno added his name to the protest, although he personally has had a triumphant season, and will be remembered as 1990's 'Man of the Year' for his consistently winning form. He began the year with victory in Milan-San Remo in March and continued with wins in the Italian Tour of Trentino in May, the Tour of Italy (including three stages) in late May-June; a stage in the Tour de France where he also finished seventh, the Wincanton Classic and finally the World Cup competition. He also took a bronze medal in the World Championship road race in Japan and the number one world FICP ranking. Ater the Tour of Lombardy he had a 25-point World Cup lead, and it would have been impossible for Dhaenens, second-placed on the World Cup ladder before the race, to even contemplate overtaking the Italian. Not even the 25 winner's points would have changed things – 18th and 19th places at Lunel were awarded two points each.

So the Final had no bearing on who would win the World Cup. In the event Bugno's eighth place left him with 133 points and the World Cup. Second and third places were also unchanged: Dhaenens, who was 17th in the final, finished with 99 points, and Kelly, who was 16th, held on to his third place with 94 points. Interest at Lunel, therefore, centred solely on who would win the time trial.

But even that suspense was quickly over when Breukink, racing eleventh, clocked the fastest splits. His performance was a repeat of his effort in the early part of the Grand Prix des Nations, the longer, hillier time trialling classic, when he faded in the final stages and surrendered victory to Wegmüller. But this time he convincingly avenged that defeat, clocking a winning time for the 50km of 1:02.48. 'The Grand Prix des Nations was another thing altogether. There are no mountains here. But this was still hard as, after crashing at Paris-Tours, I think I lost some condition,' said Breukink who, like all but Sörensen, rode with a rear disc wheel and the now customary triathlete handlebars.

Breukink's margin was 0:34 on his nearest rival who was, surprisingly, not Wegmüller or Mottet, but Rominger. Mottet's fifth place at 1:20 and Wegmüller's 11th at 2:22 were two of the biggest upsets of the day. However, Mottet's poor showing was caused by a puncture after just five kilometres, and Wegmüller started the time trial suffering from a sore throat which had sapped his legendary strength. Rominger's second place was also unexpected, because whilst he is a noted time triallist he had failed to do much preparation for the event. 'It was a surprise, yes, because I haven't really done much training at all in the last couple of weeks,' said the dark-haired Swiss later. And while Breukink was fastest at the respective 17.5km, 34km and 45km marks before securing victory with a fastest time at the 50km finishing mark, Rominger did not move up into second place until 34km, passing the in-form Spaniard Federico Echave (Clas), who eventually finished third at 0:41.

So closed the 1990 cycling season, a season full to the brim with drama, sensation, heroics, glory and even humour; all the ingredients to keep our minds ticking before 1991 marks another cycle.

Team Listings

AUSTRIA

VARTA-ELK
Sponsor: Battery manufacturer. Bicycles: Pinarello. Directeur sportif: Gerhard Schönebacher
Austrians
Wolfgang Hofer
Paul Popp
Bernhard Rassinger
Arno Wohlfahrter
Foreigners
Markus Hess (WG)
Milan Jurco (Cz)

BELGIUM

HISTOR-SIGMA
Sponsor: Paint manufacturer. Bicycles: Vitus. Directeur sportif: Willy Teirlinck. Assistants: Patrick Valcke and Frans Van Looy
Belgians
Luc Colijn
Patrick Dewaele
Etienne De Wilde
Herman Frison
Paul Haghedooren
Jan Nevens
Rudy Patry
Wilfried Peeters
Luc Roosen
Rik Van Slycke
Johan Verstreppen
Foreigners
Laurent Biondi (Fr)
Philippe Chevalier (Fr)
Rob Harmeling (Hol)
Sören Lilholt (Den)
Francis Moreau (Fr)
Laurent Pillon (Fr)
Stephen Roche (Ire)
Brian Holm (Sörensen) (Den)
Marc Thevenin (Fr)
Didier Virvaleix (Fr)

ISOGLASS-GARDEN WOOD
Sponsor: Cavity wall insulation manufacturer. Bicycles: Rossin. Directeur sportif: Luc Landuyt
Belgians
Edwin Bafcop
Philippe Cottennies
Geert Decorte
Geert De Vlaeminck
Hendrik Devos
Rudi Dexters
Danny Lippens
Peter Naessens
Franky Pattyn
Patrick Roelandt
Rudi Rogiers
Benny Van Brabant
Roger Van Den Bossche
Frank Van Himst
Peter Van Impe
Kurt Van Keirsbulck
Peter Verbeken
Foreigners
Stephan Rakers (Hol)
Paolo Ratti (It)

LA WILLIAM-SALTOS
Sponsor: Liquor distillery. Bicycles: Colnago. Directeur sportif: Paul Debaeremaecker. Assistant: Rudi Pebenage
Belgians
Jan Bogaert
Corneille Daems
Luc Desmet
Ferdi Dierickx
Ludo Giesberts
Mark Macharis
Yvan Messelis
Johan Pauwels
Chris Scharmin
Stan Tourné
Koenraad Van Rooy
Patrick Verplancke
Foreigners
Marat Ganeev (USSR)
Harry Lodge (GB)
John Nuttall (Aus)

LOTTO-SUPERCLUB
Sponsor: National lottery. Bicycles: MBK. Directeur sportif: Jean-Luc Bandenbroucke. Assistant: Jef Braeckevelt
Belgians
Wim Arras
Thierry Bock
Bruno Bruyère
Johan Bruyneel
Claude Criquielion
Peter De Clercq
Dirk DeMol
Patrick Deneut
Franck Francken
Jos Haex
Sammie Moreels
Johan Museeuw
Hendrick Redant
Peter Roes
Frank Van Den Abbeele
Wim Van Eynde
Benjamin Van Itterbeck
Koen Vekemans
Rudy Verdonck
Patrick Verschueren
Ludwig Willems

TULIP-IOC
Sponsors: Computer company and billiard table manufacturer. Bicycles: Rossin. Directeur sportif: José Decauwer. Assistants: Dirk Wayenberg and Willy Jossart
Belgians
Patrick Bar
Gino De Backer
Fons De Wolf
Frank Hoste
Peter Huyghe
Laurenzo Lapage
Roland Liboton
René Martens
Kurt Onclin
Eddy Planckaert
Patrick Schoovaerts
Noël Szostek
Eddy Van Craeynest
Wim Van de Laer
Ronny Van Holen
Flip Van Vooren
Foreigners
Henri Dorgelo (Hol)
Adri Kools (Hol)
Torjus Larsen (Nor)
Bo-André Namtvedt (Nor)
Joe Parkin (USA)
Colin Sturgess (GB)
Cayn Theakston (GB)

SEFB-GAN
Sponsors: Savings bank and insurance company. Bicycles: Look. Directeur sportif: Walter Dalgal. Assistant: Gérard Bulens
Belgians
Daniel Beelen
Jerry Cooman
Danny de Bie
Eddy de Bie
Paul de Brauwer
Alain Deschacht
Johan Devos
Bruno Geuens
Dirk Heirweg
Benny Heylen
Wim Lambrechts
Marnix Lameire
Peter Spaenhoven
Jan Van Camp
Marc Verbeeck
Jan Wijnants
Foreigners
Frank Pirard (Hol)

WEINMANN
Sponsor: Bicycle components manufacturer. Bicycles: Eddy Merckx. Directeur sportif: Walter Godefroot. Assistants: Patrick Lefevere and Jules De Wever
Belgians
Carlo Bomans
Jean-François Brasseur
Johnny Dauwe
Michel Dernies
Marc Dierickx
Jan Goessens
Ronny Pauwels
Patrick Robeet
Luc Van de Vel
Foreigners
Alfred Acchermann (Swi)
Beat Breu (Swi)
Marco Diem (Swi)
Arno Kuttel (Swi)
Kurt Steinmann (Swi)
Adrie Van Der Poel (Hol)
Jac Van Der Poel (Hol)
Thomas Wegmüller (Swi)

WESTWOOD-IBEA
Sponsors: Garden machinery manufacturers. Bicycles: Eddy Merckx. Directeur sportif: Robert Hendrickx
Belgians
Luc Govaerts
Guy Rooms
Marc Sprangers
Chris Van Dijk
Stefan Van Leeuwe
Frank Verleyen
Jean-Marie Vernie
Willem Wijnant

COLOMBIA

CAFÉ DE COLOMBIA
Sponsor: Coffee growers' cooperative. Bicycles: Vitus. Directeur sportif: Rafaël Niño. Assistant: Pedro-Pablo Valdiviesco
Colombians
Angel Alayon
Juan-Carlos Arias
Herman Buenahors
Julio-César Cadena
Alberto Camargo
Henry Cardenas
Edgar Corredor
Luis Herrera
Luis-Felipe Moreno
Pablo-Enrique Rincon
Alvaro Sierra
Augusto Triana
Foreigners
Robert Forest (Fr)
Jörgen Pedersen (Den)
Jesper Worre (Den)

PONY MALTA-AVIANCA
Sponsors: Soft drink producer and national airline. Bicycles: Battaglin. Directeur sportif: Jorge Tenjo. Assistant: Hector Mayorga
Colombians
Marco-Antonio Carreno
German-Antonio Castillo
José-Alvio Chizabas
Dametrio Cuspoca
Luis-Alberto Gonzalez
José-Enrique Lopez
Alvaro Lozano
Jorge-Nilton Ortiz
Herman Patino
Martin Ramirez
Ruban Ramirez
Fabio-Herman Rodriguez
José-Francisco Rodriguez
Celio-Roberto Roncancio
Luis-Ernesto Saavedra
Angel-Miguel Sanabria
Rafaël Tolosa
Ramon Tolosa
Pablo Wilches

POSTOBON
Sponsor: Soft drinks producer. Bicycles: Pinarello. Directeurs sportif: Raul Meza and Elkin Rendon
Colombians
Raul Acosta
Marco Bernal
Hector Betancur
Juan Castillo
Arsenio Chaparro
Omar Hernandez
Carlos Jaramillo
Alvaro Mejia
Gerardo Moncada
Javier Montoya
Reynel Montoya
Luis Mosquera
Federico Muñoz
Victor-Hugo Olarte
Jorge Otalvaro
William Palacio
Hector Patarroyo
William Pulido
Efrain Rico
Oscar Vargas
Gustavo Wilches

FRANCE

CASTORAMA
Sponsor: Hardware store chain. Bicycles: Raleigh. Directeur sportif: Cyrille Guimard. Assistant: Bernard Quilfen
French
Dominique Arnould
Vincent Barteau
Yves Bonnamour
Pascal Dubois
Jacques Durant
Laurent Fignon
Dominique Garde
Christophe Lavainne
Luc Leblanc
Yvon Ledanois
Thierry Marie
Patrick Moncassin
Fabrice Philipot
Eric Pichon
Jean-Philippe Rouxel
Gérard Rué
Pascal Simon
Foreigners
Bjarne Riijs (Den)

RMO
Sponsor: Temporary employment agency. Bicycles: Liberia-Mavic. Directeur sportif: Bernard Vallet. Assistant: Christian Rumeau
French
Jean-Claude Bagot
Philippe Bouvatier
Frédéric Brun
Eric Caritoux
Thierry Claveyrolat
Jean-Claude Colotti
Jean-Luc Jonrond
Thierry Laurent
Pascal Lino
Christophe Manin
Charly Mottet
Frank Pineau
Dante Rezze
Gilles Sanders
Foreigners
Per Pedersen (Den)
Mauro Ribeiro (Bra)
Michel Vermote (B)
Marcel Wüst (WG)

TOSHIBA
Sponsor: Electronics manufacturer. Bicycles: Raleigh. Directeur sportif: Yves Hézard. Assistant: Maurice Le Guilloux
French
Jean-François Bernard
Laurent Bezault
Thierry Bourgignon
Christian Chaubet
Sébastien Flicher
Martial Gayant
Laurent Jalabert
Pascal Lance
Roland Le Clerc
Philippe Louviot
Marc Madiot
Yvon Madiot
Thierry Richard
Denis Roux
Claude Seguy
Foreigners
John Carlsen (Den)
Andreas Kappes (WG)
Remig Stumpf (WG)

Z
Sponsor: Children's clothing manufacturer. Bicycles: LeMond. Directeur sportif: Roger Legeay. Assistant: Serge Beucherie
French
Henri Abadie
Frank Boucanville
Eric Boyer
Philippe Casado
Bruno Cornillet
Gilbert Duclos-Lassalle
François LeMarchand
Laurent Madouas
Ronan Pensec
Pascal Poisson
Jérôme Simon
Foreigners
Kim Andersen (Den)
Miguel Arroyo (Mex)
Wayne Bennington (GB)
Atle Kvalsvoll (Nor)
Johan Lammerts (Hol)
Greg LeMond (USA)
Robert Millar (GB)

HOLLAND

BUCKLER
Sponsor: Low alcohol beer. Bicycles: Colnago. Directeur sportif: Jan Raas. Assistant: Hilaire Van der Schueren
Dutch
Tom Cordes
Gerrit De Vries
Frans Maassen
Jelle Nijdam
Twan Poels
Gerrit Solleveld
Patrick Tolhoek
Marco Van Der Hulst
Wiebren Veenstra
Peter Winnen
Foreigners
Ludo De Keulenaer (B)
Fabian Fuchs (Swi)
Peter Gansler (WG)
Rolf Gölz (WG)
Jan Mattheus (B)
Noël Segers (B)
Eric Vanderaerden (B)
Edwig Van Hooydonck (B)
Gino Van Hooydonck (B)

PANASONIC-SPORTLIFE
Sponsors: Electronics manufacturer and chewing gum producer. Bicycles: Panasonic. Directeurs sportifs: Walter Planckaert, Ferdi Van den Haute. Manager: Peter Post
Dutch
Eddy Bouwmans
Michel Cornelisse
Louis De Koning
Theo De Rooy
Henk Lubberding
Steven Rooks
Harry Rozendal
John Talen
Gert-Jan Theunisse
Jos Van der Pas
Jean-Paul Van Poppel
Teun Van Vliet
Foreigners
Thomas Dürst (WG)
Viatcheslav Ekimov (USSR)
Urs Freuler (Swi)
Jozef Lieckens (B)
Olaf Ludwig (EG)
Guy Nulens (B)
Allan Peiper (Aus)
Marc Sergeant (B)
Eric Van Lancker (B)
Jean-Marie Wampers (B)

PDM
Sponsor: Video and audio tape manufacturer. Bicycles: Concorde. Directeur sportif: Jan Giesbers. Assistant: Piet Van der Kruys
Dutch
Eric Breukink
Marten Den Bakker
Johannes Draaijer
Peter Hoondert
Gert Jakobs
Frank Kersten
Jos Van Aert
John Van Den Akker
Marc Van Orsouw
Nico Verhoeven
John Vos
Foreigners
Raúl Alcalá (Mex)
Uwe Ampler (EG)
Dirk De Wolf (B)
Rudy Dhaenens (B)
Martin Earley (Ire)
Sean Kelly (Ire)
Atle Pedersen (Nor)
Uwe Raab (EG)
Gerhard Zadrobilek (Austria)

TVM-YOKO
Sponsors: Trucking company and tape manufacturer. Bicycles: Kirk. Directeur sportif: Cees Priem
Dutch
Patrick Bol
Maarten Ducrot
Jacques Hanegraaf
Rob Kleinsman
Daan Luyckx
Peter Pieters
Martin Schalkers
Eddy Schurer
Jan Siemons
Willem-Jan Van Louenhout
Foreigners
Phil Anderson (Aus)
Johan Capiot (B)
Patrick Jacobs (B)
Jörg Müller (Swi)
Dag-Erik Pedersen (Nor)
Jesper Skibby (Den)
Scott Sunderland (Aus)
Alain Van Den Bossche (B)
Jean-Philippe Vandenbrande (B)

ITALY

ARIOSTEA
Sponsor: Ceramics manufacturer. Bicycles: De Rosa. Directeur sportif: Giancarlo Ferretti. Assistant: Alfio Vandi
Italians
Moreno Argentin
Adriano Baffi
Sergio Carcano
Davide Cassani
Bruno Cenghialta
Roberto Conti
Alberto Elli
Federico Ghiotto
Massimiliano Lelli
Marco Lietti
Dario Mariuzzo
Rodolfo Massi
Giuseppe Petito
Valerio Piva
Marco Saligari
Marcello Siboni
Foreigners
Stephan Joho (Swi)
Rolf Sörensen (Den)

CARRERA
Sponsor: Jeans manufacturer. Bicycles: Battaglin. Directeur sportif: Davide Boifava. Assistants: Sandro Quintarelli and Giuseppe Martinelli
Italians
Guido Bontempi
Claudio Chiappucci
Mario Chiesa
Massimo Ghirotto
Alessandro Giannelli
Flavio Giupponi
Giancarlo Perini
Felice Puttini
Luca Rota
Max Sciandri
Enrico Zaina
Foreigners
Bruno Bonnet (Fr)
Primoz Cerin (Yug)
Acacio Da Silva (Por)
Christian Henn (WG)
Erich Mächler (Swi)
Jure Pavlic (Yug)
Laurence Roche (Ire)

CHATEAU D'AX
Sponsor: Furniture manufacturer. Bicycles: Moser. Directeur sportif: Gianluigi Stanga. Assistants: Vittorio Algeri and Claudio Corti
Italians
Roberto Amadio
Ettore Badolato
Luigi Botteon
Gianni Bugno
Giuseppe Calcaterra
Giovanni Fidanza
Roberto Gusmeroli
Camillo Passera
Mauro-Antonio Santoromita
Mario Scirea
Valerio Tebaldi
Ennio Vanotti
Alberto Volpi
Franco Vona
Stefano Zanatta
Foreigners
Mario Kummer (EG)
Toni Rominger (Swi)
Jan Schur (EG)

DEL TONGO
Sponsor: Fitted kitchen manufacturer. Bicycles: Pinarello. Directeur sportif: Enrico Paolini. Assistant: Paolo Abetoni
Italians
Marino Amadori
Franco Ballerini
Luigi Bielli
Francesco Cesarini
Franco Chioccioli
Mario Cipollini
Maurizio Fondriest
Luca Gelfi
Angelo Lecchi
Federico Longo
Fabio Roscioli
Gianluca Zanini
Marco Zen

DIANA-COLNAGO
Sponsors: Shoe manufacturer and bicycle manufacturer. Bicycles: Colnago. Directeur sportif: Pietro Algeri. Assistant: Czeslaw Lang
Italians
Emanuele Bombini
Fabrizio Bontempi
Fabio Bordonali
Gianluca Bortolami
Davide Bramati
Giorgio Furlan
Maurizio Piovani
Giuseppe Saronni
Flavio Vanzella
Foreigners
Joachim Halupczok (Pol)
Zenon Jaskula (Pol)
Marek Kulas (Pol)
Lech Piasecki (Pol)
Marek Szerszynski (Pol)

AMORE E VITA-FANINI
Sponsor: Bicycle manufacturer. Bicycles: Fanini. Directeur sportif: Giorgio Vanucci. Assistant: Giuseppe Lanzoni
Italians
Florido Barale
Simone Bruscoli
Andrea Chiurato
Fabrizio Convalle
Stefano Della Santa
Pierino Gavazzi
Claudio Golinelli
Fabrizio Margon
Ottavio Paccagnella
Roberto Pelliconi
Foreigners
Marcello Alexandre (Arg)
Daniel Castro (Arg)
Eddie Salas (Aus)
Scott Steward (Aus)

GIS
Sponsor: Ice cream manufacturer. Bicycles: Benotto. Directeur sportif: Franco Gini
Italians
Dario Bottaro
Angelo Canzonieri
Paolo Cimini
Silvano Contini
Salvatore Criscione
Alessio Di Basco
Danilo Gioia
Walter Magnago
Fabrizio Orlando
Germano Pierdomenico
Luciano Rabottini
Paolo Rosola
Maurizio Vandelli
Marco-Franco Votolo

ITALBONIFICA
Bicycles: Conti. Directeur sportif: Bruno Reverberi. Assistant: Greziano Rossi
Italians
Stefano Allocchio
Stefano Arlotti
Stefano Bianchini
Cesare Cippolini
William Dazzani
Fabiano Fontanelli
Michele Moro
Dario Rando
Luca Rigamonti
Eduardo Rocchi
Fabrizio Settembrini

JOLLY-CLUB 88
Sponsors: Kitchenware manufacturer and travel group. Bicycles: Pinarello. Directeur sportif: Enrico Paolini. Assistant: Pietro Abetoni
Italians
Stefano Cattai
Stefano Cecini
Stefano Colage
Enrico Galleschi
Stefano Giuliani
Bruno Leali
Enrico Leoni
Silvio Martinello
Maurizio Rossi
Francesco Rossignoli
Roberto Visentini

MALVOR-SIDI
Sponsors: Cosmetics company and shoe manufacturer. Bicycles: Bottecchia. Directeur sportif: Dino Zandegu
Italians
Gianni Faresin
Gianpaolo Fregonese
Daniele Gallo
Silvano Lorenzon
Michele Mara
Roberto Pagnin
Gianluca Pierobon
Daniele Pizzol
Giovanni Strazzer
Stefano Tomasini
Gianluca Tonetti

SELLE ITALIA-EUROCAR
Sponsors: Saddle manufacturer and car rental company. Bicycles: Moser. Directeur sportif: Domenico Cavallo
Italians
Sandro Bono
Stefano Breme
Andrea Demitri
Antonio-Pado Fanelli
Ivan Mantegazza
Andrea Michelucci
Claudio Savini
Sergio Scremin
Andrea Tafi
Foreigners
Severin Kurmann (Swi)
Herbert Niederberger (Swi)
Leonardo Sierra (Ven)
Daniel Wyder (Swi)

SPAIN

ORBEA
Sponsors: Bicycle manufacturer. Bicycles: Orbeo. Directeur sportif: Domingo Perurena
Spanish
Ivan Alemany
Jesus Arambarri
Jan Arrospide
Javier Carballeda
Daniel Clavero
José-Antonio Davoz
Miguel-Angelo Garcia
Javier Garciandia
Altor Garmendia
José-Luis Izaguirre
Joaquim Martinez
Iñaki Murua
José-Antonio Sanchez
Foreigners
Marcel Arntz (Hol)
René Beuker (Hol)
Dick Dekker (Hol)
Peter Harings (Hol)
Neil Stephens (Aus)
Johan Van Der Velde (Hol)
Helmut Wechselberger (Austria)

BANESTO
Sponsor: Banking corporation. Bicycles: Banesto. Directeur sportif: José-Miguel Echevarri. Assistant: Eusebio Unzue
Spanish
Marino Alonso
José-Enrique Carrera
Pedro Delgado
Juan-Carlos Gonzales
Victor Gonzalo
Julian Gorospe
Ruben Gorospe
Miguel Indurain
Javier-Luis Luquin
Juan Martinez-Oliver
Jokin Mujika
Jesus Rodriguez-Magro
Ignacio Sanroman
Javier Santamaria
Jośe Ramon Uriarte
Foreigners
Dominique Arnaud (Fr)
Armand de las Cuevas (Fr)
Abelardo Rondon (Col)

BH-AMAYA
Sponsor: Bicycle manufacturer. Bicycles: BH. Directeur sportif: Javier Minguez. Assistant: José-Luis Lopez-Cerron
Spanish
Francisco-José Antequera
Vicente Aparicid
Juan-Carlos Arribas
Miguel Aynat
Laudelino Cubino
José-Luis Diaz
Enrique Guerricagoitia
Alfonso Gutierrez
Juan-Carlos Martinez
Jesus Montoya
Javier Murguialday
Fernando Quevedo
Juan Romero
Eduardo Ruiz
Miguel-Angel Serrano
Jaïme Tomas-Florit
Foreigners
Jacques Decrion (Fr)
Patrice Esnault (Fr)
Joël Pelier (Fr)

CLAS-CAJASTUR
Sponsors: Cooperative dairy and bank. Bicycles: Colnago. Directeur sportif: Juan Fernandez. Assistant: Jesus Suarez-Cueva
Spanish
Gonzalo Aguiar
Guillermo Arenas
Angel Camarillo
Jesus Carballido
Javier Duch-Ballester
Fédérico Echave
Iñaki Gaston
Arturo Geriz-Morino
Pedro-Antonio Marquina
Francisco-Javier Mauleon
Casimiro Moreda
Carlos Muniz
Francisco-Javier Occhaita
José-Manuel Oliveira
Antonio Sampedro
Foreigner
Americo-José Da Silva-Neves (Por)

KELME
Sponsor: Shoe manufacturer. Bicycles: Eddy Merckx. Directeur sportif: Rafaël Carrasco. Assistant: Juan Suñol
Spanish
Francisco Cabello
Xavier Claramunt
Antonio-Miguel Diaz
Antonio Espejo
José-Maria Genesca
Mario Lara
Juan Reina
Jesus Rosado
Ramon-Antonio Rota
Mariano Sanchez-Martinez
Foreigners
José-Martin Farfãn (Col)
José-Dario Hernandez (Col)
Nestor Mora (Col)
Pedro-Saul Morales (Col)
Fabio Parra (Col)
Humberto Parra (Col)
Carlos Revelo (Col)
Nelson Rodriguez (Col)

LOTUS-FESTINA
Sponsor: Computer software company. Bicycles: Macario. Directeur sportif: Miguel Moreno
Spanish
Enrique Alonso
Josaba Berrojalbiz
Jesus Blanco-Villar
Manuel Carrera
Carlos Galaretta
Pedro-Luis Garcia
Ramon Gonzalez
Carlos Hernandez
José-Luis Laguia
Juan-Ramon Martin
Manuel Martinez-Costa
Juan-Tomas Martinez
Angel Ocaña
Luis Perez
Fernando Piñero
Santiago Portillo
Josaba Ruiz-Martinez
Agualin Sebastian-Alvarez
Juan Valbuena
José-Maria Yurrebaso
Foreigners
Tim Harris (GB)
Luc Suykerbuyk (Hol)
Roberto Torres (Fr)

MAVISA
Sponsor: Wooden door manufacturers. Directeur sportif: Faustino Ruperez
Spanish
José-Emilio Cuadrado
Manuel Delgado
Antonio Esparza

Manuel Guijarro
Miguel-Angel Iglesias
Rafaël Lorenzana
Fernando Martinez de Guereno
José-Luis Moran
Alejandro Muñoz
Jose Luis Otero
Clemencio Rodas
Jesus Rodriguez
Foreigners
Bryan-Lykke Bistrup (Den)
Pascal Kholveter (Lux)

ONCE
Sponsor: State lottery tickets. Bicycles: Otero and Look. Directeur sportif: Manolo Saiz
Spanish
Xavier Aldanondo
Eduardo Chozas
Luis-Maria Diaz de Otazu
Herminio Diaz-Zabala
Pedro-Luis Diaz-Zabala
Anselmo Fuerte
Santos Hernandez
Juan-Carlos Jusado
Marino Lejarreta
Miguel-Angel Martinez
Melchor Mauri-Prat
Pedro Muñoz
Celestino Prieto
Pello Ruiz-Cabestany
José-Luis Villanueva
Foreigners
Ivan Franco (USA)
Stephen Hodge (Aus)
Alex Pedersen (Den)
Johnny Weltz (Den)
Kenneth Weltz (Den)

SEUR
Sponsor: Courier Service. Bicycles: Macario. Directeur sportif: Maximino Perez-Montero
Spanish
Roque de la Cruz
Manuel Dominguez
Francisco Espinosa
José-Rafaël Garcia
Manuel Garcia
Joaquin Hernandez
Pablo Moreno
Francisco Navarro
Jorge Perez
Alvaro Piño
Vicente-Juan Ridaura
José Recio
José Rodriguez
Juan-Carlos Rozas
Jose-Salvador Sanchis
Jan Unzaga
José Urea
Miguel-Angel Vos-Garcia
Foreigners
Luis-Edgar Barroso (Ven)
Marco Giovannetti (It)
Mathieu Hermans (Hol)
Jean-Pierre Heynderickx (B)

TEKA
Sponsor: Appliances manufacturer. Bicycles: ALAN. Directeur sportif: José-Antonio Gonzales-Linares. Assistant: Julio San Emeterio
Spanish
José-Maria Ahedo-Toca
Enrique Aja
Juan-Carlo Alonso
Manuel-Angel Anton-Renard
Roberto Cordoba
Arsenio Gonzales
Alberto Leanizbarrutia
Juan-José Martinez
Bernardo Mazon
José-Fernando Pacheco
José Pedrero
Mariano Sanchez
Roberto-José Sierra
Foreigners
Reimund Dietzen (WG)
Malcolm Elliott (GB)
Nico Emonds (B)
Peter Hilse (WG)
Jaanus Kuum (Nor)

TULIP
Sponsor: Computer manufacturer. Bicycles: Rossin. Directeur sportif: Juan Hortelano
Spanish
Antonio Balboa
Manuel-Jorge Domingez
Jesus Hernandez-Ubeda
Francisco Navarro
José-Maria Palacin
Vicente Prado
José-Andres Ripoll
Luis Vicente-Otin
Jaïme Villamajo
Foreigners
Daniele Caroli (It)
Stéphane Guay
José-Rolando Ovando (Guat)
Eddy Schepers (B)

SOVIET UNION

ALFA LUM
Sponsor: Aluminium siding manufacturer. Bicycles: Colnago. Directeurs sportifs: Primo Franchini and Sergei Morozov
Soviets
Djamolidin Abdujaparov
Konstantin Bankine
Nikolai Golovatenko
Ivan Ivanov
Viktor Klimov
Dmitri Konyshev
Vladimir Pulnikov
Asiat Saitov
Igor Sumnikov
Andrei Tchmil
Alexander Troubine
Piotr Ugrumov
Sergei Uslamine
Oleg Yaroshenko
Vassily Zdanov

SWITZERLAND

FRANK-TOYOTA
Sponsor: Car dealership. Bicycles: Look. Directeur sportif: Robert Thalmann
Swiss
Jürg Bruggman
Pascal Ducrot
Bruno Holenweger
Bruno Hürlimann
Rolf Järmann
Jens Jentner
Karl Kälin
Omar Pedretti
Pius Schwartzentrüber
Daniel Steiger
Werner Stutz
Foreigners
Masatoshi Ichikawa (Jap)
Marco Vitali (It)
Sandro Vitali (It)

HELVETIA-LA SUISSE
Sponsors: Insurance company and national newspaper. Bicycles: Villiger. Directeur sportif: Paul Köchli. Assistant: Bruno Roussel
Swiss
Serge Demierre
Mauro Gianetti
Othmar Häfliger
Hans-Rüdi Märki
Pascal Richard
Niki Rüttimann
Guido Winterberg
Foreigners
Gilles Delion (Fr)
Luigi Furlan (It)
Dominik Krieger (WG)
Jean-Claude Leclercq (Fr)
Henri Manders (Hol)
Peter Stevenhaagen (Hol)
Gerard Veldscholten (Hol)
Frédéric Vichot (Fr)
Micheal Wilson (Aus)

WEST GERMANY

STUTTGART
Sponsor: City of Stuttgart. Bicycles: Eddy Merckx. Directeur sportif: Hennie Kuiper. Assistant: Werner Stauff
West Germans
Hartmut Bölts
Udo Bölts
Guido Eickelbeck
Jochen Görgen
Bernd Gröne
Josef Holzmann
Dariusz Kajzer
Uwe Nepp
Markus Schleicher
Werner Wüller
Foreigners
Marcel Arntz (Hol)
Kees Hopmans (Hol)
Ralph Moorman (Hol)
Erwin Nijboer (Hol)
Ludo Peeters (Bel)
Ad Wijnands (Hol)
Dean Woods (Aus)

UNITED KINGDOM

BANANA-FALCON
Sponsors: Banana producers and cycle manufacturer. Bicycles: Falcon. Directeur sportif: Keith Lambert
British
Glen Clarke
Rob Holden
Chris Lillywhite
Dave Rayner
Keith Reynolds
Chris Walker
Foreigner
Shane Sutton (Aus)

EVER READY-HALFORDS
Sponsors: Battery manufacturers and bicycle retail chain. Bicycles: Halfords. Directeur sportif: Mick Bennett
British
Gary Baker
Bernie Burns
Tony Doyle MBE
Ben Luckwell
Joey McLoughlin
Russell Williams
Chris Young

AIRMARSHALL-KIRK CYCLES
Sponsors: Airproducts and compressors, Kirk magnesium cycle frames. Bicycles: Kirk. Directeur sportif: Howard Marshall
British
Andy Johnson
Dave Mann
Hilton McMurdo
Ian Sanders
Steve Sefton

USA

7-ELEVEN-HOONVED
Sponsors: Convenience store chain and industrial washing machine manufacturer. Bicycles: Eddy Merckx. Directeur sportif: Noel Dejonckheere. Assistant: Richard Dejonckheere. Manager: Jim Ochowicz
Americans
Norman Alvis
Frankie Andreu
Andy Bishop
Thomas Craven
Andy Hampsten
Eric Heiden
Ron Kiefel
Roy Knickman
Tommy Matush
Scott McKinley
Davis Phinney
Jeff Pierce
Bob Roll
Tom Schuler
John Tomac
Foreigners
Steve Bauer (Can)
John Brady (Ire)
Nathan Dahlberg (NZ)
Dag-Otto Lauritzen (Nor)
Alex Stieda (Can)
Jens Veggerby (Den)
Brian Walton (Can)
Sean Yates (GB)
Urs Zimmermann (Swi)

COORS LIGHT
Sponsor: Brewery. Bicycles: Clark-Kent. Directeur sportif: Len Pettyjohn
Americans
David Farmer
Todd Gogulski
Alexi Grewal
Chris Huber
Greg Oravetz
Andy Paulin
Foreigners
Roberto Gaggioli (It)
Alan McCormack (Ire)
Stephen Swart (NZ)
Michel Zanoli (Hol)

AC-PINARELLO
Sponsor: Private company and bicycle manufacturer. Bicycles: Pinarello. Directeur sportif: Chris Wight
Americans
Michael Carter
Mike Costello
Matt Eaton
Mike Engleman
Keith Harper
Bryan Miller
Clark Sheehan
John Seibert
Don Spence
Randy Whicker
Bruce Whitesel

SPAGO
Sponsor: Restaurant. Bicycles: Giordana. Directeur sportif: Tom Kaplan
Americans
Ronnie Hinson
Gary Mulder
Doug Smith
Oliver Starr
James Urbonas
Foreigners
Arjan Jagt (Hol)

AMERICAN COMMERCE NATIONAL BANK
Sponsor: Bank. Bicycles: Canopus. Directeur sportif: Pablo Abrahams
Americans
Kenny Adams
David Brinton
Kurt Stockton
Foreigners
Peter Gylling (Den)

Results

TOUR OF THE AMERICAS *page 8*
Florida-Puerto Rico section
1 Daniel Wyder (Swi), Selle Italia 18:54.58
2 Malcolm Elliott (GB), Teka at 1:03
3 Michael Carter (USA), AC-Pinarello at 0:16
4 Hector Patarroyo (Col), Postobon st
5 Andrea Tafi (It), Selle Italia at 0:17
6 David Rayner (GB), Banana-Falcon at 0:50
7 Mike Engleman (USA), AC-Pinarrello at 0:56
8 Santos Hernandez (Sp), ONCE st
9 Robinson Merchant, Venezuelan am st
10 William Pulido (Col), Postobon st

Venezuela section
1 Daniel Wyder (Swi), Selle Italia 10:11.19
2 Johan Museeuw (B), Lotto-Superclub at 0:25
3 Hector Patarroyo (Col), Postobon at 0:36
4 Leonardo Sierra (Ven), Selle Italia at 0:41
5 Alvaro Mejia (Col), Postobon at 0:42
6 William Pulido (Col), Postobon at 0:49
7 Greg Oravetz (USA), Coors Light st
8 Pedro Diaz-Zabala (Sp), ONCE at 0:56
9 Andy Bishop (USA), American Commerce National Bank at 0:58
10 Michael Carter (USA), AC-Pinarello st

Overall Super Series (Combined points for Florida-Puerto Rico and Venezuela sections)
1 Daniel Wyder (Swi), Selle Italia 1500
2 Hector Patarroyo (Col), Postobon 1250
3 Malcolm Elliott (GB), Teka 1140
4 Michael Carter (USA), AC-Pinarello 1075
5 Alvaro Mejia (Col), Postobon 931
6 William Pulido (Col), Postobon 906
7 Mike Engleman (USA), AC-Pinarello 786
8 Andrea Tafi (It), Selle Italia 770
9 Santos Hernandez (Sp), ONCE 721
10 David Rayner (GB), Banana-Falcon 700

HET VOLK *page 12*
1 Johan Capiot (B), TVM 5:25.00
2 Edwig Van Hooydonck (B), Buckler st
3 Etienne De Wilde (B), Histor-Sigma st
4 Johan Museeuw (B), Lotto-Superclub st
5 Eddy Planckaert (B), Panasonic-Sportlife st
6 Johan Lammerts (Hol), Z st
7 Adrie Van der Poel (Hol), Weinmann st
8 Eric Vanderaerden (B), Buckler at 0:55
9 Brian Holm (Den), Histor-Sigma st
10 Carlo Bomans (B), Weinmann st

PARIS-NICE *page 14*
1 Miguel Indurain (Sp), Banesto 29:27.30
2 Stephen Roche (Ire), Histor-Sigma at 0:08
3 Luc Leblanc (Fr), Castorama at 0:42
4 Laurent Fignon (Fr), Castorama at 0:52
5 Eric Boyer (Fr), Z at 1:19
6 Pascal Simon (Fr), Castorama at 1:33
7 Claudio Chiappucci (It), Carrera at 1:41
8 Moreno Argentin (It), Ariostea at 2:14
9 Atle Kvalsvoll (Nor), Z at 2:22
10 Alex Pedersen (Den), ONCE st
Stage winners
Stage 1 (TT): Francis Moreau (Fr), Histor
Stage 2: Etienne De Wilde (B), Histor
Stage 3: Carlo Bomans (B), Weinmann
Stage 4 (TTT): Histor-Sigma (B)
Stage 5: Adriano Baffi (It), Ariostea
Stage 6: Miguel Indurain (Sp), Banesto
Stage 7: Claudio Chiappucci (It), Carrera
Stage 8a: Mauro Ribeiro (Br), RMO
Stage 8b (TT): Jean-François Bernard (Fr), Toshiba

TIRRENO-ADRIATICO *page 18*
1 Toni Rominger (Swi), Chateau d'Ax 27:19.18
2 Zenon Jaskula (Pol), Diana-Colnago at 2:31
3 Gilles Delion (Fr), Helvetia-La Suisse at 2:42
4 Jean-Claude Leclercq (Fr), Helvetia-La Suisse at 2:46
5 Maurizio Fondriest (It), Del Tongo st
6 Sean Kelly (Ire), PDM at 2:58
7 Frans Maassen (Hol), Buckler at 2:59
8 Martin Earley (Ire), PDM at 3:12
9 Daniel Steiger (Swi), Frank-Toyo at 3:22
10 Luc Roosen (B), Histor-Sigma at 3:59
Stage winners
Stage 1: John Talen (Hol), Panasonic-Sportlife
Stage 2: Toni Rominger (Swi), Chateau d'Ax
Stage 3: Jean-Claude Leclercq (Fr), Helvetia-La Suisse
Stage 4: Massimiliano Lelli (It), Ariostea
Stage 5: Eric Vanderaerden (B), Buckler
Stage 6: Jean Claude Leclercq (Fr), Helvetia-La Suisse
Stage 7: Eddy Planckaert (B), Panasonic-Sportlife
Stage 8 (TT): Eric Breukink (Hol), PDM

MILAN-SAN REMO *page 20*
1 Gianni Bugno (It), Chateau d'Ax 6:25.06
2 Rolf Gölz (WG), Buckler at 0:04
3 Gilles Delion (Fr), Helvetia-La Suisse at 0:23
4 Moreno Argentin (It), Ariostea at 0:31
5 Maurizio Fondriest (It), Del Tongo st
6 Jean-Claude Colotti (Fr), RMO st
7 Jesper Skibby (Den), TVM at st
8 Adriano Baffi (It), Ariostea at 1:02
9 Johan Museeuw (B), Lotto-Superclub st
10 William Dazzani (It), Italbonifica st

CRITERIUM INTERNATIONAL *page 24*
1 Laurent Fignon (Fr), Castorama 8:20.43
2 Gilles Delion (Fr), Helvetia-La Suisse at 0:29
3 Jean-Claude Leclercq (Fr), Helvetia-La Suisse at 0:42
4 Julian Gorospe (Sp), Banesto at 0:57
5 Rolf Gölz (WG), Buckler at 1:12
6 Stephen Roche (Ire), Histor-Sigma at 1:28
7 Miguel Indurain (Sp), Banesto at 1:32
8 Sean Kelly (Ire), PDM st
9 Tom Cordes (Hol), Buckler at 1:41
10 Luc Leblanc (Fr), Castorama at 1:57
Stage winners
Stage 1: Ron Kiefel (USA), 7-Eleven
Stage 2: Gilles Delion (Fr), Helvetia-La Suisse
Stage 3 (TT): Viatcheslav Ekimov (USSR), Panasonic-Sportlife.

TOUR OF FLANDERS *page 26*
1 Moreno Argentin (It), Ariostea 6:47.25
2 Rudy Dhaenens (B), PDM st
3 John Talen (Hol), Panasonic-Sportlife at 0:11
4 Carlo Bomans (B), Weinmann st
5 Maurizio Fondriest (It), Del Tongo at 0:14
6 Jan Schur (EG), Chateau d'Ax at 0:23
7 Niki Rüttiman (Swi), Helvetia-La Suisse st
8 Claude Criquielion (B), Lotto-Superclub at 0:37
9 Jean-Claude Colotti (Fr), RMO st
10 Franco Ballerini (It), Del Tongo st

GHENT-WEVELGEM *page 30*
1 Herman Frison (B), Histor-Sigma 4:59.00
2 Johan Museeuw (B), Lotto-Superclub st
3 Franco Ballerini (It), Del Tongo st
4 Frans Maassen (Hol), Buckler st
5 Jean-Marie Wampers (B), Panasonic-Sportlife st
6 Brian Holm (Den), Histor-Sigma at 0:02
7 Olaf Ludwig (EG), Panasonic-Sportlife at 0:04
8 Dmitri Konyshev (USSR), Alfa Lum st
9 Steve Bauer (Can), 7-Eleven st
10 Rudy Dhaenens (B), PDM st

TOUR OF TEXAS *page 32*
1 Chris Huber (USA), Coors Light 25:08.21
2 Michel Zanoli (Hol), Coors Light at 0:04
3 Jens Veggerby (Den), 7-Eleven st
4 Thomas Craven (USA), 7-Eleven st
5 Michael Carter (USA), AC-Pinarello st
6 Bobby Julich, United States am at 0:08
7 Randy Whicker (USA), AC-Pinarello st
8 Wayne Randle, Great Britain am at 0:11
9 Nate Reiss (USA), Subaru-Montgomery at 0:12
10 Thurlow Rogers (USA), Subaru-Montgomery st
Stage winners
Prologue: Chris Huber (USA), Coors Light
Stage 1: John Brady (Ire), 7-Eleven
Stage 2: Harvey Nitz (USA), Subaru-Montgomery
Stage 3: Chris Huber (USA), Coors Light
Stage 4: John Brady (Ire), 7-Eleven
Stage 5: Alex Dörper, West German am
Stage 6: Chris Boardman, Great Britain am
Stage 7: Nate Sheafor (USA), Shaklee
Stage 8: Jan Svorada, Czechoslovakian am

PARIS-ROUBAIX *page 34*
1 Eddy Planckaert (B), Panasonic-Sportlife 7:37.02
2 Steve Bauer (Can), 7-Eleven st
3 Edwig Van Hooydonck (B), Buckler st
4 Martial Gayant (Fr), Toshiba at 0:03
5 Jean-Marie Wampers (B), Panasonic-Sportlife st
6 Gilbert Duclos-Lassalle (Fr), Z st
7 Thomas Wegmüller (Swi), Weinmann at 0:07
8 Adrie Van der Poel (Hol), Weinmann at 0:10
9 Rudy Dhaenens (B), PDM st
10 John Talen (Hol), Panasonic-Sportlife st

FLECHE WALLONNE *page 38*
1 Moreno Argentin (It), Ariostea 5:21.00
2 Jean-Claude Leclercq (Fr), Helvetia-La Suisse at 0:03
3 Gert-Jan Theunisse (Hol), Panasonic-Sportlife at 0:06
4 Miguel Indurain (Sp), Banesto at 0:10
5 Steven Rooks (Hol), Panasonic-Sportlife at 0:14
6 Stephen Roche (Ire), Histor-Sigma at 0:18
7 Ron Kiefel (USA), 7-Eleven at 0:22
8 Raúl Alcalá (Mex), PDM at 0:29
9 Robert Millar (GB), Z at 0:37
10 Davide Cassani (It), Ariostea at 0:45

LIEGE-BASTOGNE-LIEGE *page 40*
1 Eric Van Lancker (B), Panasonic-Sportlife 7:10.00
2 Jean-Claude Leclercq (Fr), Helvetia-La Suisse at 0:34
3 Steven Rooks (Hol), Panasonic-Sportlife st
4 Rudy Dhaenens (B), PDM at 1:16
5 Luc Roosen (B), Histor-Sigma st
6 Moreno Argentin (It), Ariostea at 1:20
7 Gianni Bugno (It), Chateau d'Ax st
8 Gert-Jan Theunisse (Hol), Panasonic Sportlife st
9 Martin Earley (Ire), PDM st
10 Atle Kvalsvoll (Nor), Z st

AMSTEL GOLD RACE *page 44*
1 Adrie Van der Poel (Hol), Weinmann 6:17.17
2 Luc Roosen (B), Histor-Sigma st
3 Jelle Nijdam (Hol), Buckler st
4 Jan Goessens (B), Weinmann st
5 Franco Ballerini (It), Del Tongo st
6 Jean-Claude Leclercq (Fr), Helvetia-La Suisse st
7 Andreas Kappes (WG), Toshiba st
8 Gianni Bugno (It), Chateau d'Ax st
9 Johan Museeuw (B), Lotto-Superclub st
10 Phil Anderson (Aus), TVM st

FOUR DAYS OF DUNKIRK *page 46*
1 Stephen Roche (Ire), Histor-Sigma 23:51.49
2 François Lemarchand (Fr), Z at 0:19
3 Thierry Marie (R), Castorama at 1:43
4 Bruno Cornillet (Fr), Z at 2:31
5 Johan Museeuw (B), Lotto-Superclub at 2:35
6 Gilbert Duclos-Lassalle (Fr), Z at 2:40
7 Christophe Lavainne (Fr), Castorama at 2:40
8 Allan Peiper (Aus), Panasonic-Sportlife at 3:14
9 Per Pedersen (Den), RMO at 3:22
10 Eddy Schurer (Hol), TVM at 3:56

TOUR DE TRUMP *page 48*
1 Raúl Alcalá (Mex), PDM 45:20.09
2 Atle Kvalsvoll (Hol), Z at 0:48
3 Eric Breukink (Hol), PDM at 1:44
4 Dmitri Zhdanov (USSR), Du Pont am at 1:52
5 Viatcheslav Ekimov (USSR), Panasonic-Sportlife at 2:13
6 Steve Speaks (USA), Crest at 2:23
7 Clark Sheehan (USA), AC-Pinarello at 3:01
8 Ed Kaczmarczyk, Canadian am at 3:49
9 Andy Hampsten (USA), 7-Eleven at 4:02
10 Jos Van Aert (Hol), PDM at 4:43
Stage winners
Prologue: Raúl Alcalá (Mex), PDM
Stage 1: Olaf Ludwig (EG), Panasonic-Sportlife
Stage 2: Olaf Ludwig (EG), Panasonic-Sportlife
Stage 3: Vladislav Bobrik, (USSR) Du Pont am
Stage 4 (TTT): 7-Eleven
Stage 5: Nate Reiss (USA), Subaru-Montgomery
Stage 6: Pascal Poisson (Fr), Z
Stage 7: Andy Bishop (USA), Spago
Stage 8 (TT): Raúl Alcalá (Mex), PDM
Stage 9: Olaf Ludwig (EG), Panasonic-Sportlife
Stage 10: Michel Zanoli (Hol), Coors Light
Stage 11: Ed Kaczmarczyk, Canadian am
Stage 12: James Urbonas (USA), Spago
Stage 13: Michel Zanoli (Hol), Coors Light

TOUR DE ROMANDIE *page 54*
1 Charly Mottet (Fr), RMO 22:20.01
2 Robert Millar (GB), Z at 2:00
3 Luc Roosen (B), Histor-Sigma at 2:10
4 Micheal Wilson (Aus), Helvetia-La Suisse at 2:41
5 Stephen Hodge (Aus), ONCE at 3:08
6 Pascal Simon (Fr), Castorama at 3:39
7 Jérôme Simon (Fr), Z at 3:45
8 Bruno Cornillet (Fr), Z at 4:52
9 Rolf Järmann (Swi), Frank at 4:55
10 Fabian Fuchs (Swi), Buckler at 5:23
Stage winners
Prologue: Çharly Mottet (Fr), RMO
Stage 1: Rolf Järmann (Swi), Frank-Toyota
Stage 2a: Urs Freuler (Swi), Panasonic-Sportlife
Stage 2b (22km TT): Charly Mottet (Fr), RMO
Stage 3: Michel Dernies (B), Weinmann
Stage 4: Robert Millar (GB), Z
Stage 5: Urs Freuler (Swi), Panasonic-Sportlife

VUELTA A ESPAÑA *page 56*
1 Marco Giovanetti (It), Seur 94:36.40
2 Pedro Delgado (Sp), Banesto at 1:28

3 Anselmo Fuerte (Sp), ONCE at 1:48
4 Pello Ruiz-Cabestany (Sp), ONCE at 2:16
5 Fabio Parra (Col), Kelme at 3:07
6 Federico Echave (Sp), Clas at 3:52
7 Miguel Indurain (Sp), Banesto at 6:22
8 Ivan Ivanov (USSR), Alfa Lum at 6:48
9 Uwe Ampler (EG), PDM at 7:15
10 Denis Roux (Fr), Toshiba at 7:56
11 Martín Farfán (Col), Kelme at 8:27
12 Luis Herrera (Col), Café de Colombia at 9:07
13 Carlos-Maria Jamarillo (Col), Postobon at 10:38
14 Iñaki Gaston (Sp), Clas at 11:15
15 Fabio-Herman Rodriguez (Col), Pony-Malta at 11:40
16 Toni Rominger (Swi), Chateau d'Ax at 13:33
17 Alvaro Mejia (Col), Postobon at 16:52
18 Jesus Montoya (Sp), BH-Amaya at 17:45
19 Alvaro Sierra (Col), Café de Colombia at 18:41
20 Jan Unzaga (Sp), Seur at 19:45
21 Julian Gorospe (Sp), Banesto at 20:09
22 Alberto Camargo (Col), Café de Colombia at 20:24
23 José Luis Laguia (Sp), Lotus at 20:30
24 Pablo Wilches (Col), Pony-Malta at 23:11
25 Gerardo Moncada (Col), Postobon at 24:39
26 Dariusz Kasjer (WG), Stuttgart at 27:12
27 Javier Murguialdy (Sp), BH-Amaya at 28:06
28 Johnny Weltz (Den), ONCE at 29:05
29 Jesus Rodriguez-Magro (Sp), Banesto at 30:42
30 Pedro Saul Morales (Col), Kelme at 32:46
31 Carlos Hernandez (Sp), Lotus at 37:30
32 Henry Cardenas (Col), Café de Colombia at 38:32
33 Eduardo Chozas (Sp), ONCE at 42:47
34 Dametrio Cuspoda (Col), Pony-Malta at 43:05
35 Nico Emonds (B), Teka at 45:21
36 Mariano Sanchez (Sp), Teka at 47:16
37 Thierry Bourguignon (Fr), Toshiba at 48:36
38 Santos Hernandez (Sp), ONCE at 49:01
39 William Palacio (Col), Postobon at 49:57
40 Enrique Aja (Sp), Teka at 50:54
41 Arsenio Chaparro (Col), Postobon at 51:08
42 Nestor Mora (Col), Kelme at 52:14
43 Yvon Madiot (Fr), Toshiba at 53:15
44 Fernando Quevedo (Sp), BH-Amaya at 53:18
45 Martin Ramirez (Col), Pony-Malta at 53:33
46 Abelardo Rondon (Col), Banesto at 1:00.50
47 Javier Mauleon (Sp), Clas at 1:01.39
48 Philippe Louviot (Fr), Toshiba at 1:05.44
49 Javier Luquin (Sp), Banesto at 1:06.54
50 Nikolai Golovatenko (USSR), Alfa Lum at 1:12.29

Teams classification
1 ONCE
Mountains prize
1 Martín Farfán (Col), Kelme
Best sprinter
1 Uwe Raab (EG), PDM
Flying sprint
1 Miguel Angel Iglesias (Sp), Mavisa
Special sprint
1 Asiat Satov (USSR), Alfa Lum
Combined points jersey
1 Federico Echave (Sp), Clas
Special prize
1 Uwe Ampler (EG), PDM
Stage winners
Stage 1 (TTT): ONCE (Sp)
Stage 2a: José-Emilio Cuadrado (Sp), Mavisa
Stage 2b (TTT): Lotus (Sp)
Stage 3: Silvio Martinello (It), Jolly
Stage 4: Erwin Nijboer (Hol), Stuttgart
Stage 5: Patrice Esnault (Fr), BH
Stage 6: Jesper Worre (Den), Café de Colombia
Stage 7: Benny Van Brabant (B), Isoglass
Stage 8: Atle Pedersen (Nor), PDM
Stage 9: Nestor Mora (Col), Kelme
Stage 10: Uwe Raab (EG), PDM
Stage 11: Carlos Hernandez (Sp), Lotus
Stage 12: Alberto Camargo (Col), Café de Colombia
Stage 13: Nico Edmonds (B), Teka
Stage 14: Bernd Gröne (WG), Stuttgart
Stage 15 (TT): Jean-François Bernard (Fr), Toshiba
Stage 16: Uwe Raab (EG), PDM
Stage 17: Federico Echave (Sp), Banesto
Stage 18: Martín Farfán (Col), Kelme
Stage 19: Asiat Saitov (USSR), Alfa Lum
Stage 20 (TT): Pello Ruiz-Cabestany (Sp), ONCE
Stage 21: Denis Roux (Fr), Toshiba
Stage 22: Uwe Raab (EG), PDM

DAUPHINÉ LIBÉRÉ *page 62*
1 Robert Millar (GB), Z 33:42.00
2 Thierry Claveyrolat (Fr), RMO at 1:35
3 Alvaro Mejia (Col), Postobon at 1:56
4 Toni Rominger (Swi), Chateau d'Ax at 2:35
5 Fabio Parra (Col), Kelme at 5:06
6 Bruno Cornillet (Fr), Z at 6:05
7 Stephen Roche (Ire), Histor-Sigma at 6:48
8 Andy Hampsten (USA), 7-Eleven at 6:53
9 Denis Roux (Fr), Toshiba at 9:39
10 Oliverio Rincon, Colombian am at 10:42

GIRO D'ITALIA *page 66*
1 Gianni Bugno (It), Chateau d'Ax 91:51.08
2 Charly Mottet (Fr), RMO at 6:33
3 Marco Giovannetti (It), Seur at 9:01
4 Vladimir Pulnikov (USSR), Alfa Lum at 12:19
5 Federico Echave (Sp), CLAS at 12:25
6 Franco Chioccioli (It), Del Tongo at 12:36
7 Marino Lejarreta (Sp), ONCE at 14:31
8 Piotr Ugrumov (USSR), Alfa Lum at 17:02
9 Massimiliano Lelli (It), Ariostea at 17:14
10 Leonardo Sierra (Ven), Selle Italia at 19:12
11 Eduardo Chozas (Sp), ONCE at 20:15
12 Claudio Chiappucci (It), Carrera at 25:28
13 Fabrice Philipot (Fr), Castorama at 25:47
14 Angelo Lecchi (It), Del Tongo at 26:01
15 Gert-Jan Theunisse (Hol), Panasonic Sportlife at 28:43
16 Enrico Zaina (It), Carrera at 30:29
17 Flavio Giupponi (It), Carrera at 31:01
18 Jean-Claude Bagot (Fr), RMO at 31:58
19 Stephen Hodge (Aus), ONCE at 33:54
20 Zenon Jaskula (Pol), Diana-Colnago at 37:10
21 François Lemarchand (Fr), Z at 37:43
22 Maurizio Vandelli (It), Gis-Benotto at 40:48
23 Eric Boyer (Fr), Z at 43:06
24 Gilbert Duclos-Lasalle (Fr), Z at 46:19
25 Javier Mauleon (Sp), CLAS at 47:01
26 Roberto Visentini (It), Jolly at 47:25
27 Jure Pavlic (Yug), Carrera at 53:22
28 Marino Amadori (It), Del Tongo at 55:37
29 Roberto Conti (It), Ariostea at 57:54
30 Dmitri Konyshev (USSR), Alfa Lum at 59:52
31 Franco Vona (It), Chateau d'Ax 1:01.04
32 Andrea Chiurato (It), Amore & Vita 1:02.27
33 Phil Anderson (Aus), TVM at 1:02.45
34 Massimo Ghirotto (It), Carrera 1:04.48
35 Rodolfo Massi (It), Ariostea at 1:06.32
36 Giancarlo Perini (It), Carrera 1:10.14
37 Massimo Podenzana (It), Italbonifica at 1:13.03
38 Alberto Volpi (It), Chateau d'Ax at 1:14.36
39 Nathan Dahlberg (NZ), 7-Eleven at 1:14.42
40 Carmillo Passera (It), Chateau d'Ax at 1:16.45
41 Emanuele Bombini (It), Diana-Colnago at 1:16.59
42 Luca Gelfi (It), Del Tongo at 1:17.14
43 Angel Camarillo (Sp), CLAS at 1:18.13
44 Gianni Fresin (It), Malvor-Sidi at 1:18.22
45 Giuseppe Saronni (It), Diana-Colnago at 1:21.41
46 Juan-Carlos Rozas (Sp), Seur at 1:23.23
47 Francisco Espinosa (Sp), Seur at 1:2.00
48 Henri Abadie (Fr), Z-Sanson at 1:32.15
49 Acacio Da Silva (Por), Carrera at 1:32.58
50 Masatoshi Ichikawa (Jap), Frank-Toyo at 1:33.29
Stage winners
Stage 1 (TT): Gianni Bugno (It), Chateau d'Ax
Stage 2: Giovanni Fidanza (It), Chateau d'Ax
Stage 3: Eduardo Chozas (Sp), ONCE
Stage 4a: Stefano Allocchio (It), Italbonifica
Stage 4b: Phil Anderson (Aus), TVM
Stage 5: Fabrizio Convalle (It), Amore & Vita
Stage 6: Luca Gelfi (It), Del Tongo
Stage 7: Gianni Bugno (It), Chateau d'Ax
Stage 8: Stefano Allocchio (It), Italbonifica
Stage 9: Vladimir Pulnikov (USSR), Alfa Lum
Stage 10: Luca Gelfi (It), Del Tongo
Stage 11: Adriano Baffi (It), Ariostea
Stage 12: Eric Boyer (Fr), Z
Stage 13: Cesare Cipollini (It), Italbonifica
Stage 14: Allan Peiper (Aus), Panasonic-Sportlife
Stage 15: Eric Boyer (Fr), Z
Stage 16: Charly Mottet (Fr), RMO
Stage 17: Leonardo Sierra (Ven), Sella Italia
Stage 18: Adriano Baffi (It), Ariostea
Stage 19: Gianni Bugno (It), Chateau d'Ax
Stage 20: Cesare Cipollini (It), Italbonifica
Points
Gianni Bugno (It), Chateau d'Ax
Mountains
Claudio Chiappucci (It), Carrera
InterGiro
Phil Anderson (Aus), TVM
Teams
ONCE (Sp)

MILK RACE *page 74*
1 Shane Sutton (Aus), Banana-Falcon 48:26.22
2 Rob Holden (GB), Banana-Falcon at 2:40
3 Miroslav Vasicek, Czechoslovakian am at 2:41
4 Didier Thueux, French am at 2:53
5 Chris Walker (GB), Banana-Falcon at 3:28
6 Ruud Poels, Dutch am at 4:02
7 Miroslav Liptak, Czechoslovakian am at 4:54
8 Jim Van de Laer (B), IOC-Tulip at 4:56
9 Steve Farrell, Great Britain am at 4:57
10 Gerd Audehm, East German am at 4:57
Stage winners
Prologue: Cayn Theakston (GB), Tulip
Stage 1: Chris Walker (GB), Banana-Falcon
Stage 2: Jan Bogaert (B), La William-Saltos
Stage 3: Shane Sutton (Aus), Banana-Falcon
Stage 4: Paul Curran (GB), Crown Printers
Stage 5A: Steve Farrell, Great Britain am
Stage 5B: Jan Bogaert (B), La William-Saltos
Stage 6: Pavel Tonkov, USSR am
Stage 7: Frank Augustin, East German am
Stage 8: Uwe Preissler, East German am
Stage 9: Jan Bogaert (B), La William-Saltos
Stage 10: Shane Sutton (Aus), Banana-Falcon
Stage 11: Frank Augustin, East German am
Stage 12: Jan Bogaert (B), La William-Saltos
King of the Mountains
Gary Baker
Leyland DAF Points
Joey McLoughlin
Milk In Action Combine Competition
Shane Sutton
Hot Spot Sprint Competition
Simeon Hempsall
Most Aggressive Rider Overall
Bruno Huger
Most Unfortunate Rider Overall
Tom Bamford

CORESTATES CHAMPIONSHIP *page 76*
1 Paolo Cimini (It), Gis-Benotto 6:01.54
2 Laurent Jalabert (Fr), Toshiba st
3 Kurt Stockton (USA), American Commerce st
4 Angelo Canzonieri (It), Gis-Benotto st
5 Andy Bishop (USA), 7-Eleven st
6 Kenny Adams (USA), American Commerce st
7 John Tomac (USA), 7-Eleven st
8 Gary Mulder (USA), Spago st
9 Oliver Starr (USA), Spago st
10 James Urbonas (USA), Spago st

TOUR OF SWITZERLAND *page 78*
1 Sean Kelly (Ire), PDM 43:50.36
2 Robert Millar (GB), Z at 0:41
3 Andy Hampsten (USA), 7-Eleven at 1:04
4 Daniel Steiger (Swi), Frank-Toyo at 1:13
5 Zenon Jaskula (Pol), Diana-Colnago at 2:17
6 Atle Kvalsvoll (Nor), Z at 3:08
7 Eddy Bouwmans (Hol), Panasonic-Sportlife at 3:39
8 Laurent Madouas (Fr), Z at 5:19
9 Marco Vitali (It), Italbonifica at 5:44
10 Greg LeMond (USA), Z at 5:54
Stage winners
Stage 1: Nathan Dahlberg (NZ), 7-Eleven
Stage 2: Olaf Ludwig (EG), Panasonic-Sportlife
Stage 3: Luc Roosen (B), Histor-Sigma
Stage 4: Sean Kelly (Ire), PDM
Stage 5 (TT): Eric Breukink (Hol), PDM
Stage 6: Thierry Bock (B), Lotto-Superclub
Stage 7: Andy Hampsten (USA), 7-Eleven
Stage 8: Rolf Järmann (Swi), Frank-Toyota
Stage 9: Moreno Argentin (It), Ariostea
Stage 10: Uwe Ampler (EG), PDM
Stage 11: Kim Andersen (Den), Z

TOUR DE FRANCE *page 80*
1 Greg LeMond (USA), Z 90:43.20
2 Claudio Chiappucci (It), Carrera at 2:16
3 Eric Breukink (Hol), PDM at 2:29
4 Pedro Delgado (Sp), Banesto at 5:01
5 Marino Lejarreta (Sp), ONCE at 5:05
6 Eduardo Chozas (Sp), ONCE at 9:14
7 Gianni Bugno (It), Chateau d'Ax at 9:39
8 Raúl Alcalá (Mex), PDM at 11:14
9 Claude Criquielion (B), Lotto-Superclub at 12:04
10 Miguel Indurain (Sp), Banesto at 12:47
11 Andy Hampsten (USA), 7-Eleven at 12:54
12 Pello Ruiz-Cabestany (Sp), ONCE at 13:39
13 Fabio Parra (Col), Kelme at 14:35
14 Fabrice Philipot (Fr), Castorama at 15:49
15 Gilles Delion (Fr), Helvetia-la Suisse at 16:57
16 William Palacio (Col), Postobon at 19:43
17 Johan Bruyneel (B), Lotto-Superclub at 20:04
18 Roberto Conti (It), Ariostea at 20:43
19 Eric Boyer (Fr), Z at 22:09
20 Ronan Pensec (Fr), Z at 22:54
21 Thierry Claveyrolat (Fr), RMO at 20:33
22 Jérôme Simon (Fr), Z 27:23
23 Pascal Lino (Fr), RMO at 30:38
24 Anselmo Fuerte (Sp), ONCE at 31:18
25 Dimitri Konyshev (USSR), Alfa-Lum at 31:21
26 Atle Kvalsvoll (Nor), Z at 32:03
27 Steve Bauer (Can), 7-Eleven at 34:05

28 Abelardo Rondon (Col), Banesto at 35:37
29 Miguel Martinez Torres (Sp), ONCE at 38:39
30 Sean Kelly (Ire), PDM at 38:42
31 Jörg Müller (Swi), TVM at 39:50
32 Nelson Rodriguez (Col), Kelme-Ibexpress at 39:56
33 Steven Rooks (Hol), Panasonic-Sportlife at 42:09
34 Stephen Hodge (Aus), ONCE at 44:22
35 Pascal Simon (Fr), Castorama at 45:47
36 Patrick Robeet (B), Weinmann at 46:59
37 Reynel Montoya (Col), Ryalcao-Postobon at 50:16
38 Oscar de Jesus Vargas (Col), Ryalcao-Postobon at 52:11
39 Bruno Cornillet (Fr), Z at 53:00
40 Gerardo Moncada, Ryalcao-Postobon at 53:36
41 Jesus Rodriguez-Magro (Sp), Banesto at 53:44
42 Beat Breu (Swi), Weinmann at 59:13
43 Rudy Dhaenens (B), PDM at 59:51
44 Stephen Roche (Ire), Histore-Sigma at 1:00:07
45 Piotr Ugrumov (USSR), Alfa-Lum at 1:01:42
46 Omar Hernandez (Col), Ryalcao-Postobon at 1:02:46
47 Philippe Louviot (Fr), Toshiba at 1:03:18
48 Alvaro Mejia (Col), Ryalcao-Postobon at 1:05:04
49 Charly Mottet (Fr), RMO at 1:06:57
50 Jean-Claude Colotti (Fr), RMO at 1:08:31

Stage winners
Prologue: Thierry Marie (Fr), Castorama
Stage 1: Frans Maassen (Hol), Buckler
Stage 2 (TTT): Panasonic-Sportlife (Hol)
Stage 3: Moreno Argentin (It), Ariostea
Stage 4: Johan Museeuw (B), Lotto-Superclub
Stage 5: Gerrit Solleveld (Hol), Buckler
Stage 6: Jelle Nijdam (Hol), Buckler
Stage 7: Raúl Alcalá (It), PDM
Stage 8: Olaf Ludwig (EG), Panasonic-Sportlife
Stage 9: Massimo Ghirotto (It), Carrera
Stage 10: Thierry Claveyrolat (Fr), RMO
Stage 11: Gianni Bugno (It), Chateau d'Ax
Stage 12: Eric Breukink (Hol), PDM
Stage 13: Eduardo Chozas (Sp), ONCE
Stage 14: Marino Lejarreta (Sp), ONCE
Stage 15: Charly Mottet (Fr), RMO
Stage 16: Miguel Indurain (Sp), Banesto
Stage 17: Dmitri Konyshev (USSR), Alfa Lum
Stage 18: Gianni Bugno (It), Chateau d'Ax
Stage 19: Guido Bontempi (It), Carrera
Stage 20: Eric Breukink (Hol), PDM
Stage 21: Johan Museeuw (B), Lotto-Superclub

Teams classification
Z (France)

Points (Green jersey)
Olaf Ludwig (WG), Panasonic-Sportlife

Mountains Grand Prix
Thierry Claveyrolat (Fr), RMO

Best Young Rider (under 25)
Gilles Delion (Fr), Helvetia-La Suisse

WINCANTON CLASSIC *page 100*
1 Gianni Bugno (It), Chateau d'Ax 6:09.51
2 Sean Kelly (Ire), PDM at 0:13
3 Rudy Dhaenens (B), PDM st
4 Claudio Chiappucci (It), Carrera st
5 Marc Sergeant (B), Panasonic-Sportlife st
6 Michel Dernier (B), Weinmann st
7 Sammie Moreels (B), Lotto-Superclub st
8 Federico Echave (Sp), Clas st
9 Dirk De Wolf (B), PDM st
10 Marino Lejarreta (Sp), ONCE st

KELLOGG'S TOUR OF BRITAIN *page 102*
1 Michel Dernies (B), Weinmann 29:11.20
2 Robert Millar (GB), Z at 0:04
3 Maurizio Fondriest (It), Del Tongo at 1:38
4 Federico Echave (Sp), Clas at 1:56
5 Jörg Müller (Swi), TVM at 2:03
6 Emanuele Bombini (It), Diana-Colnago st
7 Leonardo Sierra (Ven), Selle Italia at 2:37
8 Martial Gayant (Fr), Toshiba at 2:54
9 Laurent Jalabert (Fr), Toshiba at 3:14
10 Phil Anderson (Aus), TVM at 3:19

Stage winners
Stage 1: Malcolm Elliott (GB), Teka
Stage 2: Andrea Tafi (It), Selle Italia
Stage 3: Michel Dernies (B), Weinmann
Stage 4: Sören Lilholt (Den), Histor-Sigma
Stage 5: Gianluca Bortalami (It), Diana-Colnago
Stage 6: Maurizio Fondriest (It), Del Tongo

CLASICO SAN SEBASTIAN *page 106*
1 Miguel Indurain (Sp), Banesto 6:19.59
2 Laurent Jalabert (Fr), Toshiba at 2:24
3 Sean Kelly (Ire), PDM st
4 Tony Rominger (Swi), Chateau d'Ax st
5 Federico Echave (Sp), Clas at 2:29
6 Steve Bauer (Can), 7-Eleven st
7 Enrique Aja (Sp), Teka st
8 Jesus Rodriguez Magro (Sp), Banesto st
9 Pascal Richard (Swi), Helvetia-La Suisse st
10 Marino Lejarreta (Sp), ONCE st

CHAMPIONSHIP OF ZÜRICH *page 108*
1 Charly Mottet (Fr), RMO 6:07.08
2 Greg LeMond (USA), Z st
3 Claudio Chiappucci (It), Carrera st
4 Marino Lejarreta (Sp), ONCE st
5 Gianni Bugno (It), Chateau d'Ax at 0:39
6 Rolf Sörensen (Den), Ariostea st
7 Franco Ballerini (It), Del Tongo st
8 Iñaki Gaston (Sp), Clas st
9 Gilles Delion (Fr), Helvetia-La Suisse st
10 Pedro Delgado (Sp), Banesto st

COORS LIGHT NORBA NATIONAL SERIES *page 110*
1 Ned Overend, Specialized 178
2 Dave Wiens, Diamond Back 150
3 Tim Rutherford, Ritchey 139
4 John Weissenrieder, KHS 132
5 John Tomac, Tioga-Yeti 129
6 Rishi Grewal, Coors Light-GT 124
7 Max Jones, Mongoose 110
8 Daryl Price, Specialized 92
9 Lance Lollar, Fat Chance-Campagnolo 86
10 Martin Stenger, Slingshot 84

GRUNDIG WORLD CUP CHALLENGE SERIES *page 112*
1 Mike Kluge (WG), Specialized 228
2 Mike Kloser (USA), AlpineStars 228
3 Volker Krukenbaum (WG), Cilo 208
4 Jörgen Sprich (WG), Scott 186
5 Andrej Glajza (Cz), Fuji 178
6 Robert Martin (WG), MTB-Troger 164
7 Rune Hoydahl (Nor), Fisher 161
8 Uli Rottler (WG), Centurion 160
9 Bruno D'Arsie (Swi), Mondia-Kuwahara 155
10 Jürgen Eckmann (WG), Scott 130

WORLD MOUNTAIN BIKE CHAMPIONSHIPS *page 114*

Men's cross-country
1 Ned Overend (USA), Specialized 2:28.31
2 Thomas Frischknecht (Swi), Ritchey at 2:36
3 Tim Gould (GB), Peugeot at 3:24
4 Paul Thomasberg (USA), Giant at 3:52
5 Max Jones (USA), Mongoose at 4:29
6 John Tomac (USA), Tioga-Yetei at 4:31
7 Mario Noris (It), unatt. at 4:40
8 Tom Rogers (USA), GT at 6:07
9 Dryl Price (USA), Specialized at 6:31
10 Travis Brosn (USA), Durango Wheel Club at 7:52
11 Tom Collins (USA) Marin at 8:15
12 Don Myrah (USA), Fat Chance-Campagnolo at 9:02
13 Mike Kloser (USA), AlpineStars at 9:16
14 John Weissenrieder (USA), KHS at 10:02
15 Albert Itan (Swi), Cilo-Ciclolinea at 10:34
16 Marc Schnyder (Swi), Scott-Lipton at 11:32
17 Bruno D'Arsie (Swi), Mondia-Kuwahara at 11:50
18 Steve Tilford (USA), KHS at 12:33
19 Jan Wiejak (Pol), Scott at 13:17
20 Riccardo De Bertolis (It), unatt. at 13:24

Women's cross-country
1 Julie-Furtado (USA), Yeti 2:09.27
2 Sara Ballantyne (USA), Specialized at 2:27
3 Ruthie Matthes (USA), Ritchey at 3:25
4 Susi Buchwieser (WG), Scott at 3:55
5 Susan DeMattei (USA), Diamond Back at 5:33
6 Julia Ingersoll (USA), KHS at 6:50
7 Chantal Daucourt (Fr), Scott-Lipton at 7:41
8 Cindy Whitehead (USA), Klein-Campagnolo at 10:18
9 Susan DiBiase (USA), GT at 10:44
10 Kathy Lynch (NZ), Fisher at 10:52
11 Silvia Fürst (Swi), Scott-Lipton at 11:52
12 Darcy Wright (USA), Cannondale at 12:35
13 Helen Gilroy (NZ), unatt. at 14:34
14 Judy Kohin (USA), Ross Indians at 15:23
15 Elladee Brown (Can), Canadian Club-Specialized at 15:50
16 Kathleen Fitzsimmons (USA), Trimble-Cool Tool at 17:02
17 Teresa Williams (USA), Slingshot at 18:50
18 Giovanna Bonazzi (It), unatt. at 19:48
19 Deb Murrell (GB), Daihatsu-Offroad at 20:08
20 Anne-Marie Dozois (Can), Canadian Club at 20:27

Men's downhill:
1 Greg Herbold (USA), Miyata-Bula 6:37.75
2 Mike Kloser (USA), AlpineStars 6:40.93
3 Paul Thomasberg (USA), Giant 6:46.00
4 John Tomac (USA), Tioga-Yeti 6:46.63
5 Marc Schnyder (Swi), Scott-Lipton 6:50.39
6 Dave Wonderly (USA), GT 6:52.98
7 Filip Meirhaege (B), MBK 6:53.60
8 Tom Rogers (USA), GT 6:54.30
9 Jürgen Sprich (WG), unatt. 6:54.36
10 Casey Kunselmen (USA), KHS 6:54.45
11 Jimmy Kight (USA), T.J. Frisbee-Uniback 6:57.47
12 Glen Adams (USA), Northshore-Bingham's 6:59.27
13 Christian Taillefer (Fr), Lapierre 6:59.56
14 Guido Visser (Can), Altitude-Rocky Mountain 7:04.69
15 Andy Tout (Can), Canadian Club-Rocky Mountain 7:05.13
16 Tom Collins (USA), Marin 7:05.87
17 Wayne Croasdale (USA), KHS 7:05.89
18 Daryl Price (USA), Specialized 7:06.55
19 Greg Johnson (USA), Cook Brothers-Powerbar 7:08.43
20 Mike Jordan (USA), Marin 7:08.81

Women's downhill:
1 Cindy Devine (Can), Klein-Campagnolo 7:34.39
2 Elladee Brown (Can), Specialized 7:34.74
3 Penny Davidson (USA), Klein-Campagnolo 7:36.39
4 Cindy Whitehead (USA), Klein-Campagnolo 7:41.41
5 Julie Furtado (USA), Yeti 7:52.89
6 Kathleen Fitzsimmons (USA), Trimble-Cool Tool 7:55.13
7 Melissa Giove (USA), Team Holsten-Yeti 8:01.12
8 Giovanna Bonazzi (It), unatt. 8:02.74
9 Helen Gilroy (NZ), unatt. 8:02.68
10 Chantal Daucourt (Swi), Scott-Lipton 8:02.74
11 Denise Mueller (USA), Mammoth-Answer 8:06.18
12 Kathy Lynch (NZ), Fisher 8:07.74
13 Silvia Fürst (Swi), Scott-Lipton 8:07.92
14 Susan DiBiase (USA), GT 8:07.99
15 Wendy Ward (USA), Metalsmith 8:14.79
16 Kim Sonier (USA), Team Rhino 8:15.62
17 Sara Ballantyne (USA), Specialized 8:32.60
18 Nathalie Fiat (Fr), Marin 8:34.50
19 Deb Murrell (GB), Daihatsu-Offroad 8:40.87
20 Lee Ann Fiolka (USA), Yeti 8:46.25

WORLD ROAD CHAMPIONSHIPS *page 116*

Men's professional road race
1 Rudy Dhaenens (B) 6:51.59
2 Dirk De Wolf (B) st
3 Gianni Bugno (It) at 0:08
4 Greg LeMond (USA) st
5 Sean Kelly (Ire) st
6 Laurent Jalabert (Fr) st
7 Johnny Weltz (Den) st
8 Andreas Kappes (WG) st
9 Maurizio Fondriest (It) st
10 Claude Criquielion (B) st
11 Piotr Ugrumov (USSR) st
12 Miguel Indurain (Sp) st
13 Marek Szerszynski (Pol) st
14 Federico Echave (Sp) st
15 Pello Ruiz-Cabestany (Sp) st
16 Joachim Halupczok (Pol) st
17 Iñaki Gaston (Sp) st
18 Martial Gayant (Fr) st
19 Steve Bauer (Can) st
20 Pedro Delgado (Sp) st
21 Marino Lejarreta (Sp) at 0:14
22 Alberto Leanizbarrutia (Sp) st
23 Claudio Chiappucci (It) at 0:45
24 Zenon Jaskula (Pol) st
25 Mario Kummer (EG) st
26 Gilbert Duclos-Lassalle (Fr) st
27 Atle Pedersen (Nor) st
28 Miguel-Angel Martinez (Sp) st
29 Jesus Rodriguez (Sp) st
30 Dmitri Konyshev (USSR) st
31 Peter Hilse (WG) st
32 Marek Kulas (Pol) st
33 Uwe Ampler (EG) st
34 Hans-Rüdi Märki (Swi) st
35 Alex Pedersen (Den) st
36 Robert Millar (GB) st
37 Michel Dernies (B) st
38 Thierry Claveyrolat (Fr) st
39 Dag-Otto Lauritzen (Nor) st
40 Laudelino Cubino (Sp) at 0:50
41 Sammie Moreels (B) st
42 Stephen Hodge (Aus) at 1:06
43 Gerard Rué (Fr) st
44 Eric Breukink (Hol) st
45 Thomas Wegmüller (Swi) at 3:06
46 Bruno Cornillet (Fr) at 4:56
47 Franco Ballerini (It) st
48 Eduardo Chozas (Sp) at 13:12
49 Dariusz Kajzer (WG) at 13:14
50 Pascal Richard (Swi) st

Men's amateur road race
1 Mirko Gualdi (It) 4:39.17
2 Roberto Caruso (It) at 0:54
3 Jean-Philippe Dojwa (Fr) at 0:56
4 Jens Heppner (EG) at 1:22
5 Fabian Jeker (Swi) at 2:20
6 Peter Meinert (Den) at 2:42
7 Falk Boden (EG) at 3:28
8 Richard Virenque (Fr) at 3:29
9 Gianluca Tarocco (It) at 3:50
10 Bjorn Stenersen (Nor) at 4:12
11 Lance Armstrong (USA) at 4:13
12 Andrzej Sypytkowski (Pol) at 5:23
13 Dario Nicoletti (It) st
14 Claus Moller (Den) st
15 Alexander Chefer (USSR) at 5:30
16 Roland Meier (Swi) st
17 Gerd Audehm (EG) st
18 Christian Andersen (Den) at 6:13
19 Armin Meier (Swi) st
20 Eric Spüler (Swi) st

Women's road race
1 Catherine Marsal (Fr) 2:00.07
2 Ruthie Matthes (USA) at 3:24
3 Luisa Seghezzi (It) st
4 Karen Holliday (NZ) st
5 Luzia Zberg (Swi) st
6 Natalia Bakanova (USSR) st
7 Kristel Werckx (B) st
8 Cynthia Lutke-Schipholt (Hol) st
9 Kathleen Shannon (Aus) st
10 Imelda Chiappa (It) st
1 Sylvie Slos (B) st
12 Cécile Odin (Fr) st
13 Karina Skibby (Den) st
14 Evelyne Müller (Swi) st
15 Kathrin Watt (Aus) st
16 Corinne Le Gal (Fr) st
17 Eva Orvosova (Cz) st
18 Belen Cuevas (Sp) st
19 Monica Bandini (It) st
20 Tea Vikstedt-Nyman (Fin) st

Men's team time trial
1 USSR (Oleg Galkine, Alexander Markovnitchenko, Igor Patenko, Rouslane Zotov) 1:56.50
2 East Germany (Uwe Berndt, Falk Boden, Maik Landsmann, Uwe Peschel) 1:57.05
3 West Germany (Rolf Aldag, Kai Hundertmark, Raimund Lehnert, Michael Rich) 1:57.09
4 France 1:58.22
5 Sweden 1:58.24
6 Bulgaria 1:58.29
7 USA 1:59.18
8 Italy 1:59.45
9 Switzerland 1:59.54
10 Poland 2:00.09

Women's team time trial
1 Holland (Monique Knol, Astrid Schop, Leontien Van Moorsel, Cora Westland) 1:03.51
2 USA (Phyllis Hines, Maureen Manley, Eve Stephenson, Inga Thompson) 1:04.07
3 USSR (Natalia Chipaeva, Nadejda Kibardina, Natalaya Melekhina, Valentina Polkhanova) 1:04.21
4 France 1:05.40
5 Sweden 1:06.12
6 Spain 1:06.51
7 Canada 1:07.09
8 Italy 1:07.10
9 West Germany 1:07.22
10 Japan 1:10.28

WORLD TRACK CHAMPIONSHIPS *page 120*
PROFESSIONALS
Sprint
Quarter-finals: Michael Hübner (EG) *beat* Yuichiro Kamiyama (Jap) 2-0
Claudio Golinelli (It) *beat* Patrick Da Rocha (Fr) 2-9
Stephen Pate (Aus) *beat* Nelson Vails (USA) 2-0
Hideyuki Matsui (Jap) *beat* Carey Hall (Aus) *was out*
Semi-finals: Hübner *beat* Matsui 2-0
Golinelli *beat* Pate 2-1
Third place: Pate *beat* Matsui 2-0
Final: Hübner *beat* Golinelli 2-0

5000m pursuit
Quarter-finals: Armand De Las Cuevas (Fr) 5:43.66
beat Shaun Wallace (GB) 5:48.63
Dean Woods (Aus) 5:45.07
beat Colin Sturgess (GB) 5:56.46
Francis Moreau (Fr) 5:37.40
caught Tony David (Aus) in 11 laps
Viatcheslav Ekimov (USSR) 5:44.01
caught Noriyuki Ijima (Jap) in 12 laps
Semi-finals: Moreau 5:42.95
beat Woods 5:47.78
Ekimov 5:42.56
beat De Las Cuevas 5:44.06
Final: Ekimov 4:39.04
beat Moreau 5:40.66
Final position:
1 Viatcheslav Ekimov (USSR)
2 Francis Moreau (Fr)
3 Armand De Las Cuevas (Fr)
4 Dean Woods (Aus)
5 Shaun Wallace (GB)

Keirin
1 Michael Hübner (EG) 11.085
2 Michel Vaarten (B)
3 Claudio Golinelli
4 Noboyuki Tawara (Jap)
5 Gibby Hatton (USA)
6 Urs Freuler (Swi)
7 Marcello Alexandre (Arg)
8 Patrick Da Rocha (Fr)

Points race
1 Laurent Biondi (Fr) 38pts
2 Michael Marcussen (Den) 15
3 (at one lap) Danny Clark (Aus) 54
4 Urs Freuler (Swi) 45
5 Silvio Martinello (It) 34
6 Francis Moreau 25
7 Colin Sturgess (GB) 24
8 Shaun Wallace (GB) 21
9 Patrick Naessens (B) 16
10 Michael Hess (WG) 14

Motor-Paced
1 Walter Brugna (It) 1:0.493
2 Peter Steiger (Swi)
3 Danny Clark (Aus)
4 (at one lap) Aleksandr Romanov (USSR)
5 Luigi Bielli
6 (at two laps) Giovanni Renosto
7 Torsten Rellensmann (WG)
8 (at 11 laps) Hideyuki Murakami (Jap)

AMATEUR MEN
Kilometre TT
1 Aleksandr Kiritchenko (USSR) 1:03.565
2 Martin Vinnicombe (Aus) 1:03.919
3 Jens Glücklich (EG) 1:04.210
4 Frédéric Magne (Fr) 1:04.705
5 Rocco Travella (Swi) 1:05.184
6 José-Manuel Moreno (Sp) 1:05.575
7 Markus Nagel (WG) 1:05.594
8 Silvano Boarin (It) 1:05.671
9 Tom Steels (B) 1:05.717
10 Koigi Kojima (Jap) 1:05.733
11 Erin Hartwell (USA) 1:05.883
12 Kenneth Ropke (Den) 1:06.037

Sprint
Quarter-finals: Bill Huck (EG) *beat* Fabrice Colas (Fr) 2:00
Curt Harnett (Can) *beat* Uwe Buchtmann (WG) 2-0
Jens Fiedler (EG) *beat* Ken Carpenter (USA) 2-0
Nikolai Kovche (USSR) *beat* Gary Neiwand (Aus) 2-0
Semi-finals: Huck *beat* Kovche 2-0
Harnett *beat* Fiedler 2-1
Third place: Fiedler *beat* Kovche 2-1
Final: Huck *beat* Harnett 2-0
Final placings:
1 Bill Huck (EG)
2 Curt Harnett (Can)
3 Jens Fiedler (EG)
4 Nikolai Kovche (USSR)
5 Gary Neiwand (Aus)
6 Ken Carpenter (USA)

Tandem sprint
Semi-finals: Japan (Toshinobu Saito-Narihiro Inamura) *beat* France (Frédéric Magne-Fabrice Colas) 2-0
Italy (Gianluca Capitano-Federico Paris) *beat* West Germany (Uwe Buchtmann-Markus Nagel) 2-0
Third place: West Germany *beat* France 2-1
Final: Italy bt. Japan 2-0

4000m pursuit
Quarter-finals: Valeri Baturo (USSR) 4:36.304
beat Cédric Mathy (B) 4:38.501
Eugeni Berzin (USSR) 4:32.869
beat Mark Kingsland (Aus) 4:42.915
Steve Hegg (USA) 4:32.980
beat Chris Boardman (GB) 4:38.061
Mike McCarthy (USA) 4:32.33
beat Jens Lehmann (EG) 4:34.14
Semi-finals: Berzin 4:33.48
beat Hegg 4:35.87
Baturo 4:31.87
beat McCarthy 4:32.62
Final:Berzin 4:33.01
beat Baturo 4:42.91
Final placings:
1 Eugeni Berzin (USSR)
2 Valeri Baturo (USSR)
3 Mike McCarthy (USA)
4 Steve Hegg (USA)

4000m team pursuit
Quarter-finals: Australia 4:15.56
beat France 4:17.88
Soviet Union 4:09.87
beat Czechoslovakia 4:19.13
West Germany 4:12.72
beat Denmark 4:18.44
East Germany 4:12.93
beat New Zealand 4:18.57
Semi-finals: West Germany 4:11.91
beat East Germany 4:14.95
Soviet Union 4:11.66
beat Australia 4:14.07
Final: Soviet Union 4:09.28
beat West Germany 4:15.91
Final placings:
1 Soviet Union (Eugeni Berzin, Valeri Baturo, Dmitri Neljubin, Alexander Gonchenkov)
2 West Germany (Michael Glöchner, Stefan Steinweg, Andreas Walzer, Erik Weispfennig)
3 Australia (Brett Aitken, Darren Winter, Mark Kingsland, Stephen McGlede)
4 East Germany (Carsten Wolf, Guido Fulst, Thomas Liese, Jan Kuehnert)
5 France
6 Denmark
7 New Zealand
8 Czechoslovakia

Points race
1 Stephen McGlede (Aus) 42pts
2 Bruno Risi (Swi) 32
3 Jan Bo Petersen (Den) 24
4 Giovanni Lombardi (It) 22
5 Eugeni Berzin (USSR) 19
6 Gary Anderson (NZ) 5
7 Leo Peelen (Hol) 2
8 (at one lap) Dmitri Neljubin (USSR) 31
9 Eric Magnin (Fr) 23
10 Manuel Youshimatz (Mex) 23

Motor-paced
1 Roland Königshofer (Austria) 39:18.877
2 (at one lap) Davide Solari (It)
3 Andrea Bellati (Swi)
4 (at three laps) Vincenzo Colamartino (It)
5 Carsten Podlesch (WG)
6 (at four laps) Thomas Königshofer (Austria)
7 (at six laps) Viktor Egorov (USSR)
8 (at 12 laps) Luigi Dessi (It)
9 (at 13 laps) Lieven Braeckman (B)

WOMEN
Sprint
Quarter-finals: Felicia Ballanger (Fr) *beat* Isabelle Gautheron (Fr) 2-0
Rita Razmaite (USSR) *beat* Kin Jin Yung (Kor) *w/o*
Renée Duprel (USA) *beat* Sinett Wolke (EG) 2-0
Connie Young *beat* Galina Enukhina (USSR) 2-0
Semi-finals: Young *beat* Ballanger 2-0
Duprel beat Razmaite 2-1
Third place: Razmaite beat Ballanger 2-0
Final: Young *beat* Duprel 2-1
Final positions:
1 Young
2 Duprel
3 Razmaite
4 Ballanger
5 Gautheron
6 Enukhina
7 Wolke
8 Kim

3000m pursuit
Quarter-finals: Madonna Harris (NZ) 3:45.723
beat Tea Vikstedt-Nyman (Fin) 3:46.077
Kelly-Ann Carter-Erdman (Can) 3:47.139
beat Janie Eickhoff (USA) 3:52.128
Barbara Ganz-Erdin (Swi) 3:46.956
beat Kelly-Ann Way (Can) 3:50.242
Leontien Van Moorsel (Hol) 3:46.836
beat Kendra Kneeland (USA) 3:47.745
Semi-finals: Van Moorsel 3:42.17
beat Ganz-Erdin 3:44.30
Harris 3:45.18
beat Carter-Erdman 3:48.32
Final: Van Moorsel 3:44.34
beat Harris 3:46.98
Final placings:
1 Van Moorsel
2 Harris
3 Ganz-Erdin
4 Carter-Erdman
5 Vikstedt-Nyman
6 Kneeland
7 Way
8 Eickhoff

Points race

1	Karen Holliday (NZ)	33
2	Svetlana Samokhavalova (USSR)	26
3	Kristel Werckx (B)	25
4	Petra Rossner (WG)	23
5	Petra Grimbergen (Hol)	18
6	Julie Speight (Aus)	12
7	Madonna Harris (NZ)	12
8	Barbara Ganz-Erdin	10
9	Janie Eickhoff (USA)	9
10	Katrin Ranger (WG)	8

GRAND PRIX DE LA LIBÉRATION *page 128*

1	PDM (Hol)	1:41.03
2	ONCE (Sp)	1:41.27
3	Buckler (Hol)	1:41.56
4	Histor-Sigma (B)	1:42.24
5	Chateau d'Ax (It)	1:43.13
6	TVM-Yoko (Hol)	1:43.31
7	Weinmann (B)	1:44.00
8	Stuttgart (WG)	1:44.01
9	Helvetia-La Suisse (Swi)	1:44.03
10	Panasonic-Sportlife (Hol)	1:44.12

PARIS-BRUSSELS *page 130*

1	Franco Ballerini (It), Del Tongo	6:07
2	Michel Dernies (B), Weinmann	st
3	Danny Neskens (B), La William	at 0:05
4	Jelle Nijdam (Hol), Buckler	st
5	Adrie Van der Poel (Hol), Weinmann	st
6	Johan Museeuw (B), Lotto-Superclub	st
7	Jesper Skibby (Den), TVM	st
8	Stefano Zanatta (It), Chateau d'Ax	st
9	Sören Lilholt (Den), Histor-Sigma	st
10	Peter Spaenhoven (B), SEFB	st

GRAND PRIX DES NATIONS *page 132*

1	Thomas Wegmüller (Swi), Weinmann	1:57.57
2	Eric Breukink (Hol), PDM	1:59.44
3	Toni Rominger (Swi), Chateau d'Ax	2:00.12
4	Stephen Hodge (Aus), ONCE	2:00.40
5	Marino Lejarreta (Sp), ONCE	2:01.22
6	Viatcheslav Ekimov (USSR), Panasonic-Sportlife	2:01.57
7	Micheal Wilson (Aus), Helvetia-La Suisse	2:02.15
8	Brian Holm (Den), Histor-Sigma	2:02.44
9	Thierry Marie (Fr), Castorama	2:02.58
10	Zenon Jaskula (Pol), Diana-Colnago	2:03.05

GRAND PRIX DES AMÉRIQUES *page 134*

1	Franco Ballerini (It), Del Tongo	6:02.46
2	Thomas Wegmüller (Swi), Weinmann	at 1:22
3	Sammie Moreels (B), Lotto-Superclub	at 1:42
4	Claudio Chiappucci (It), Carrera	at 1:53
5	Steve Bauer (Can), 7-Eleven	at 2:49
6	Sean Kelly (Ire), PDM	st
7	Louis De Koning (Hol), Panasonic	st
8	Rudy Dhaenens (B), PDM	st
9	Marco Lietti (It), Ariostea	at 3:41
10	Rudi Verdonck (B), Lotto-Superclub	at 3:47

NISSAN CLASSIC *page 136*

1	Eric Breukink (Hol), PDM	24:32.11
2	Johan Museeuw (B), Lotto-Superclub	at 0:15
3	Sean Yates (GB), 7-Eleven	at 0:23
4	Viatcheslav Ekimov (USSR), Panasonic-Sportlife	at 0:32
5	Raúl Alcalá (Mex), PDM	at 0:56
6	Frans Maassen (Hol), Buckler	at 1:00
7	Herman Frison (B), Histor-Sigma	at 1:02
8	Steve Bauer (Can), 7-Eleven	at 1:09
9	Johan Lammerts (Hol), Z	at 1:12
10	Sean Kelly (Ire), PDM	at 1:13

Stage winners

Stage 1: Johan Lammerts (Hol), Z
Stage 2a: Eric Breukink (Hol), PDM
Stage 2b: Bruno Cornillet (Fr), Z
Stage 3: Johan Musseuw (B), Lotto-Superclub
Stage 4: Markus Schleicher (Ger), Stuttgart
Stage 5: Olaf Ludwig (Ger), Panasonic-Sportlife

PARIS-TOURS *page 142*

1	Rolf Sörensen (Den), Ariostea	7:9.32
2	Phil Anderson (Aus), TVM	st
3	Maurizio Fondriest (It), Del Tongo	st
4	Kim Andersen (Den), Z	st
5	Andreas Kappes (Ger), Toshiba	st
6	Carlo Bomans (B), Weinmann	at 0:04
7	Weibren Veenstra (Hol), Buckler	st
8	Sean Kelly (Ire), PDM	st
9	Frédéric Moncassin (Fr), Castorama	st
10	Adriano Baffi (It), Ariostea	st

TOUR OF LOMBARDY *page 144*

1	Gilles Delion (Swi), Helvetia-La Suisse	at 6:11.45
2	Pascal Richard (Fr), Helvetia-La Suisse	st
3	Charly Mottet (Fr), RMO	st
4	Robert Millar (GB), Z	st
5	Federico Echave (Sp), Clas	st
6	Claude Criquielion (B), Lotto-Superclub	at 3.35
7	Leonardo Sierra (Ven), Sella Italia	st
8	Marino Lejarreta (Sp), ONCE	at 3.38
9	Thomas Wegmüller (Swi), Weinmann	at 3.56
10	Sean Kelly (Ire), PDM	at 4.06

WORLD CUP FINAL *page 150*

1	Eric Breukink (Hol), PDM	1:2.48
2	Toni Rominger (Swi), Chateau d'Ax	at 0:34
3	Federico Echave (Sp), Clas	at 0:41
4	Eric Van Lancker (B), Panasonic-Sportlife	at 1:06
5	Charly Mottet (Fr), RMO	at 1:20
6	Steve Bauer (Can), 7-Eleven	at 1:29
7	Rolf Sörensen (Den), Ariostea	at 1:43
8	Gianni Bugno (It), Chateau d'Ax	at 1:56
9	Marino Lejarreta (Sp), ONCE	at 2:08
10	Adrie Van der Poel (Hol), Weinmann	at 2:16
11	Thomas Wegmüller (Swi), Weinmann	at 2:22
12	Gilles Delion (Fr), Helvetia-La Suisse	at 2:29
13	Franco Ballerini (It), Del Tongo	at 2:31
14	Maurizio Fondriest (It), Del Tongo	at 2:37
15	Claude Criquielion (B), Lotto-Superclub	at 2:40
16	Sean Kelly (Ire), PDM	at 2:55
17	Rudy Dhaenens (B), PDM	at 3:12
18	Claudio Chiappucci (It), Carrera	at 4:05
19	Robert Millar (GB), Z	at 4:41

Perrier World Cup Classification

Individual classification	Milan-San Remo	Tour of Flanders	Paris-Roubaix	Liège-Bastogne-Liège	Amstel Gold	Wincanton Classic	Clasico San Sebastian	Championship of Zürich	Grand Prix des Amériques	Paris-Tours	Tour of Lombardy	World Cup Final	Total
1 Gianni Bugno (It), Chateau d'Ax	25	9		14	13	25		16	10		8	13	**133**
2 Rudy Dhaenens (B), PDM		22	12	18	8	20	1		13	1		4	**99**
3 Sean Kelly (Ire), PDM						22	20	8	15	13	11	5	**94**
4 Franco Ballerini (It), Del Tongo		11	2		16			14	25	3	10	8	**89**
5 Gilles Delion (Fr), Helvetia-La Suisse	20	7		3		6		12			25	9	**82**
6 Claudio Chiappucci (It), Carrera					10	18	9	20	18			3	**78**
7 Steve Bauer (Can), 7-Eleven			22				15		16			15	**68**
8 Thomas Wegmüller (Swi), Weinmann			14					9	22		12	10	**67**
9 Rolf Sörensen (Den), Ariostea	7					5		15		25		14	**66**
10 Fédérico Echave (Sp), Clas						13	16				16	20	**65**
10 Marino Lejarreta (Sp), ONCE						11	11	18			13	12	**65**
12 Moreno Argentin (It), Ariostea	18	25		15	4								**62**
12 Maurizio Fondriest (It), Del Tongo	16	16					3			20		7	**62**
14 Charly Mottet (Fr), RMO								25			20	16	**61**
15 Adrie Van der Poel (Hol), Weinmann			13		25							11	**49**
16 Claude Criquielion (B), Lotto		13		7	5						16	5	**46**
17 Eric Van Lancker (B), Panasonic				25								18	**43**
17 Andreas Kappes (WG), Toshiba	10	3			14					16			**43**
19 Robert Millar (GB), Z				6		7		8			18	2	**41**
20 John Talen (Hol), Panasonic	8	20	11										**39**
21 Jean-Claude Leclercq (Fr), Helvetia-La Suisse				22	15								**37**
22 Pascal Richard (Swi), Helvetia-La Suisse							12				22		**34**
22 Martial Gayant (Fr), Toshiba			18				10				6		**34**
24 Phil Anderson (Aus), TVM					11					22			**33**
24 Carlo Bowmans (B), Weinmann		18								15			**33**
26 Edwig Van Hooydonck (B), Buckler			20			9							**29**
27 Eric Breukink (Hol), PDM									1			25	**26**
28 Jan Goessens (B), Weinmann					18					4			**22**
28 Marc Sergeant (B), Panasonic						16	6						**22**
30 Jesper Skibby (Den), TVM	14									5			**19**
31 Michel Dernies (B), Weinmann				1		15							**16**
32 Brian Holm (Den), Histor	9		4										**13**
33 Marco Lietti (It), Ariostea									10	2			**12**
34 Atle Kvalsvoll (Nor), Z				11									**11**
34 Rudy Verdonck (B), Lotto									11				**11**
34 Mauro Gianetti (Swi), Helvetia-La Suisse					1	8		2					**11**
34 Marc Madiot (Fr), Toshiba		4							7				**11**
38 Peter De Clerq (B), Lotto						10							**10**
39 Hans-Rüdi Märki (Swi), Helvetia-La Suisse									9				**9**
39 Angelo Lecchi (It), Del Tongo											9		**9**
41 Yvon Madiot (Fr), Toshiba				8									**8**
42 Alberto Volpi (It), Chateau d'Ax					7								**7**
42 Johnny Weltz (Den), ONCE								7					**7**
44 José Ramon Uriarte Zubero (Sp), Banesto									6				**6**
44 Johan Lammerts (Hol), Z										6			**6**
46 Guido Bontempi (It), Carrera		5											**5**
47 Steven Hodge (Aus), ONCE											4		**4**
47 Raúl Alcalá (Mex), PDM				4									**4**
47 Frans Maassen (Hol), Buckler								4					**4**
50 Dag-Otto Lauritzen (Nor), 7-Eleven								3					**3**
51 Sören Lilholt (Den), Histor										2			**2**
51 Mauro Ribeiro (Bra), RMO									2				**2**

Team classification	Milan-San Remo	Tour of Flanders	Paris-Roubaix	Liège-Bastogne-Liège	Amstel Gold	Wincanton Classic	Clasico San Sebastian	Championship of Zürich	Grand Prix de la Libération	Grand Prix des Amériques	Paris-Tours	Tour of Lombardy	Total
1 PDM (Hol)		2	8	9	5	12	9	8	18	9	8	4	**92**
2 Helvetia-La Suisse (Swi)	4	9		7	9	8	6	7	8	4	3	12	**77**
3 Panasonic (Hol)		6	12	12	6	5	1		7	7		3	**59**
4 Ariostea (It)	12	5		1	4	4		9		5	9	6	**55**
5 Weinmann (B)		7	9		12	3		4	10		7		**52**
6 Chateau d'Ax (It)	2	12		6	1		7		12		5	7	**52**
7 ONCE (Sp)	1					7	5	2	15			9	**39**
8 Lotto (B)			1	4		9				12	6		**32**
9 Z (Fr)			3	8	8			12					**31**
10 Toshiba (Fr)	5	4	7	2	7		3					2	**30**
11 Histor (B)			5	5		6			13				**29**
12 TVM (Hol)	3								11		12		**26**
13 Buckler (Hol)		3	2	3	3			1	14				**26**
14 RMO (Fr)	8	1	4							3	1	8	**25**
15 Del Tongo (It)	7	8			2					2	2		**21**
16 Carrera (It)	6					2	2	5		6			**21**
17 7-Eleven (USA)									4	8			**12**